IMAGES
of America

HISTORIC DAYTONA BEACH

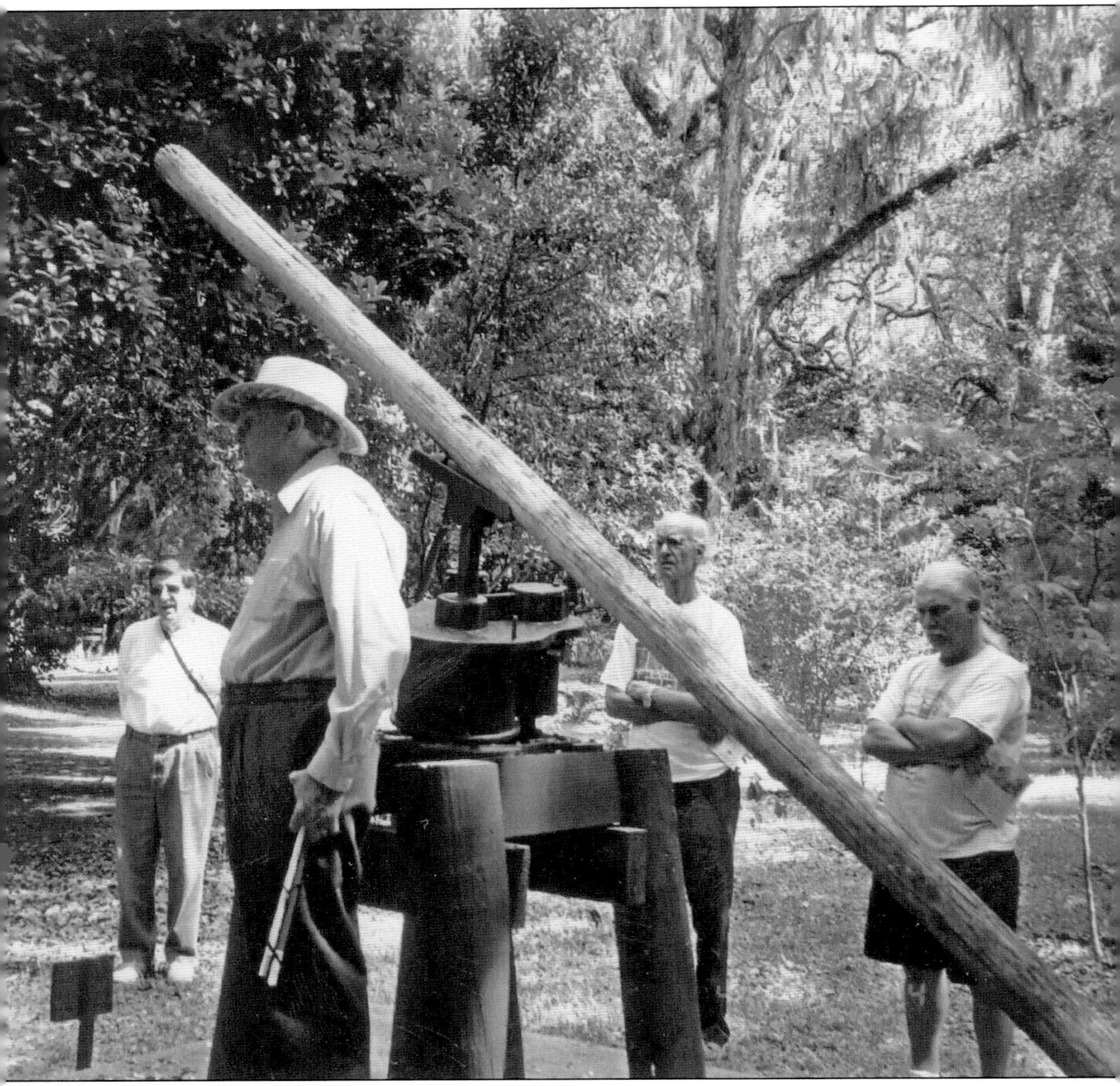

LEADING A TOUR. Author Harold Cardwell leads a history tour in Daytona Beach, Florida. (Courtesy of Cardwell Family Collection.)

IMAGES
of America

HISTORIC DAYTONA BEACH

Harold D. Cardwell Sr. and Priscilla D. Cardwell

ARCADIA
PUBLISHING

ISBN 978-0-7385-1675-2

Published by Arcadia Publishing
Charleston, South Carolina

Printed in the United States of America

Library of Congress Catalog Card Number: 2004107952

For all general information contact Arcadia Publishing at:
Telephone 843-853-2070
Fax 843-853-0044
E-mail sales@arcadiapublishing.com
For customer service and orders:
Toll-Free 1-888-313-2665

Visit us on the Internet at www.arcadiapublishing.com

This book is dedicated to all the members of the Daytona Beach Historic Preservation Board and the Halifax Historical Society, who had the vision to preserve our history and manage our heritage resources for the future.

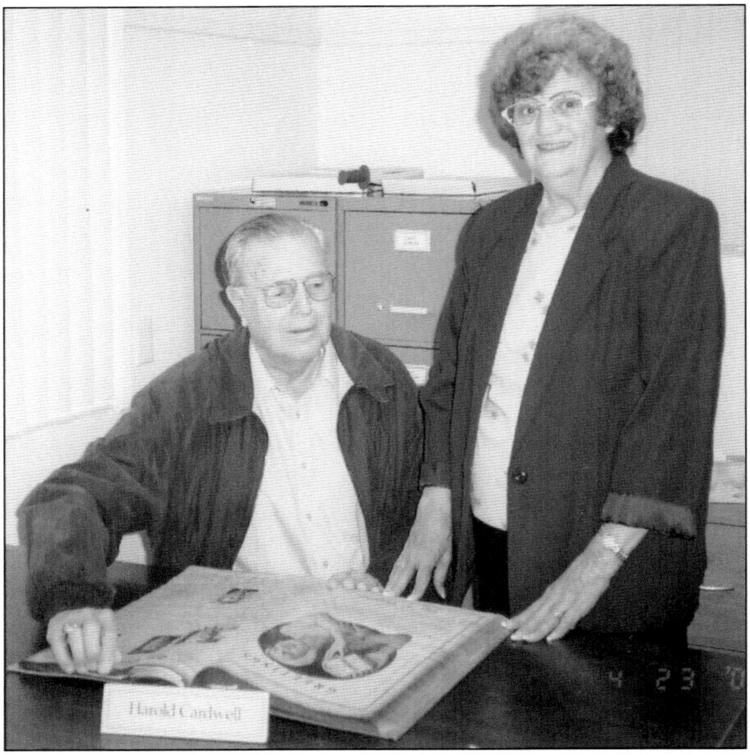

THE CARDWELLS. Authors Harold and Priscilla Cardwell are at work in their office in Daytona Beach. (Courtesy of Cardwell Family Collection.)

CONTENTS

ACKNOWLEDGMENTS

Thanks go to the following individuals and organizations: John Gontner; Diane M. Bara; Shirley Sheppard; Mary N. Poage; Cheryl Atwell; Leonard Lempel, Ph.D.; Halifax Historical Society; Florida Anthropological Society; P.K. Yonge Library at the University of Florida; Florida Historical Society; Port Orange Historical Trust; City of Daytona Beach; and Daytona Beach/Halifax Area Chamber of Commerce.

BIBLIOGRAPHY

Adams, William R., Ph.D. *Historic Properties Survey of South Beach Street, Daytona Beach, Florida.* St. Augustine, FL: Historic Property Associates, 1985.

Booth, Fred. *Early Days in Daytona Beach, Florida: How a City was Founded.* Daytona Beach, FL: News-Journal Corporation, 1951.

Cardwell Family Papers, Port Orange Historical Trust Archives. Port Orange, FL: 1997.

Cardwell, Harold D., Sr. *Daytona Beach: 100 Years of Racing.* Charleston, SC: Arcadia, 2002.

Daytona Beach, Florida Historic Preservation Board. *Minutes: 1985–2003.* (Daytona Beach, 2003).

Daytona Beach, Florida Municipal Government. *Minutes: 1876–2004.* (Daytona Beach, 2004).

Fitzgerald, T.E. *Volusia County: Past and Present.* Daytona Beach, FL: The Observer Press, 1937.

Gold, P.D. *History of Volusia County, Florida.* DeLand, FL: E.O. Painter, 1927.

Hebel, I.B. *Centennial History of Volusia County, Florida: 1854–1954.* Daytona Beach, FL: College Publishing Company, 1955.

Schene, Michael G. *Hopes, Dreams, and Promises: A History of Volusia County, Florida.* Daytona Beach, FL: News-Journal Corporation, 1976.

Ste. Claire, Dana. *True Natives: The Prehistory of Volusia County.* Daytona Beach, FL: The Museum of Arts and Science, 1992.

Works Progress Administration. *Spanish Land Grants in Florida. Confirmed Claims A.B.C.* Vol. 1–5. Tallahassee, FL: State Library Board, 1940.

Introduction

In 1513 Juan Ponce de Leon, a Spanish explorer, discovered the land he named Florida and claimed for the Spanish crown. A Spanish colony was established at St. Augustine in 1565. The Spanish ruled the Florida territory for more than 200 years, until they ceded it to England in 1763. In 1783 the English returned the territory to Spain with the Treaty of Paris. In 1804 Samuel Williams received a royal land grant from the Spanish crown for the 3,000 acres that make up the main part of Daytona Beach today. He built a sugar mill with slave labor and grew crops of sugar cane, rice, and cotton. After the death of Samuel Williams, his son Samuel Hill Williams took over operation of the plantation and ownership of the slaves. Spain sold the Florida territory to the United States in 1821. In 1836 during the Second Seminole War, Samuel Hill Williams escaped with his life after Seminole hostilities destroyed his plantation, and he returned to St. Augustine. The only other activity on the old plantation before the Civil War was a logging camp, operated by the Swift brothers of Falmouth, Massachusetts. They cut hand-hewn, live oak timbers from the nearby forest for the shipyards of the North.

Matthias Day Jr. of Mansfield, Ohio, was an entrepreneur and visionary. He had been associated with several companies and had invented the arc lamp. Prior to 1870 he sold his patent to a group of investors to pursue his life's dream. He traveled to Florida to buy land to develop into a settlement or community. On Day's arrival at Jacksonville, Florida, he met Dr. John Milton Hawks, who invited Day to accompany him on a steamboat trip down Florida's East Coast to look at several abandoned Territorial-Period plantations. They entered the Halifax River and anchored at the riverfront of the old Samuel Williams Plantation. Amidst the old fields and the beautiful forest areas, Day was convinced he had found his subtropical paradise. In 1871 Matthias Day bought 2,144.5 acres of the Samuel Williams Plantation from Christina S. Relf, the former owner's daughter, for the sum of $8,000.

Day had James H. Fowler and R. Hodgman survey the property. He imported 14 workers, including his cousin Calvin Day, and a steam-powered sawmill, operated by Webber and Skelton from Ohio. The sawmill was erected at the edge of the settlement, and a two-story frame building was constructed, which Day named the Colony House. However, thanks to a mix-up in a shipment of roofing shingles, a temporary roof was made of palmetto fronds. Hence the name was changed to Palmetto House.

By 1873 there were 20 homes, a mercantile business established by William Jackson, and a post office operated by Mrs. Elizabeth Maley. Unfortunately, Day's dream was not fulfilled; land and lot sales were slow, and he was unable to meet his mortgages. Christina Relf then repossessed the property and resold the acreage to P.W. Burr and Charles E. Jackson. By public notice a town meeting was called on July 26, 1876, at 2:00 p.m. Twenty-five attended the meeting; 23 voted "yes" and two opposed regarding incorporation. John Tolliver and Thadeus Goodin, two African Americans, were among the "yes" vote. The group adopted a council, selected a seal, and named the settlement Daytona in honor of its founder, Matthias Day. In the 1880s the new town grew with boarding houses, stores, and a large new sawmill on Orange Isle.

Utley White and his company, St. Johns and Halifax Railway Company, brought the narrow-gauge railroad to Daytona. On December 2, 1886, the first passengers arrived in cars pulled by the steam locomotive *Bulow*. In 1888 Henry Flagler acquired the railroad and laid new standard-gauge tracks along the entire line, allowing trains to travel from Daytona to all points in the North. In the late 1890s Northern industrialists came down and established winter homes, and hotels were built to accommodate tourists. The railroad also accommodated the citrus, vegetable, and timber commerce that enhanced the growth of Florida's east coast.

After the turn of the century the horseless carriage appeared and electricity became available. In 1908 the first bond issue was authorized for city water. By 1914 improvements for a sewer and drainage system were completed, and in 1916 the shell-marl–based primary streets were paved with bricks or asphalt. After World War I a land boom flourished in the Daytona area. In 1926 the three towns of Daytona, Seabreeze, and Daytona Beach decided that this new growth warranted one town. Thus the new Daytona Beach was born.

Unfortunately, the stock market failed, banks closed, land values went down, and after 1929 the Depression hit Daytona Beach. Although the economy was boosted in March 1935 by the racing era when Sir Malcolm Campbell broke the world ground speed record at 276.82 miles per hour on the "World's Most Famous Beach," times were still difficult until the Public Works Administration (PWA) and the Works Progress Administration (WPA) helped save the area by giving work to hundreds of men. Some projects built by the WPA were the band shell, boardwalk, and armory. In 1939 the tourist industry started growing and Daytona Beach began recovering from the Depression. When the United States entered World War II, Daytona Beach had to make drastic changes. The addition of a U.S. Navy Air Base, a Women's Army Corps (WAC) Training Center, a U.S. Army Convalescent Hospital, and a boat-building business brought better times to Daytona Beach during this war period.

Following the war the local Daytona Beach economy started growing. To fulfill this need, new subdivisions were built, as well as recreation and beach facilities. Today the city flourishes with special events such as the Daytona 500, Bike Week, and college reunions, as well as cultural events like the visiting London Symphony Orchestra (LSO).

One

Early History of Our Settlement 1513–1875

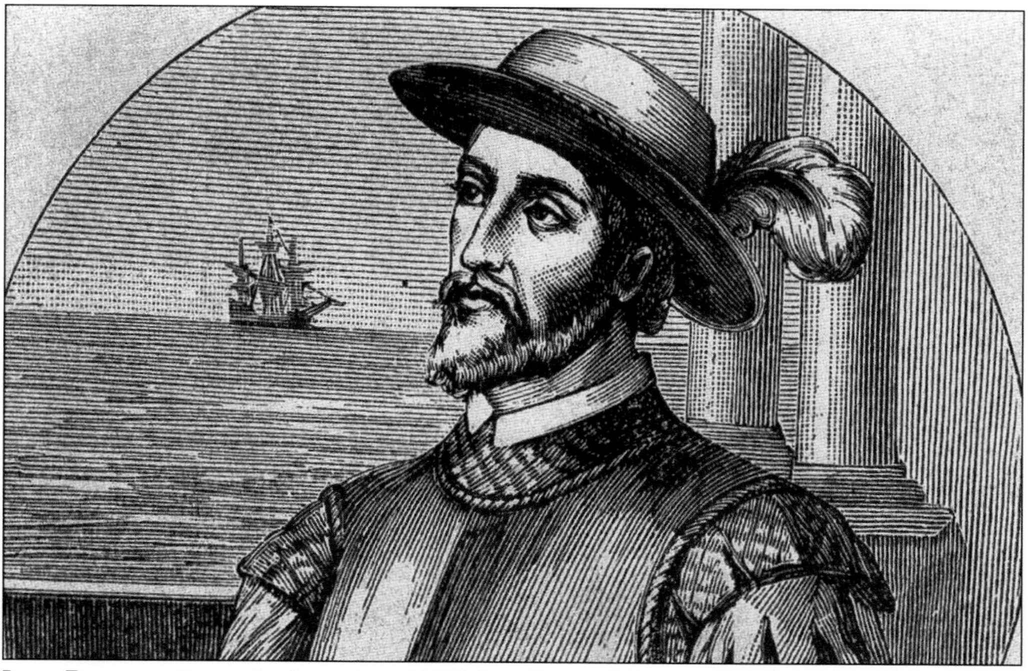

Juan Ponce de Leon. In the spring of 1513, Juan Ponce de Leon sailed along the Atlantic Coast of what is now Volusia County. Some historians believe he landed at the inlet that now bears his name. The river, which he called Rio de la Cruz (River of the Cross), was at the confluence of Spruce Creek, Halifax River, and Indian River. Ponce de Leon named this territory Florida after the beautiful flora he saw on his journey. (Courtesy of Florida State Archives.)

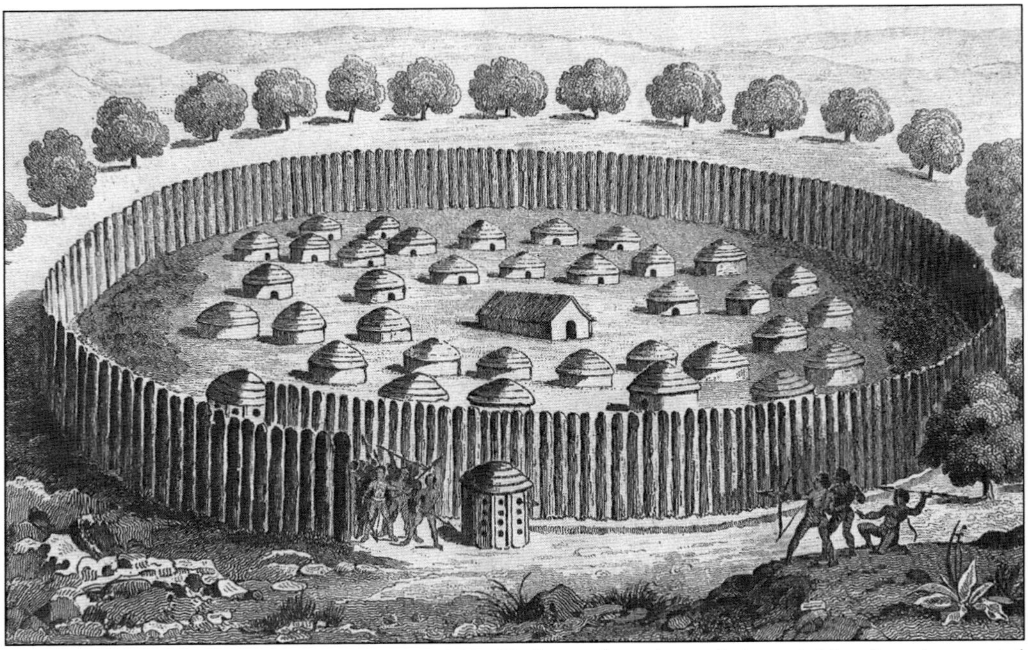

A Timucuan Fortified Village in 1562. Today archaeological sites yield cultural material that verifies the early existence of these natives. These early aborigines lived along the Halifax River and the Tomoka Basin. Notice the topography of the area. The huts are round in appearance and are built of small logs or poles. (Courtesy of Florida State Archives.)

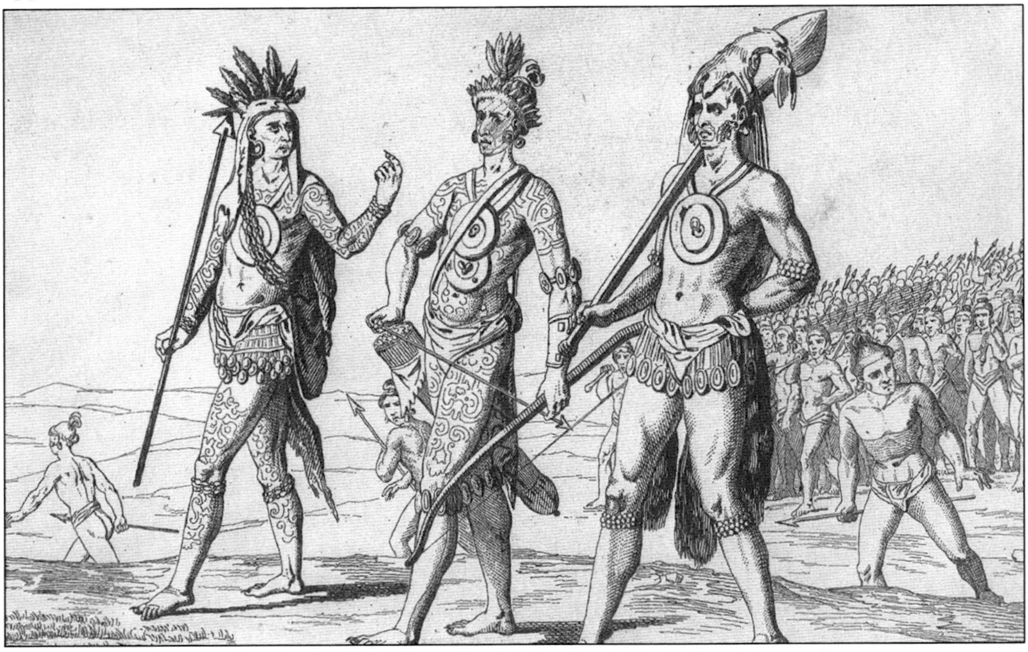

Timucuans Going off to War in 1562. Several Native American villages once existed along the Tomoka Basin, Halifax River, and Spruce Creek. Warring and disease contributed to the demise of the Timucuan culture. The Europeans brought diseases that spread throughout the natives, and by 1763 the population had decreased to approximately 100 survivors living near St. Augustine. (Courtesy of Florida State Archives.)

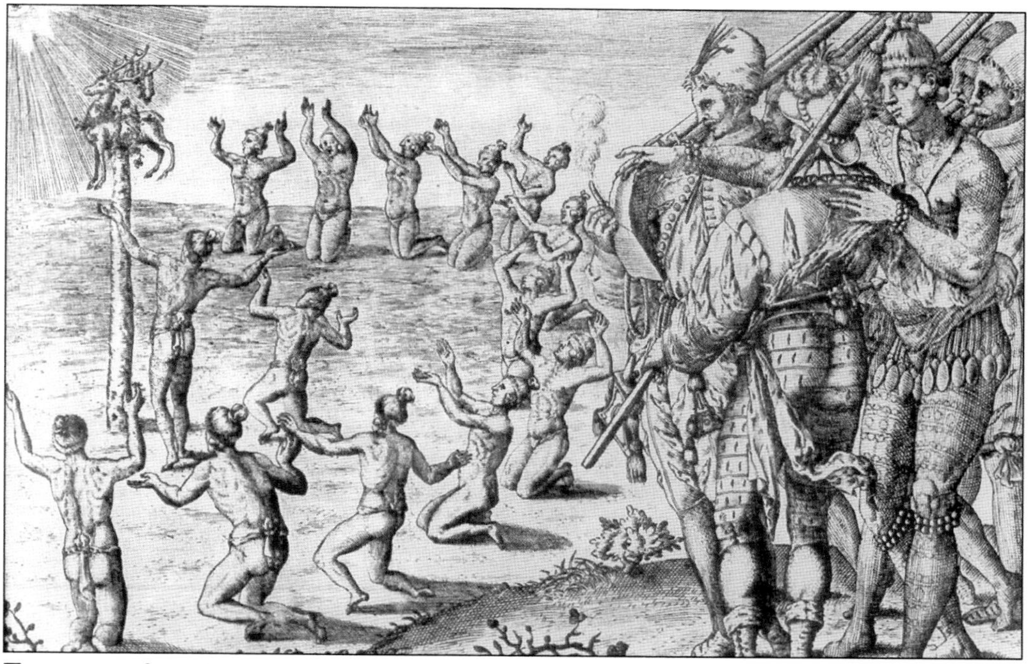

TIMUCUAN SUN WORSHIPPERS IN 1615. A young European cartographer described the Timucuan culture, with groups worshipping the sun. However, this rendering wasn't completed until he returned to Europe, and the Timucuan people took on European characteristics because of artistic influence. The nearby Timucuan village of Nocoroco was located within the present-day boundaries of Tomoka State Park. (Courtesy of Florida State Archives.)

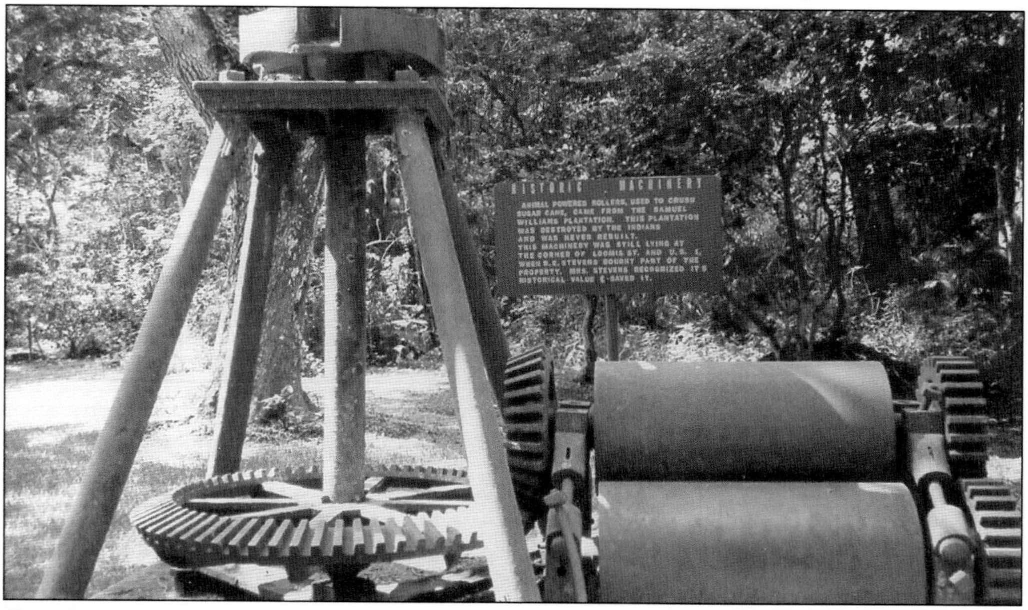

THE CANE CRUSHER FROM SAMUEL WILLIAMS'S PLANTATION, 1803–1835. These are the only physical remains of the plantation that once stood near modern Loomis and Ridgewood Avenues in Daytona Beach. The plantation was destroyed during the Second Seminole War, between 1835 and 1842. The machinery can be seen at the Sugar Mill Botanical Gardens in Port Orange, Florida. (Courtesy of Cardwell Family Collection.)

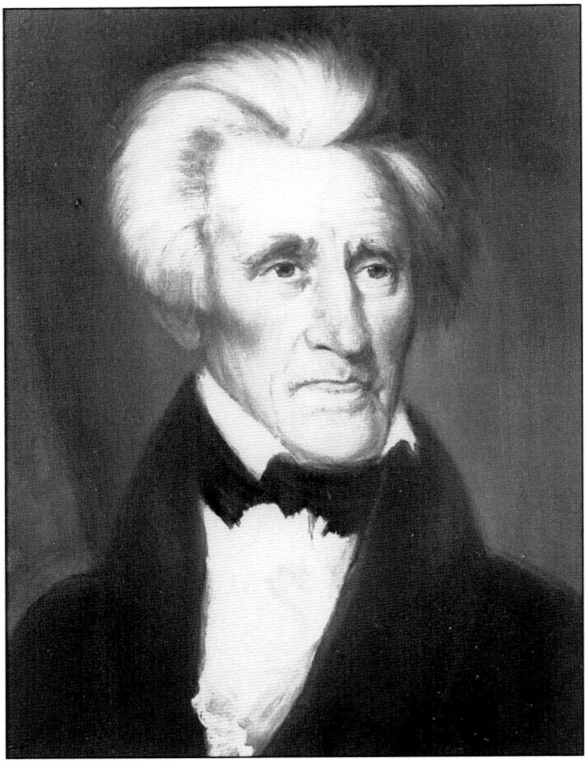

GEN. ANDREW JACKSON, MILITARY GOVERNOR OF FLORIDA FROM MARCH 10, 1821, TO DECEMBER 31, 1821. He was the first territorial governor, a former Indian fighter, and victor over the British at the Battle of New Orleans. Later he became the seventh president of the United States, serving from 1829 to 1837. (Courtesy of Florida State Archives.)

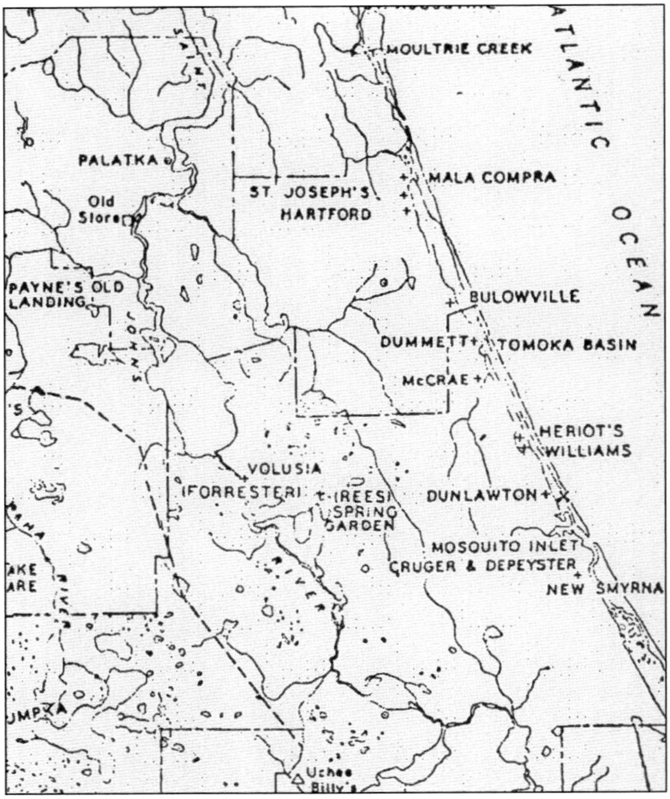

FLORIDA TERRITORIAL-PERIOD MAP, 1821–1845. This map depicts Territorial-Period plantations, which grew crops of sugar, rice, and cotton. The Heriot and Williams Plantations were located in present Daytona Beach boundaries. Note the adjoining Dunlawton and Cruger-DePeyster Plantations to the south with McCrae, Dummett, and Bulowville to the north. Nearly all the plantations were destroyed in the Second Seminole War, between 1835 and 1842. (Courtesy of Cardwell Family Collection.)

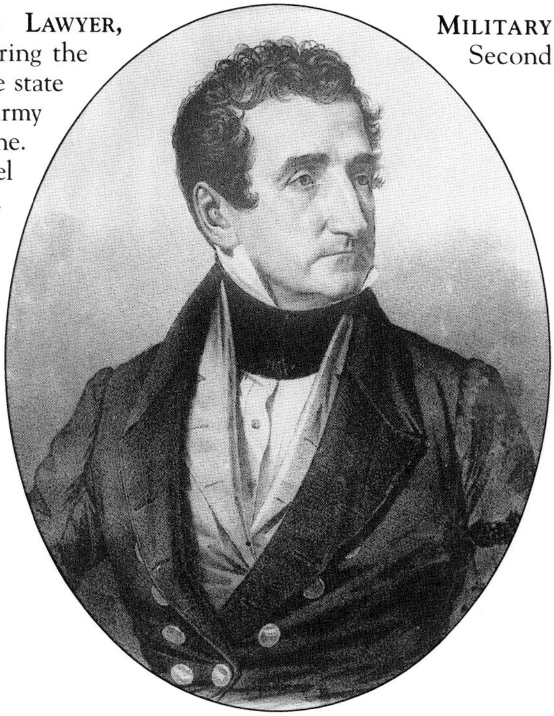

BRIG. GEN. JOSEPH M. HERNANDEZ: LAWYER, OFFICER, AND PLANTATION OWNER. During the Seminole War, Hernandez commanded the state militia; later he commanded the U.S. Army Regulars, headquartered at St. Augustine. Hernandez married the widow of Samuel H. Williams after Williams's death in St. Augustine. The Williams Plantation was in the vicinity of present-day Beach Street and Loomis Avenue in Daytona Beach. (Courtesy of Florida State Archives.)

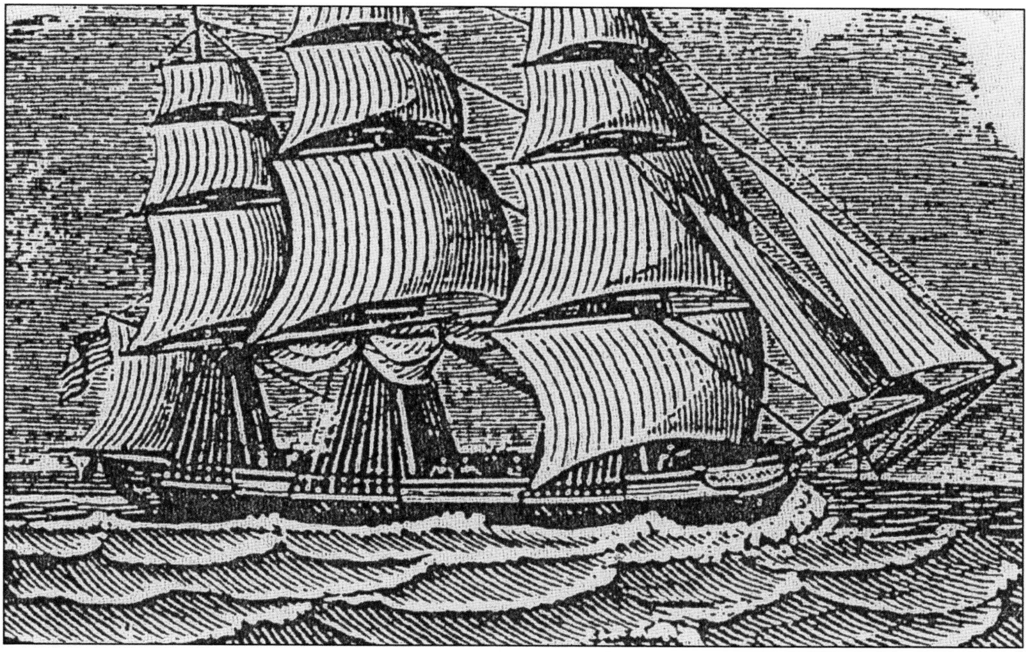

THE SWIFT BROTHERS OF FALMOUTH AND NEW BEDFORD, MASSACHUSETTS, 1828–1861. The Swift Brothers brought crews each year, from November to May, to the Halifax River area to remove hand-hewn, live oak timbers for construction of sailing ships. Large shipments of timber were removed from the Samuel Williams Plantation and other nearby properties, loaded onto flat boats, and reloaded onto sea-going schooners at Mosquito Inlet, today's Ponce Inlet, for Northern shipyards. (Courtesy of Cardwell Family Collection.)

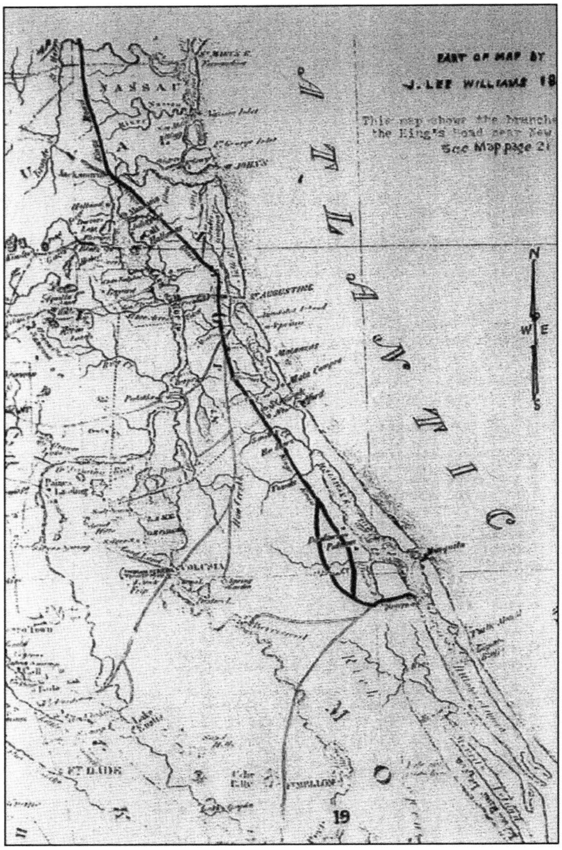

A Map by J. Lee Williams from 1837. This map depicts the branches of the Old Kings Road through present-day Daytona Beach. The Old Kings Road went from St. Augustine to New Smyrna and was originally constructed during the English Period of 1763–1783. At the time it was considered an engineering marvel because of the rivers and marsh crossings. (Courtesy of Port Orange Historical Trust.)

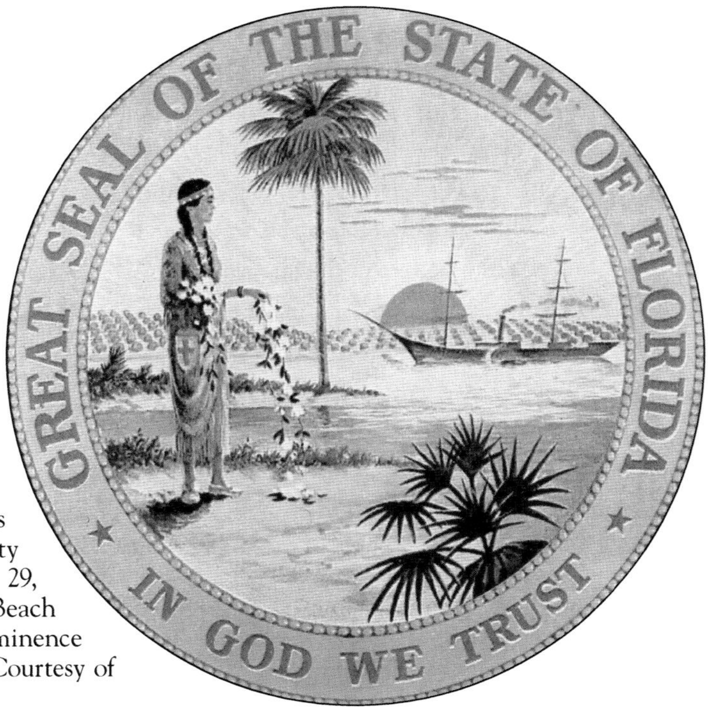

Florida State Seal. Florida gained statehood in 1845, and the territorial days were over. Volusia County came into being December 29, 1854, and today Daytona Beach has gained its rightful prominence in this progressive county. (Courtesy of Florida State Archives.)

THE REVEREND L.D. HUSTON. Huston arrived in Volusia County in 1868. Elected as Daytona's first mayor on July 26, 1876, he was actively involved in community affairs in Daytona and Volusia County. Between 1868 and 1887 he held many positions, including Methodist-Episcopal minister, superintendent of public instruction for Volusia County, county commissioner, and justice of the peace. (Courtesy of Halifax Historical Society.)

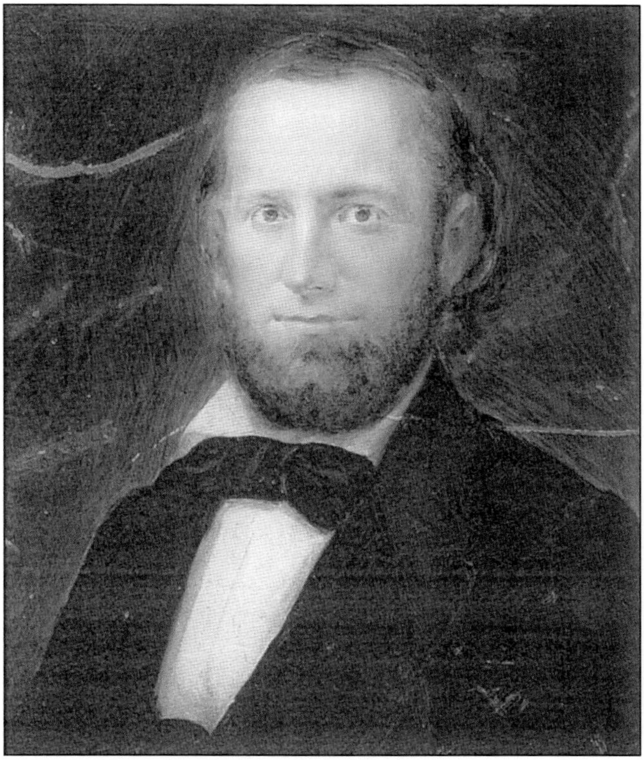

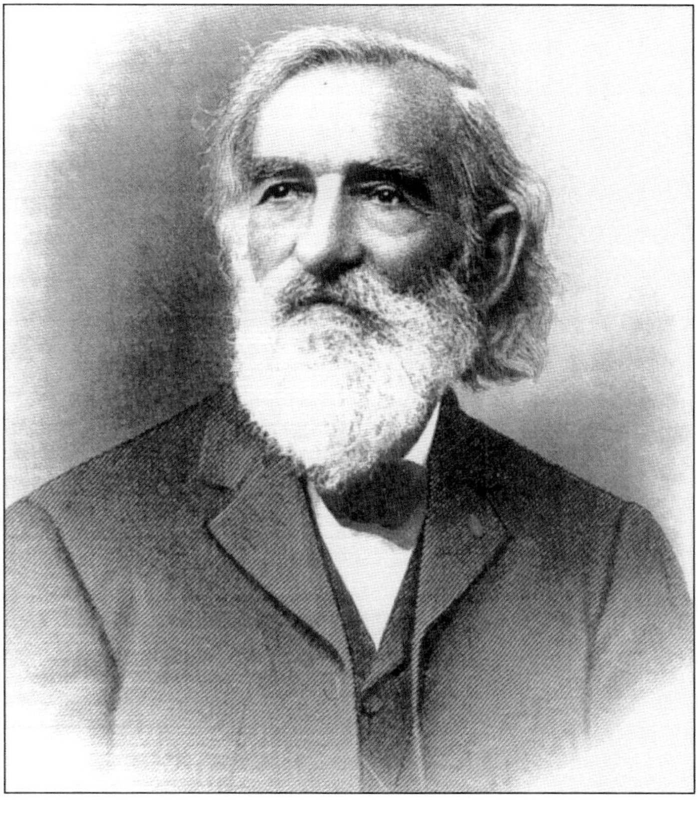

DR. JOHN MILTON HAWKS, 1870. Matthias Day met Dr. Hawks in a Jacksonville hotel in 1870 while Day was looking for a large tract of land on the east coast of Florida to establish a town. Dr. Hawks invited Day to join him on an inspection tour of the old Samuel Williams Plantation on the Halifax River. During their trip aboard the steamboat *Rover*, Matthias Day looked at the shoreline and told Dr. Hawks, "That's just what I've been looking for." (Courtesy of Florida State Archives.)

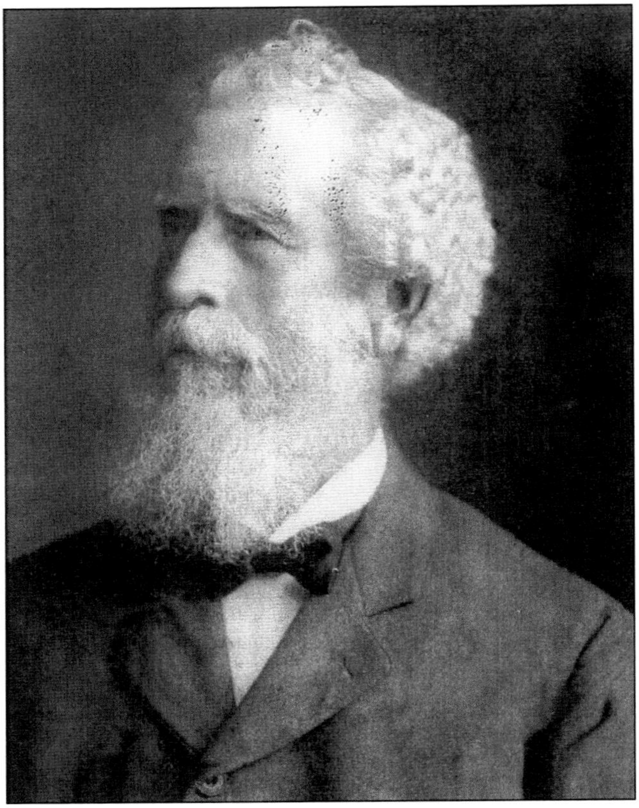

Matthias Day, Founder of Daytona. Day arrived in Florida from Mansfield, Ohio, in 1870. In March 1871 he bought 2,144.5 acres of the old Samuel Williams Plantation from Williams's only daughter, Christina Relf, for $8,000. James H. Fowler was hired to survey the tract and layout lots and streets for this new settlement. In 1872, after building the Palmetto House and several homes, this venture failed. In 1876 the settlement grew and the town was named Daytona in honor of Matthias Day. (Courtesy of Halifax Historical Society.)

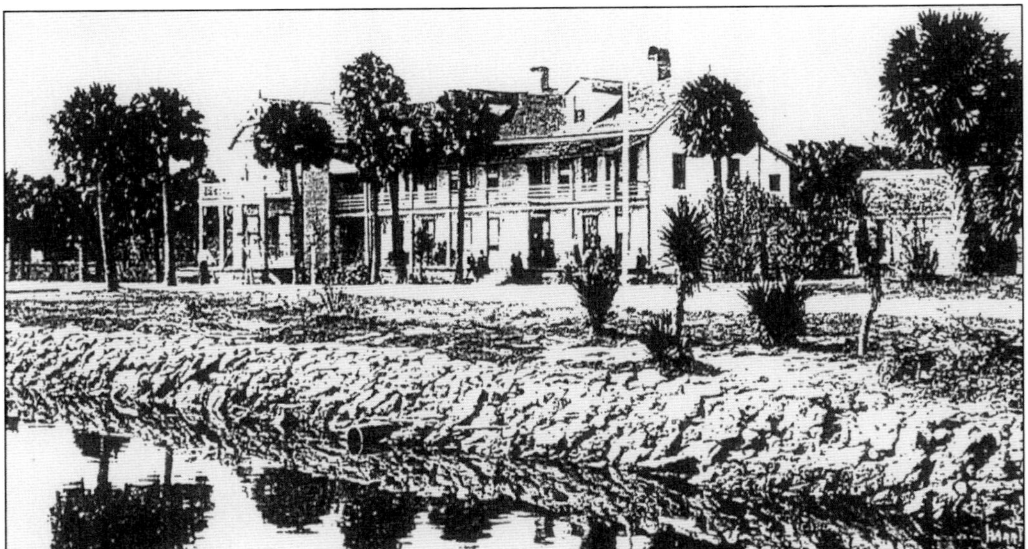

The Palmetto House in 1872. Matthias Day built this hotel, called the Colony House. However, a shipment of roofing shingles failed to arrive, and he decided to temporarily use palm fronds for a thatch roof; hence, the name Palmetto House was coined. The original Palmetto House burned in the early 1920s. (Courtesy of Cardwell Family Collection.)

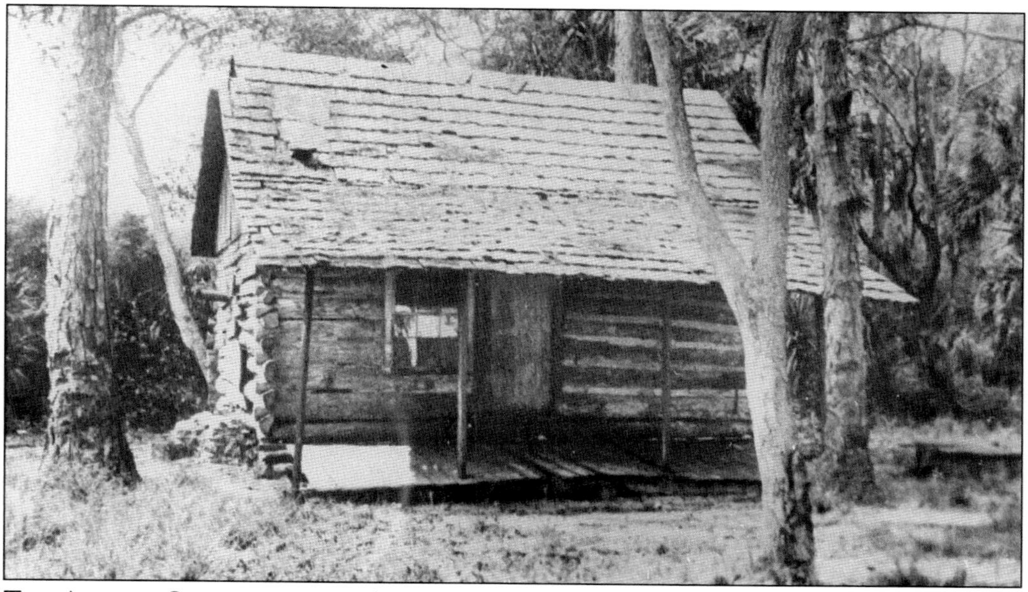

THE ARCHER CABIN IN 1875. This hand-hewn log cabin was one of the first structures on Beach Street. It stood about where 154 South Beach Street is today. The Archer family was one of three different families to live in this structure. Logs were used in building structures until Matthias Day brought a sawmill to South Beach Street, making rough-sawn lumber available to build homes. At first finished materials had to be shipped to Daytona from Jacksonville, Florida, or Savannah, Georgia; after finished lumber was available, the old log structures disappeared. (Courtesy of John Gontner.)

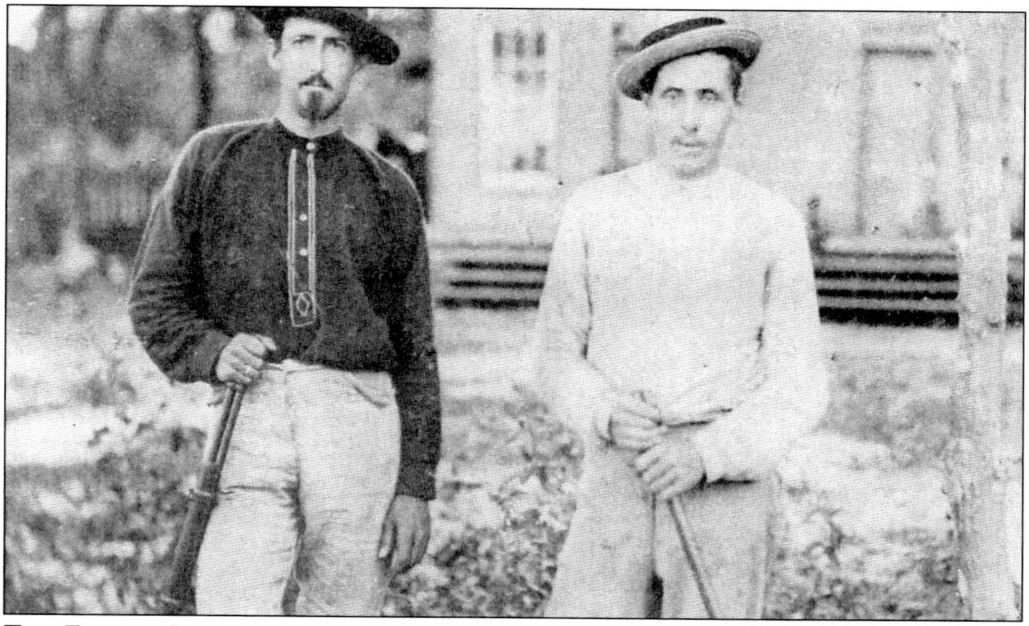

TWO FRIENDS LEAVING ON A HUNTING TRIP C. 1880S. Charles Dougherty, at left, was a lawyer, state representative, and congressman. William Jackson, at right, was a local merchant and a Daytona city councilman who was influential in Volusia County politics. Daytona was incorporated at Jackson's first store. Both men were active in politics from the early 1870s to the early 1900s. (Courtesy of Halifax Historical Society.)

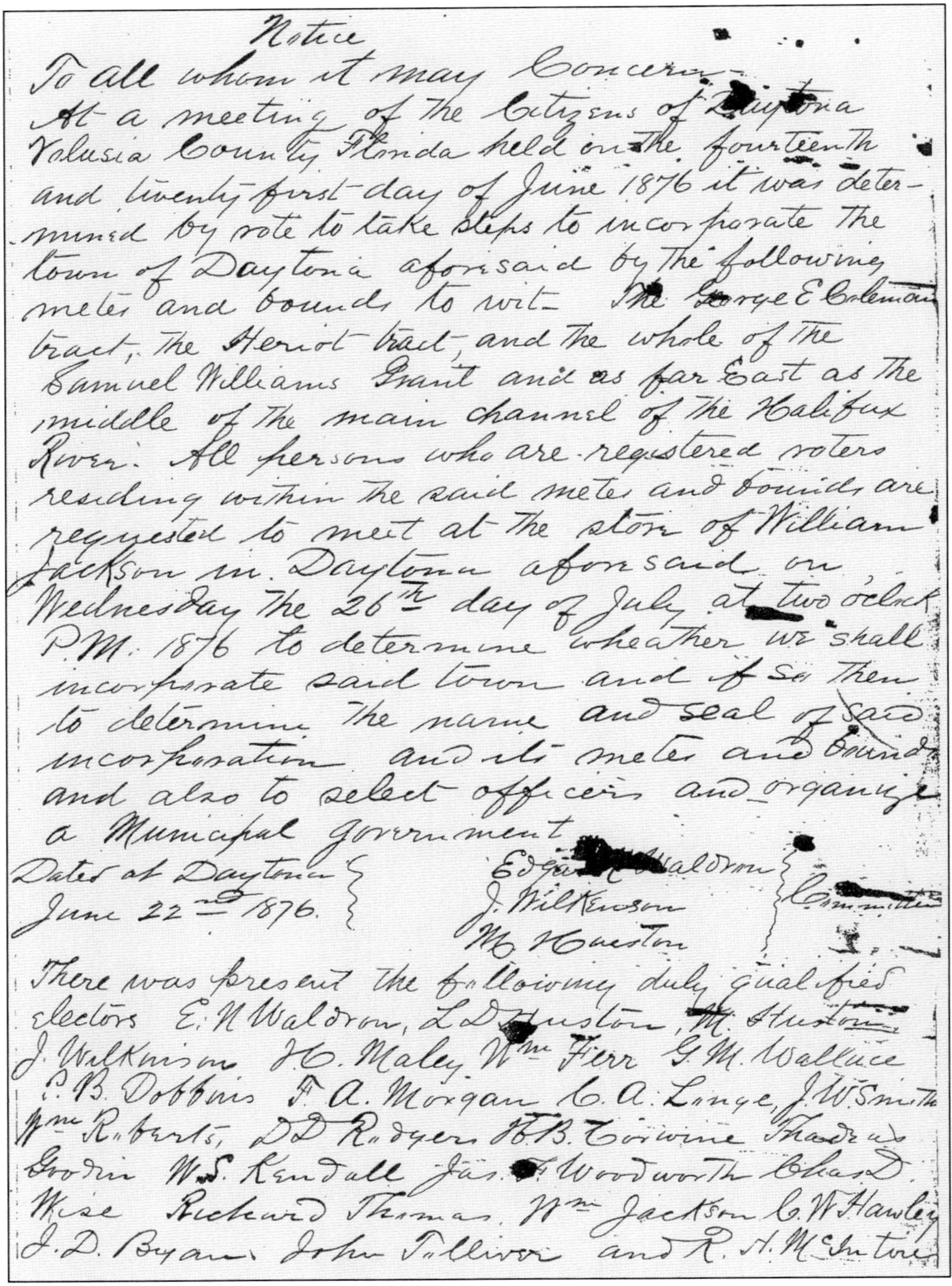

Notice

To all whom it may Concern

At a meeting of the Citizens of Daytona Volusia County Florida held on the fourteenth and twenty first day of June 1876 it was determined by vote to take steps to incorporate the town of Daytona aforsaid by the following metes and bounds to wit— The George E Coleman tract, the Heriot tract, and the whole of the Samuel Williams Grant and as far East as the middle of the main channel of the Halifax River. All persons who are registered voters residing within the said metes and bounds are requested to meet at the store of William Jackson in Daytona aforsaid on Wednesday the 26th day of July at two o'clock P.M. 1876 to determine wheather we shall incorporate said town and if so then to determine the name and seal of said incorporation and its metes and bounds and also to select officers and organize a Municipal government

Dated at Daytona June 22nd 1876.

Edgar [illegible] Waldron
J. Wilkinson
M. Huston
Committee

There was present the following duly qualified electors E. N. Waldron, L. D. Huston, M. Huston, J. Wilkinson, J. C. Maley, Wm Kerr, G. M. Wallace, P. B. Dobbins, F. A. Morgan, C. A. Lange, J. W. Smith, Wm Roberts, D. D. Rodgers, R. B. Corwine, Thadeus Godwin, W. S. Kendall, Jas. F. Woodworth, Chas. D. Wise, Richard Thomas, Wm Jackson, C. W. Hawley, J. D. Bryan, John Tolliver and R. H. McIntire

TOWN MEETING OF THE INCORPORATION OF DAYTONA ON JULY 26, 1876. The Reverend Dr. L.D. Huston was made chairman of the meeting. The town was named Daytona, and a seal was established. There were 25 citizens in attendance, and the vote was 23 for incorporation and 2 against. Rev. L.D. Huston was elected mayor. William Jackson, James Wilkinson, G.R. Puckett, D.D. Rogers, Menefee Huston, John C. Maley, and Dr. G.M. Wallace were elected to the Common Council. Charles E. Jackson was elected town clerk, and J. Bryan was elected marshall. The town was born. (Courtesy of Cardwell Family Collection.)

Two

A Town is Born 1876–1900

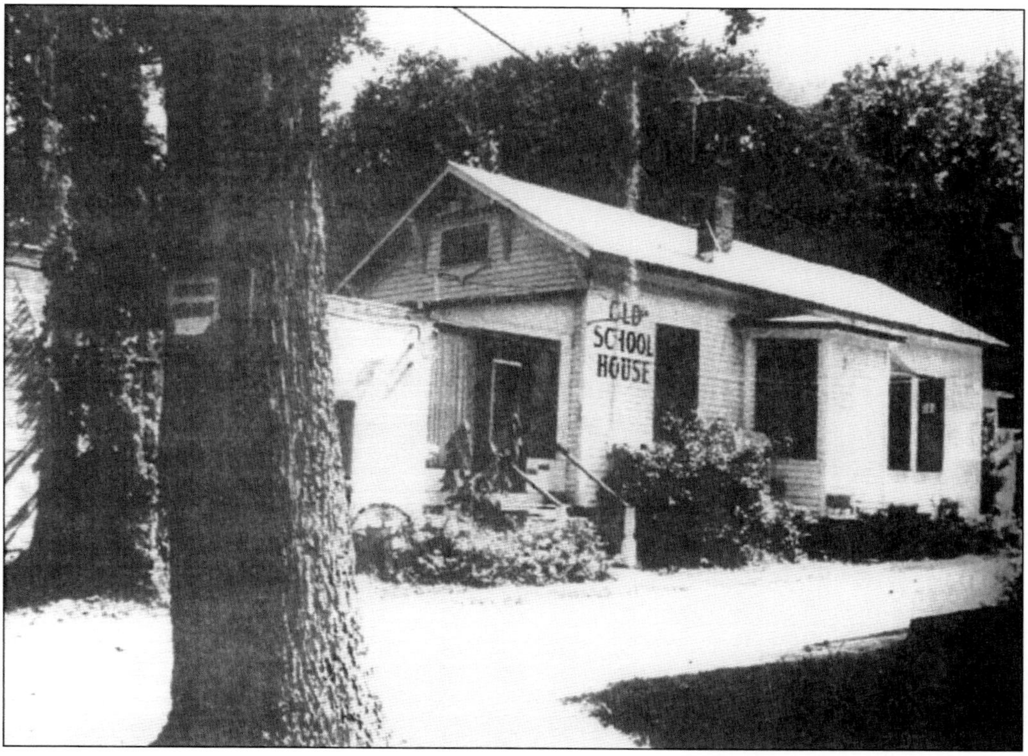

The First Public School, 1876. This "Old School House" had many uses; mainly it was used by an early prominent church. The building was constructed of hard pine with a shingle roof. For many years the school bell hanger was visible on the north gable. The old school house was later adapted to an office, apartment, and business, and sadly met its demise c.1990. The old school was located at 220 South Palmetto Avenue. (Courtesy of Halifax Historical Society.)

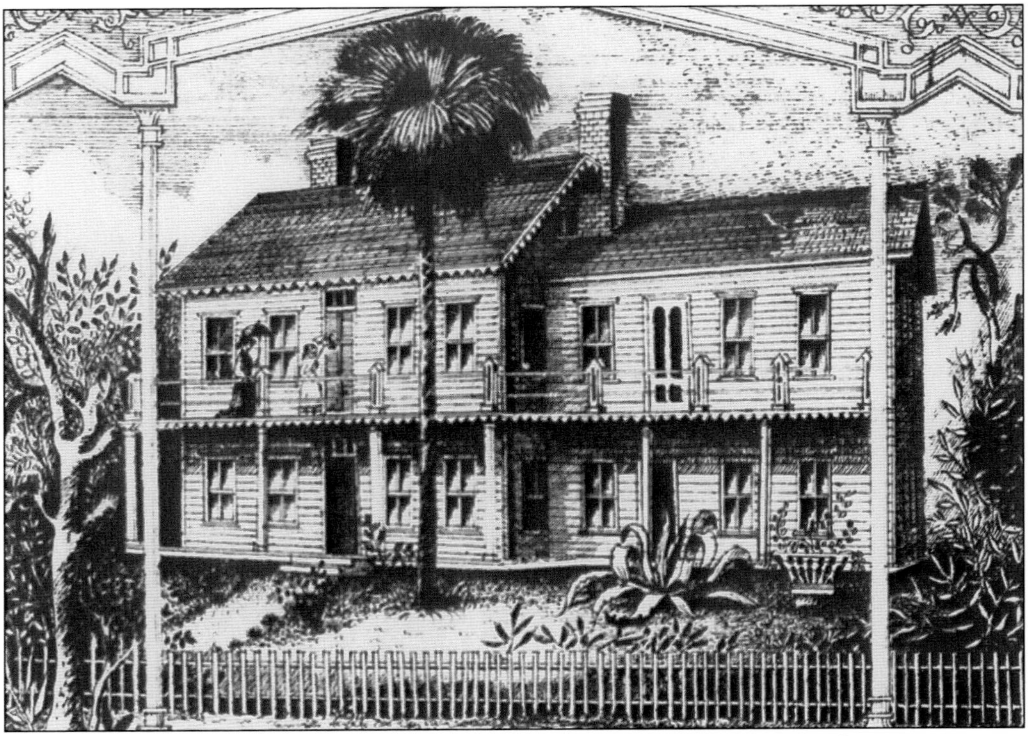

DAYTONA INSTITUTE FOR YOUNG LADIES, 1880. Miss Lucy A. Cross, a former instructor at Wellesley College in Massachusetts, opened this institute, the first of its kind south of St. Augustine. She operated the school for almost 20 years in this building at 440 South Beach Street. Around 1904 this building was demolished, and a new, coquina-stone structure was built by Sumner Hale Gove for Peter J. Seims. (Courtesy of Florida State Archives.)

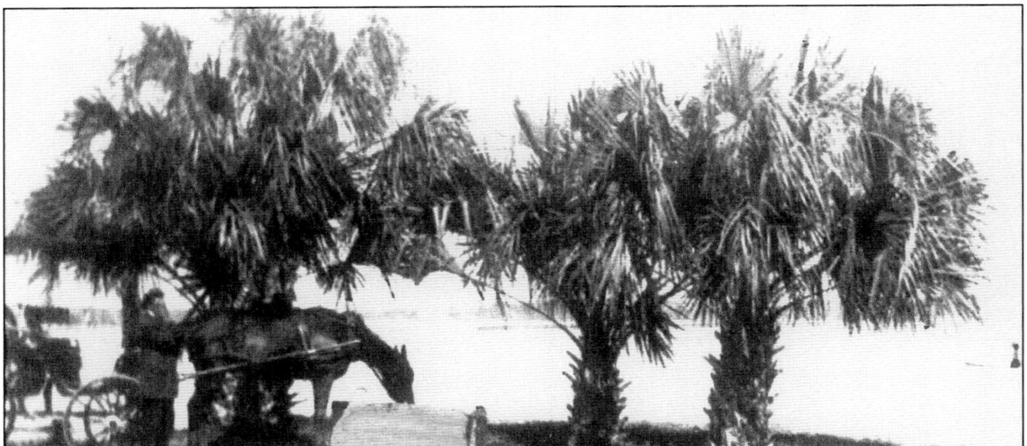

THE ARTESIAN WELL, C. 1877. This artesian well was drilled in front of William Jackson's first store on the Halifax riverfront. The well flowed into a trough for use by oxen and horses. As the first available drinking water for the community, it flowed until c. 1947, when it was capped for Beach Street improvements. (Courtesy of Cardwell Family Collection.)

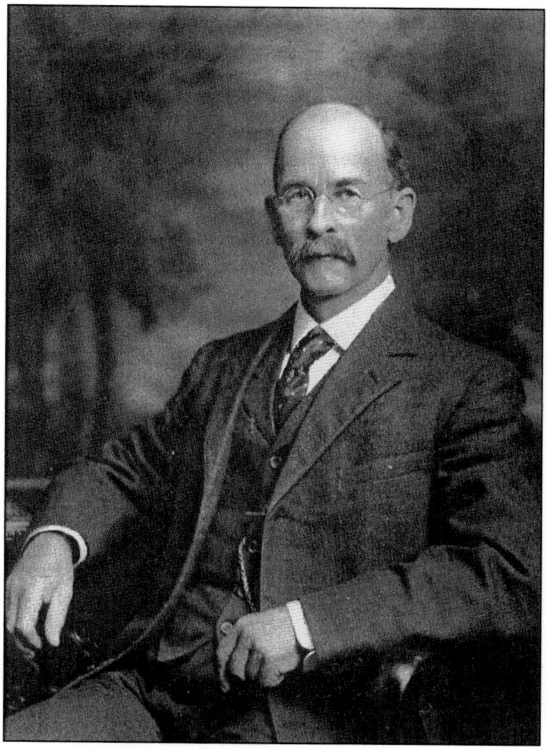

LAURENCE THOMPSON, 1848–1920. Mr. Thompson came to the area in 1875 and soon made a name for himself. When C.E. Jackson failed to perform his duties as town clerk, Thompson was appointed to take his place by the town council. Later he was elected to the council and served several terms. He operated the Thompson Brothers store at 426 South Beach Street, and in 1901 he established the real-estate and insurance firm of Bingham and Thompson. His home, Lilian Place, still stands at 111 Silver Beach Avenue. (Courtesy of Cardwell Family Collection.)

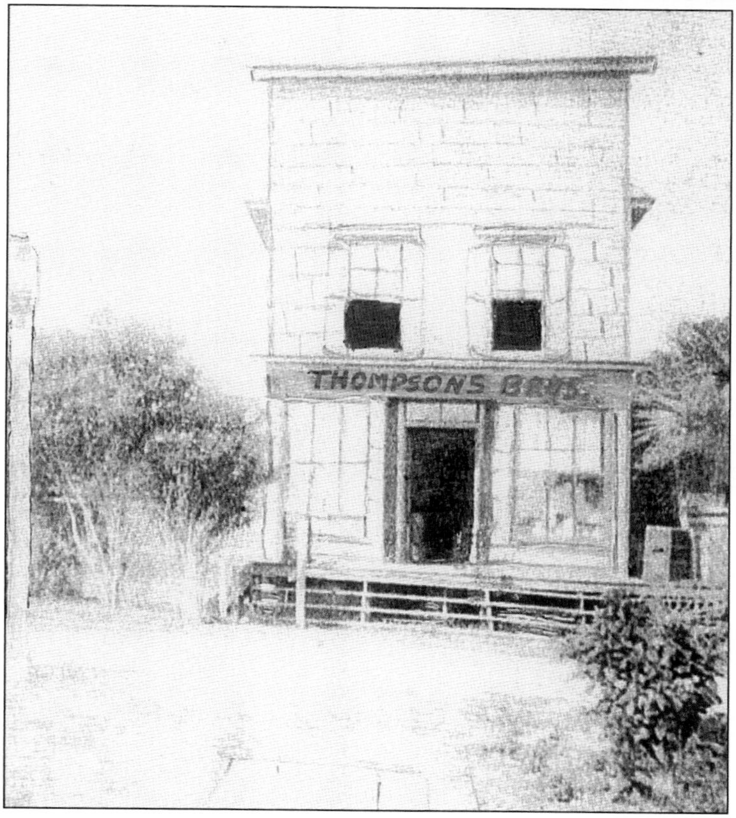

THOMPSON BROTHERS STORE C. 1879. Laurence and Graham Thompson operated this store at 426 South Beach Street for several years. Later, Graham Thompson took over sole proprietorship of the store. The store was later renovated as the winter home of playwright and author Harrison Garfield Rhodes. In the late 1970s Dr. William Doremus moved into the Rhodes home and lived there until his death in 2002. (Courtesy of Cardwell Family Collection.)

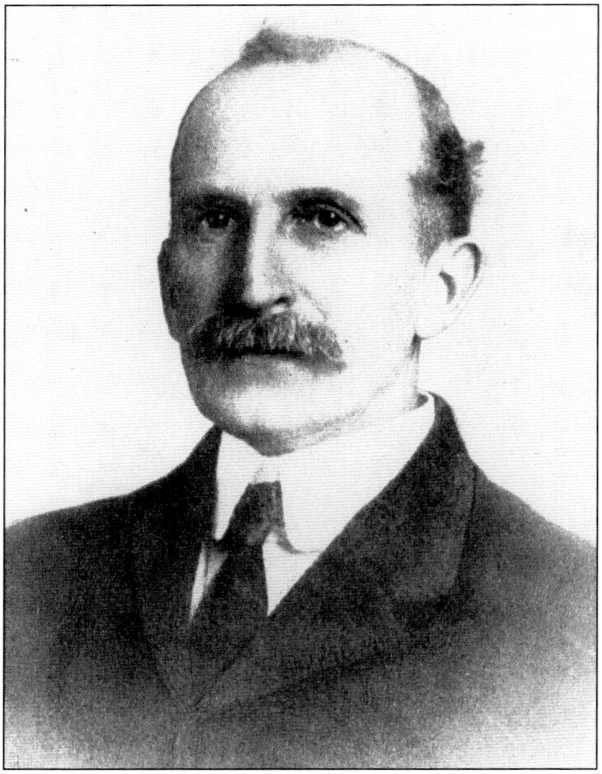

DAVID D. ROGERS, 1850–1919. D.D. Rogers came to this settlement before it was named Daytona. He was among the 25 who incorporated the town of Daytona on July 26, 1876. A civil engineer, he surveyed many tracts of land and laid out subdivisions in Daytona, Seabreeze, and Daytona Beach. His children were C.M. Rogers, a civil engineer; Dr. Mary Josie Rogers, a physician; Mable T. Rogers; and W.D. Rogers. He was truly one of Daytona's town fathers. (Courtesy of Cardwell Family Collection.)

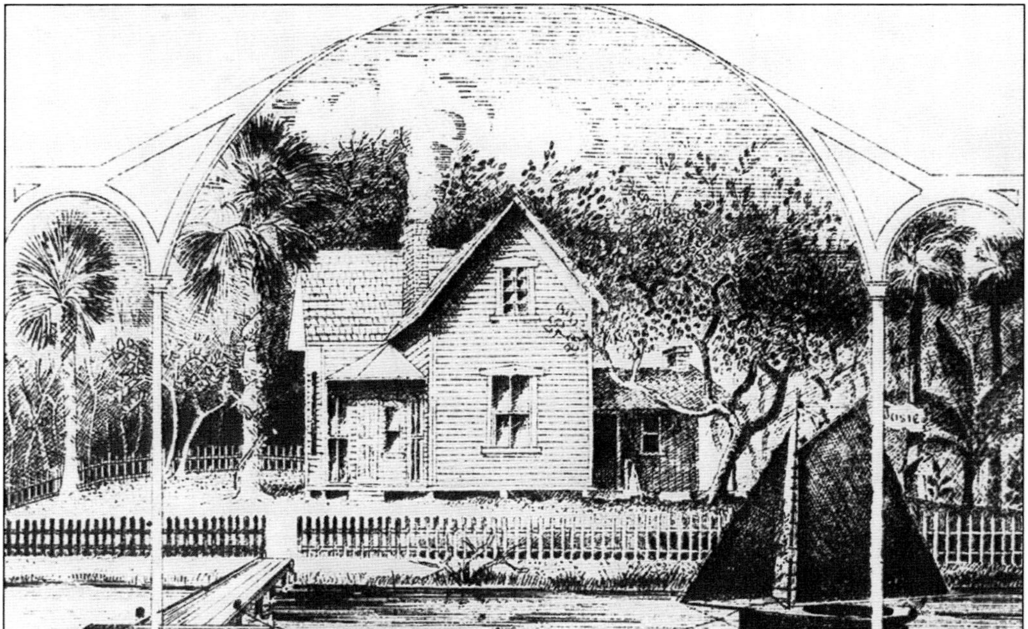

D.D. ROGERS'S HOME ON BEACH STREET C. 1904. This riverfront home was built in 1878 and was moved in 1919 from the Halifax riverfront on the east side of Beach Street to Michigan Avenue and Beach Street. Dr. Josie Rogers, D.D. Rogers's daughter, made her home in this building and also practiced medicine here. (Courtesy of Florida State Archives.)

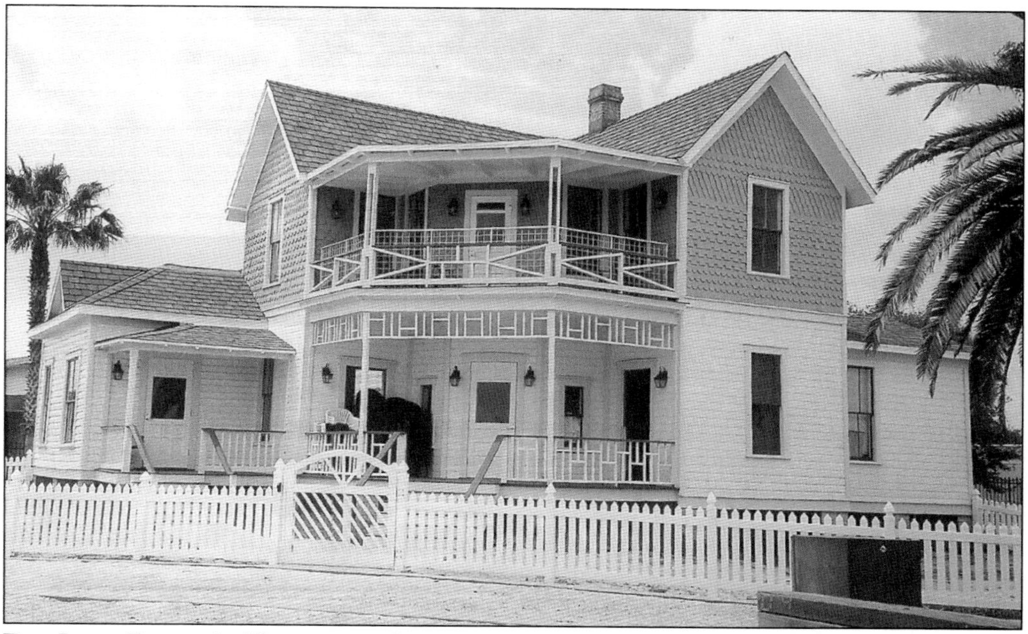

DR. JOSIE ROGERS'S HOME AND OFFICE C. 1904. In 2003 this building was moved from Michigan Avenue and Beach Street back to the riverfront near the site where it was originally located. The City of Daytona Beach completely restored this historic home and office. The re-adaptive use is for a city police office, gift shop, Daytona Partnership office, and a restored period medical waiting room. (Courtesy of Cardwell Family Collection.)

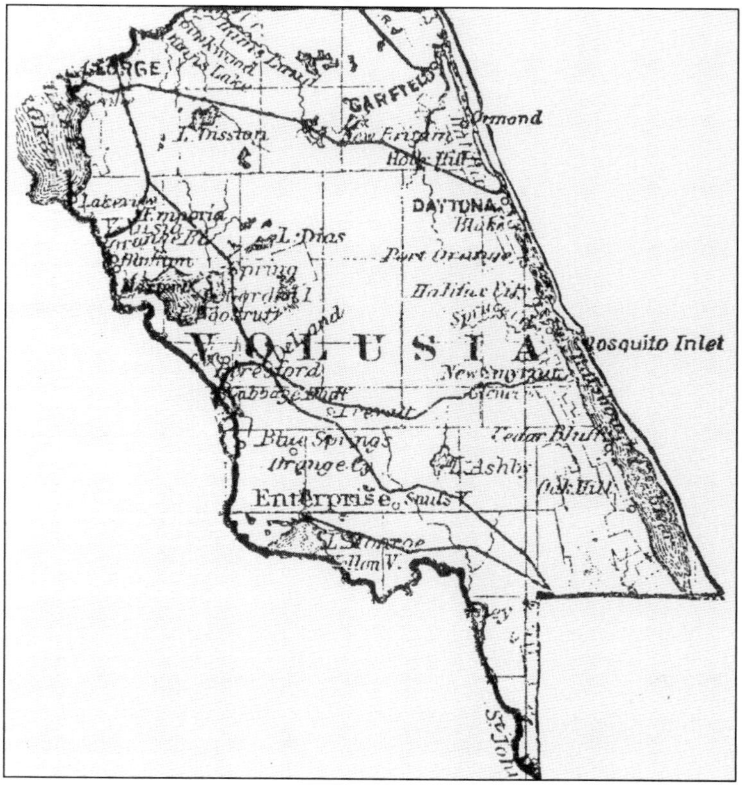

A MAP OF VOLUSIA COUNTY IN 1885. This map depicts early Volusia County from Ormond to Oak Hill on the east coast of Florida. Note the small settlements that are listed. Many have disappeared over time, but Daytona has stood the test of time. (Courtesy of Cardwell Family Collection.)

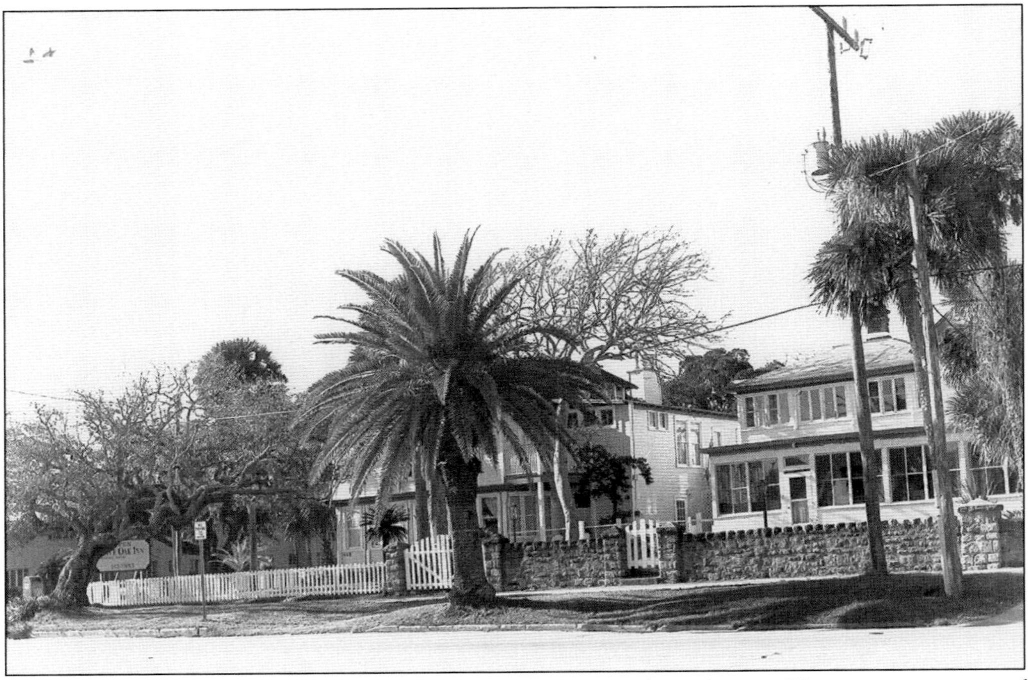

LIVE OAK INN IN 1994. This structure is a combination of two homes. The restaurant part of this bed-and-breakfast was built in 1881, but the rear portion was built in 1871. According to a Historic Property Associates survey, this is the oldest wood structure still standing in Daytona Beach. The combined bed-and-breakfast is known historically as the Riley Peck property. (Courtesy of John Gontner.)

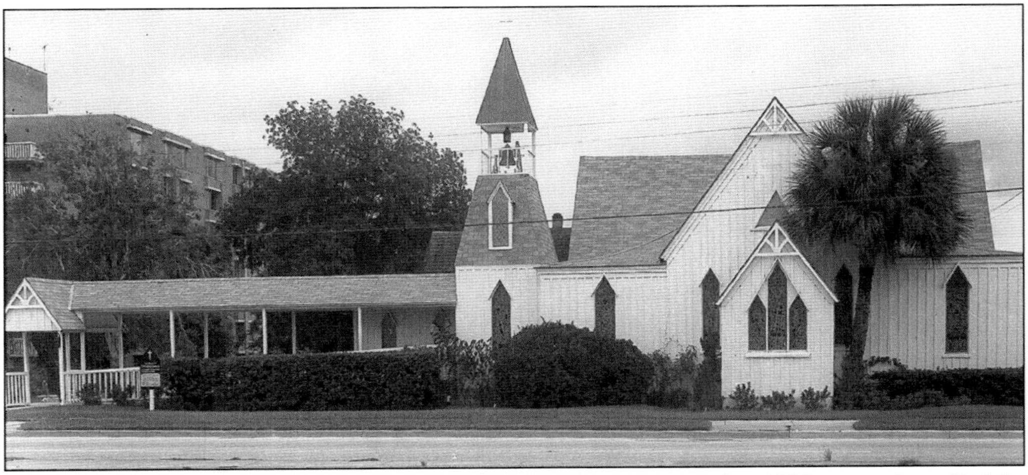

ST. MARY'S EPISCOPAL CHURCH IN 1976. This church, constructed in 1883, was to be called St. Mark's Episcopal Church. However, when the cornerstone arrived, it read, "St. Mary's Episcopal Church." When ordering building supplies, it often took months because everything had to come in by steamboat. The congregation decided to keep the cornerstone because it would cause too long of a delay in construction, and renaming the church was the easiest solution. (Courtesy of John Gontner.)

EDWARD G. HARRIS, AN EARLY PIONEER PHOTOGRAPHER WHO BROUGHT HIS FAMILY TO HOLLY HILL IN 1883. Harris operated a studio at 300 South Beach Street until 1906. His early photographs, especially the photographs of early racecars, are still used today in magazines and journals. He died in 1938. (Courtesy of Halifax Historical Society.)

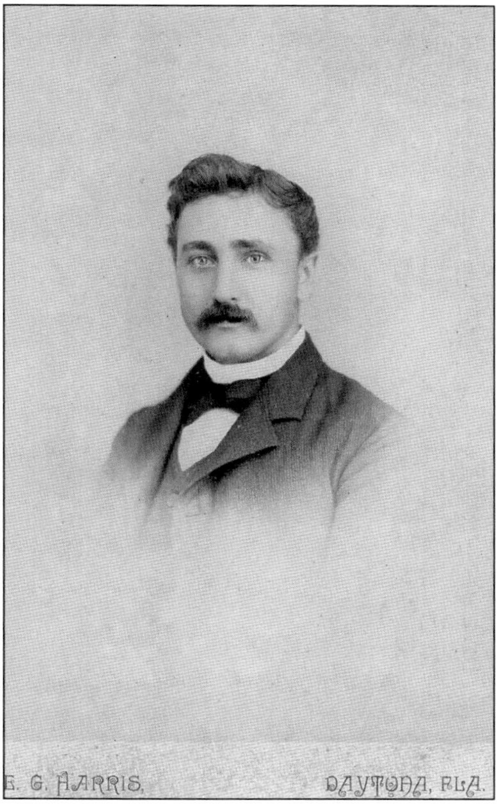

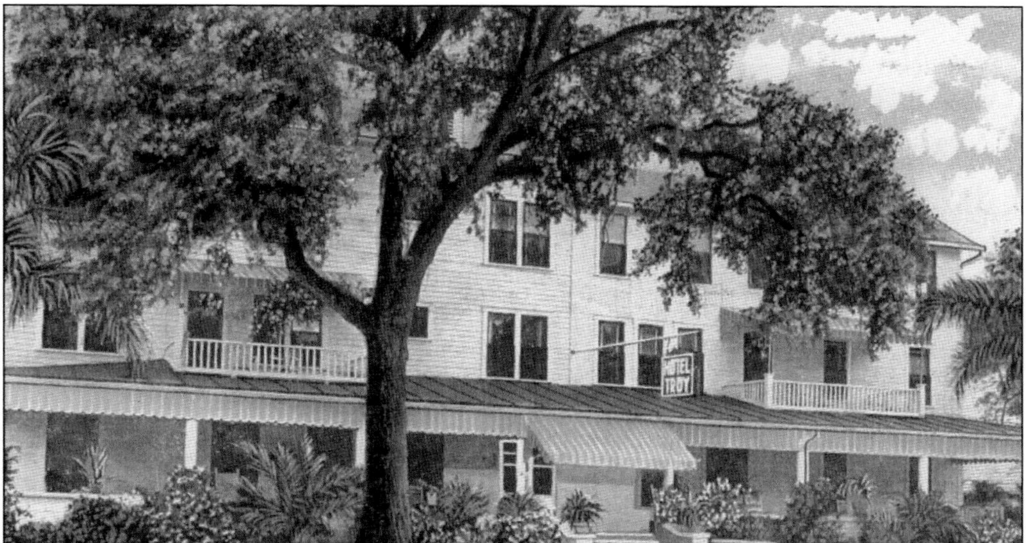

HOTEL TROY IN 1885. William and Mary Troy built this hotel from earnings William received from grafting citrus trees and selling them to many successful citrus-grove owners. This hotel was a favorite place for tourists to stay because of its central location on Volusia Avenue, now 217 West International Speedway Boulevard. (Courtesy of Cardwell Family Collection.)

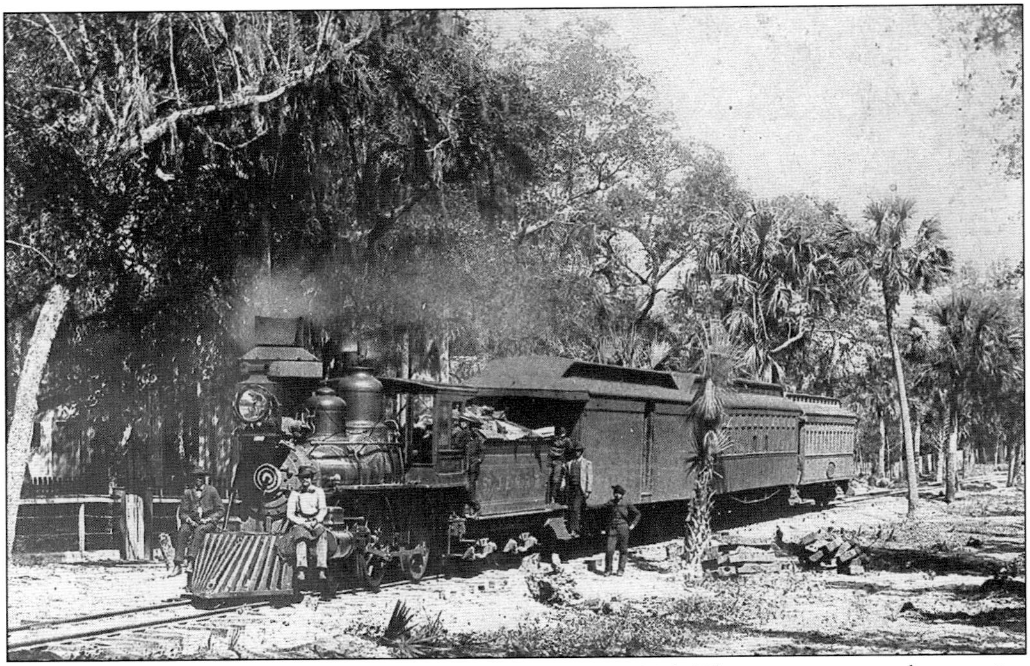

First Train to Arrive in Daytona, December 2, 1886. This narrow-gauge locomotive was named *Bulow*. In 1888 Henry Flagler bought the railroad from St. Johns and Halifax River Railway Company and replaced the narrow-gauge track with standard gauge. This allowed trains to travel all the way to New York without having to change to narrow-gauge equipment. It was reported that when the railroad arrived, citizens went to church to give thanks for the railroad giving them a way to travel to the North. It would also open up markets for produce and citrus. (Courtesy of Florida State Archives.)

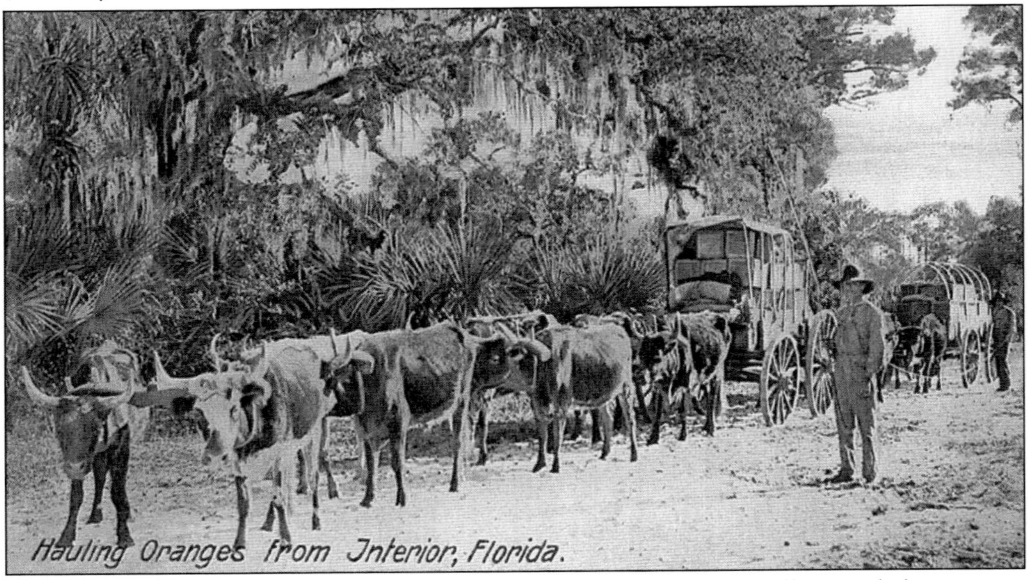

Ox-Drawn, Four-Wheeled Covered Wagons. Teams of oxen pull citrus-laden wagons to the railhead in 1888 for the Northern market. Henry Flagler built his railroad south from Daytona in 1892. Eventually the railroad reached Miami and Key West. (Courtesy of Cardwell Family Collection.)

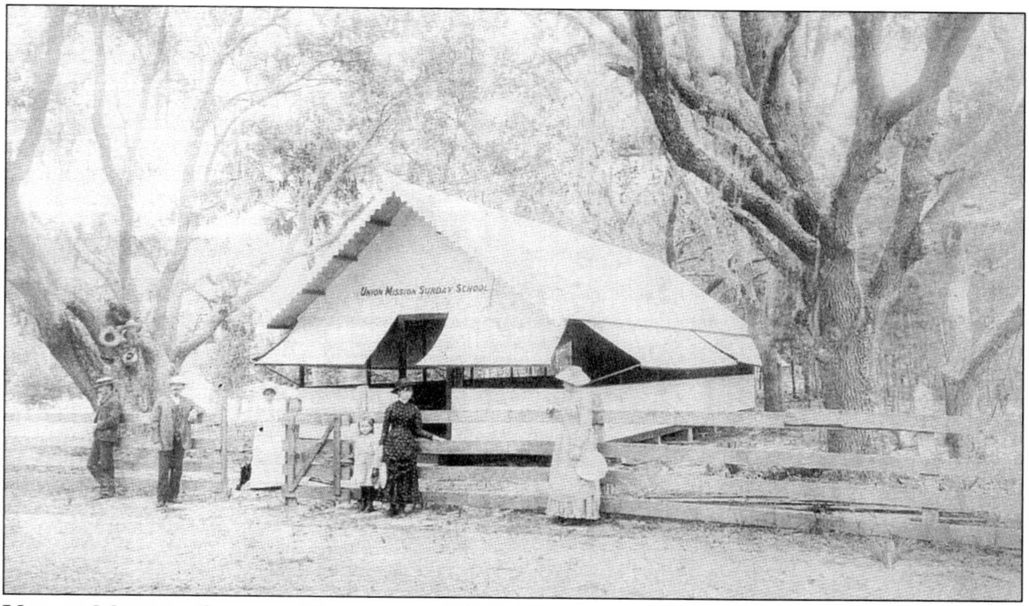

Union Mission Sunday School in 1887. This rare and unusual photograph, taken by E.G. Harris, shows the early construction of the Tabernacle, located on the north side of Fairview Avenue just east of Ridgewood Avenue. Mrs. M.A. Rogers (far right) and other unidentified people are gathered at the Union Mission Sunday School. (Courtesy of Halifax Historical Society.)

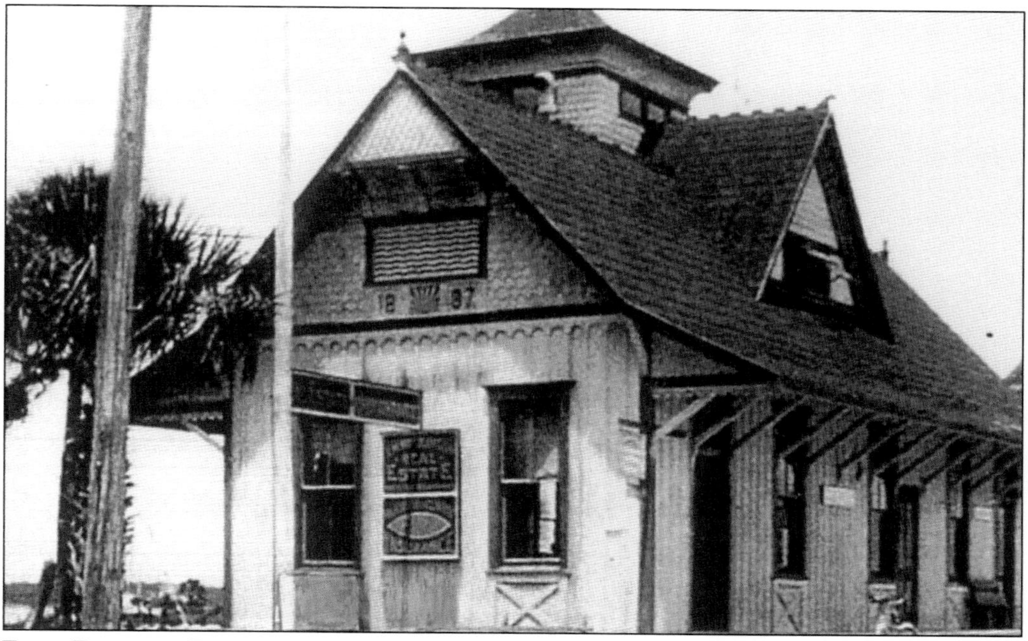

First Daytona Railway Depot, 1887. The railroad was constructed to Daytona in 1886 and had an extension that ran down the middle of Orange Avenue to the Halifax River, where Henry Flagler built a deep-water dock for steamboats. The depot, built on the corner of Orange Avenue and Beach Street, was turned over to the City in 1896 and used as the city hall and a fire station until 1920. After 1896 the depot was located between Magnolia and Volusia Avenues, where the present Florida East Coast Railroad is today. (Courtesy of Cardwell Family Collection.)

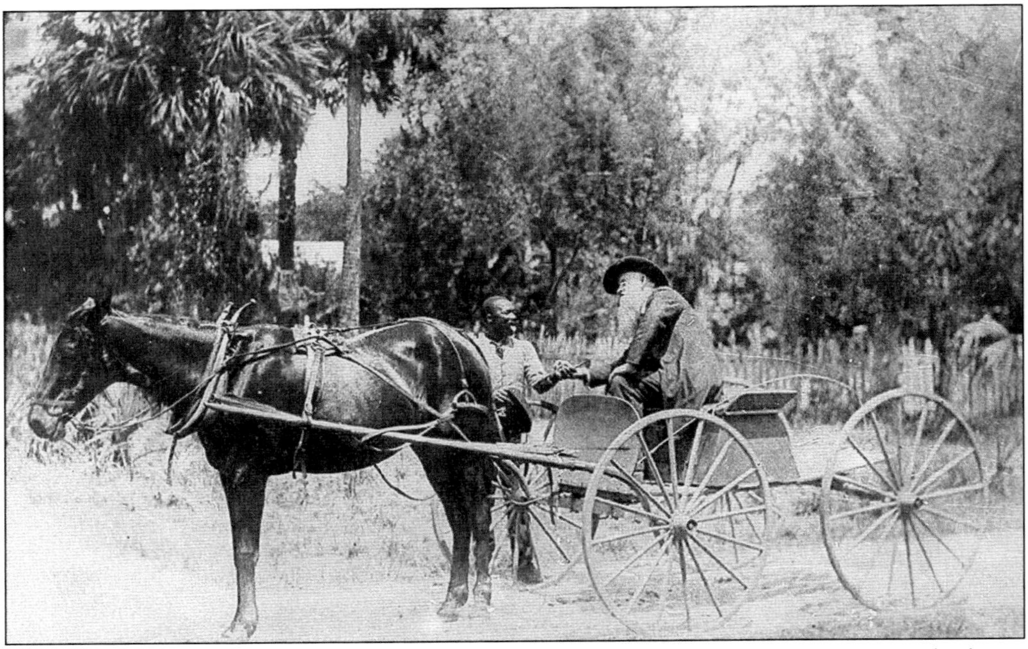

Dr. George M. Wallace c. 1900. This local physician went to see his patients by horse and buggy and often accepted vegetables and poultry as payment for services rendered. He was elected mayor on May 30, 1877, when Rev. L.D. Huston resigned after one year. Dr. Wallace remained mayor until 1887. (Courtesy of John Gontner.)

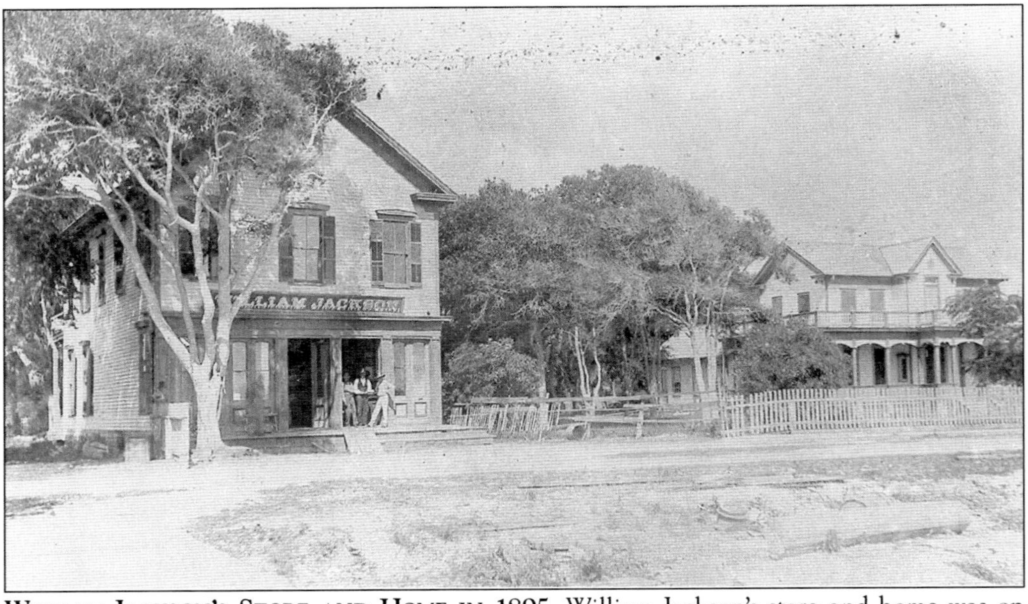

William Jackson's Store and Home in 1895. William Jackson's store and home was on South Beach Street between Orange Avenue and Cottage Lane facing the Halifax riverfront. Many town meetings were held in the hall above the store. Today the Florida Court of Appeals stands on the original site at 300 South Beach Street. This was Jackson's new store and second location, opening in 1880. (Courtesy of John Gontner).

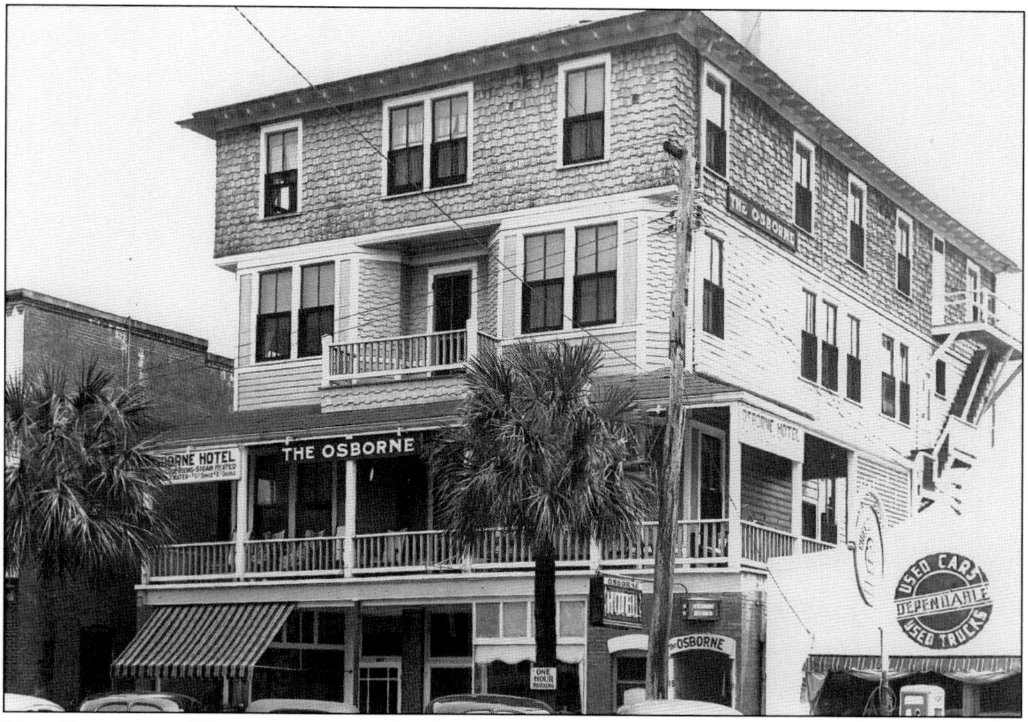

The Osbourne Hotel in 1896. This historic hotel opened as the European House. In 1898 two more floors were added, with shops on the street level, and the name changed to the Osborne in honor of the owner, Joseph Osborne. This old hotel, located at 115 Orange Avenue, met its demise in the mid-1940s. This picture was taken in 1940. (Courtesy of Cardwell Family Collection.)

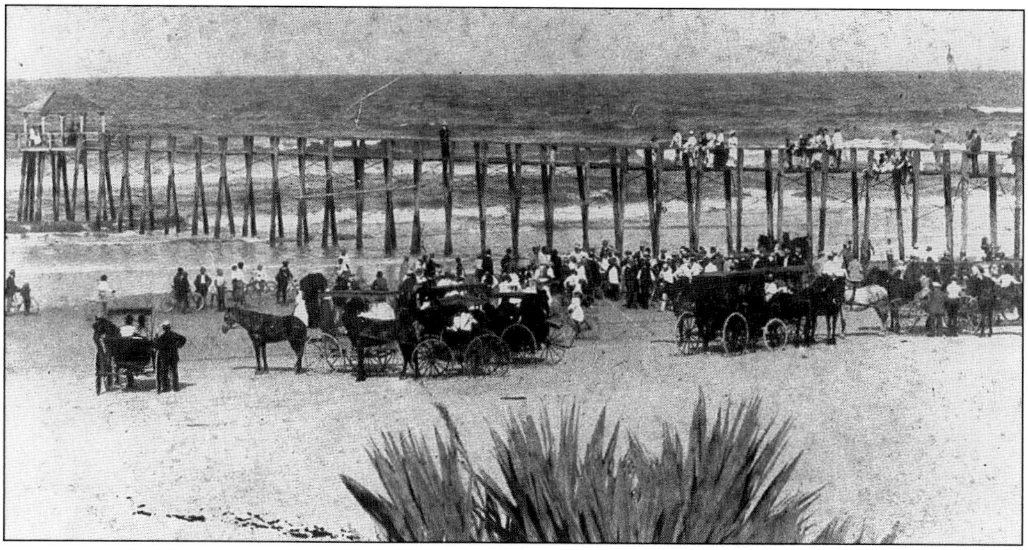

Beachgoers at the Ocean Pier in 1896. Visitors gather at the old Ocean Pier. The mode of transportation was horse and carriage, and the bicycle was a secondary type of transportation. Some appear to be overdressed for the beach. Wool suits and derbies may not be the proper attire for strolling on the beach. (Courtesy of John Gontner.)

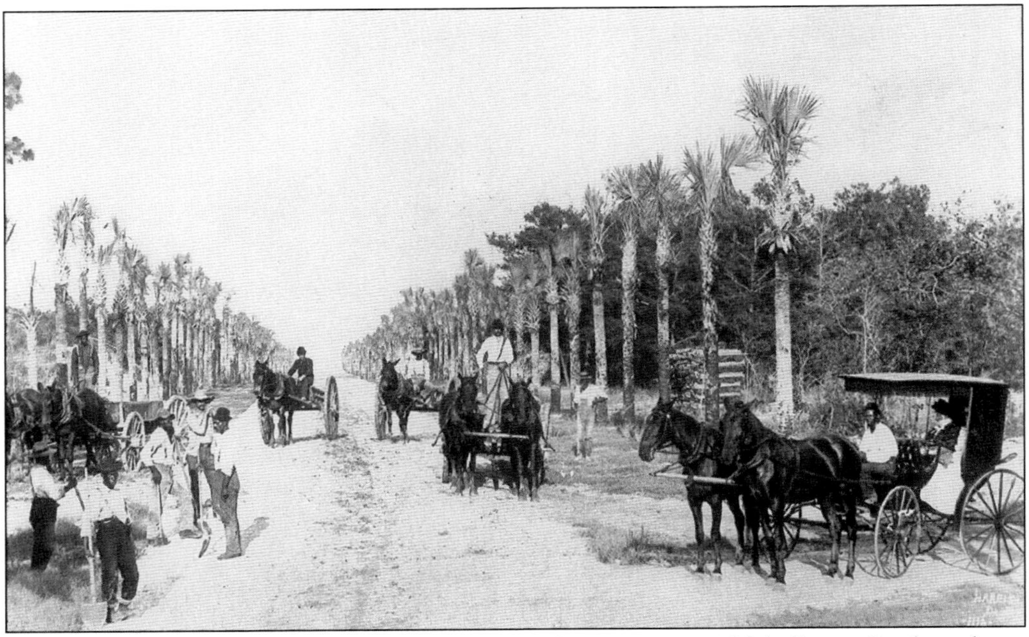

AN EARLY PICTURE OF OCEAN BOULEVARD IN SEABREEZE C. 1896. Ocean Boulevard was undeveloped in the late 1890s, before the name was changed to Seabreeze Boulevard. By the turn of the century, new homes, hotels, and an opera house were built. This was the fashionable section on the peninsula known as the town of Seabreeze. In 1926 Seabreeze became a part of Daytona Beach, along with Daytona and Daytona Beach. Workmen can be seen in the left foreground posing for this picture. (Courtesy of Florida State Archives.)

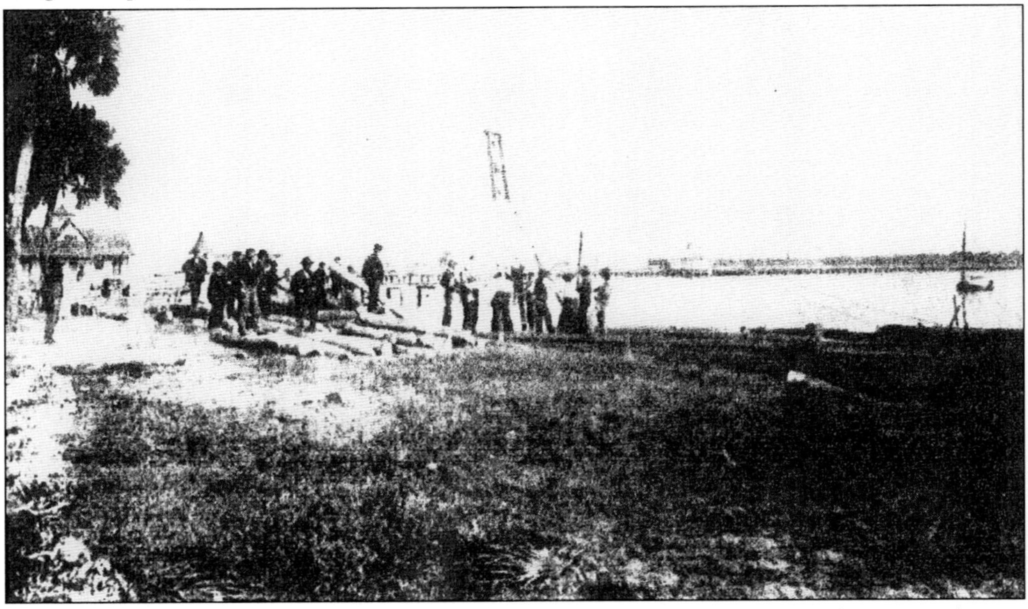

THE HALIFAX RIVER YACHT CLUB UNDER CONSTRUCTION IN 1896. Workmen are driving the first piling for the clubhouse. The historic building, listed on the National Register of Historic Places, is in the Beach Street Historic District on the river. In the left background, the first railroad depot is visible. When the Florida East Coast (FEC) Railway vacated the depot building, it became the first city hall and a fire station. (Courtesy of Florida State Archives.)

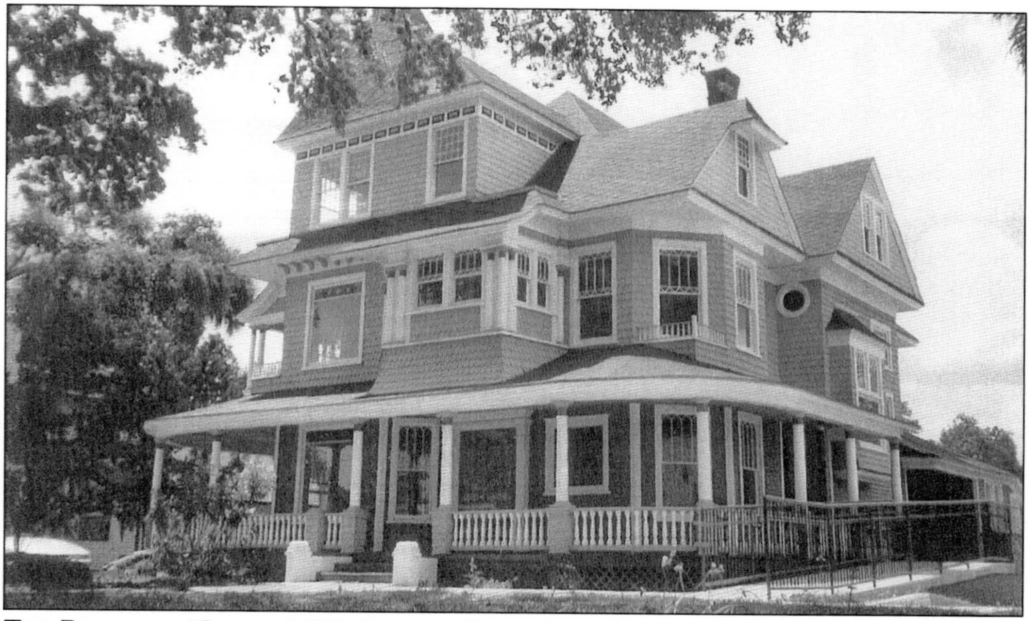

THE BLODGETT HOUSE, 1896. This excellent, Queen Anne–style home was built by Delos A. Blodgett (1825–1908). He was a wealthy lumber and furniture manufacturer from Oswego County, New York. In 1908 the Blodgett House was moved from the north side of Live Oak Street to its present site at 404 Ridgewood Avenue, on the southwest corner of Ridgewood Avenue and Live Oak Street. This restored adaptive-use building is currently the offices of ACT, Inc. Administrative Services. This photo was taken in 2003. (Courtesy of Halifax Historical Society.)

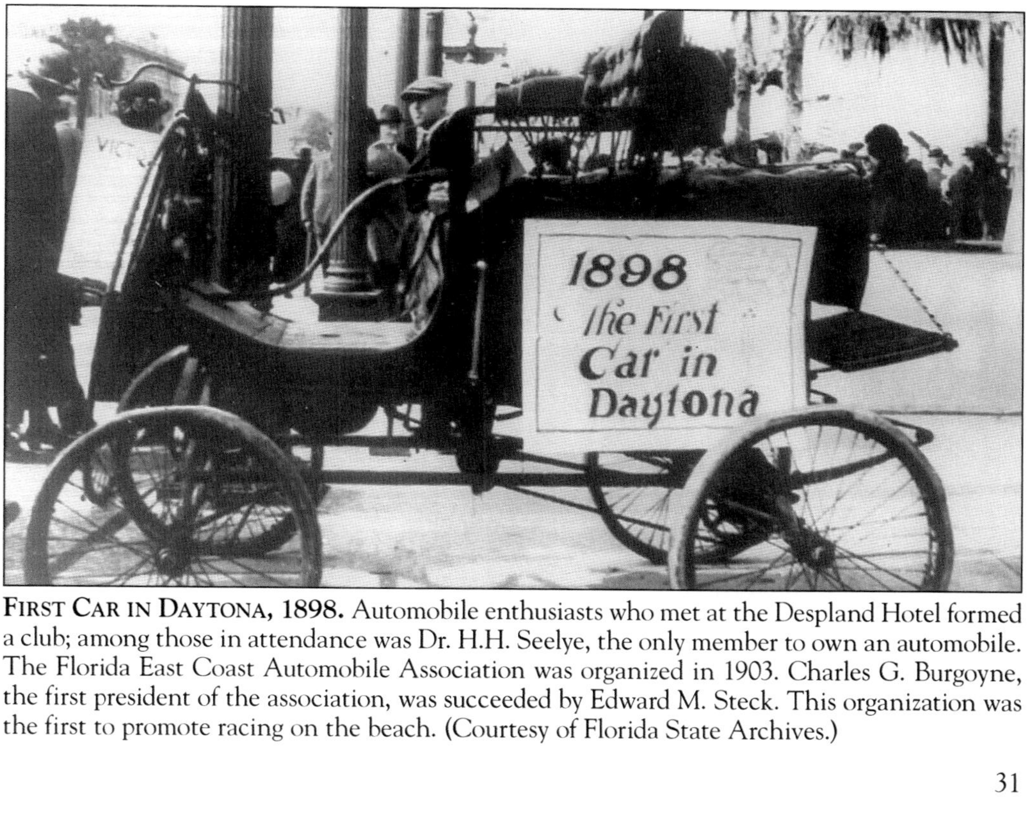

FIRST CAR IN DAYTONA, 1898. Automobile enthusiasts who met at the Despland Hotel formed a club; among those in attendance was Dr. H.H. Seelye, the only member to own an automobile. The Florida East Coast Automobile Association was organized in 1903. Charles G. Burgoyne, the first president of the association, was succeeded by Edward M. Steck. This organization was the first to promote racing on the beach. (Courtesy of Florida State Archives.)

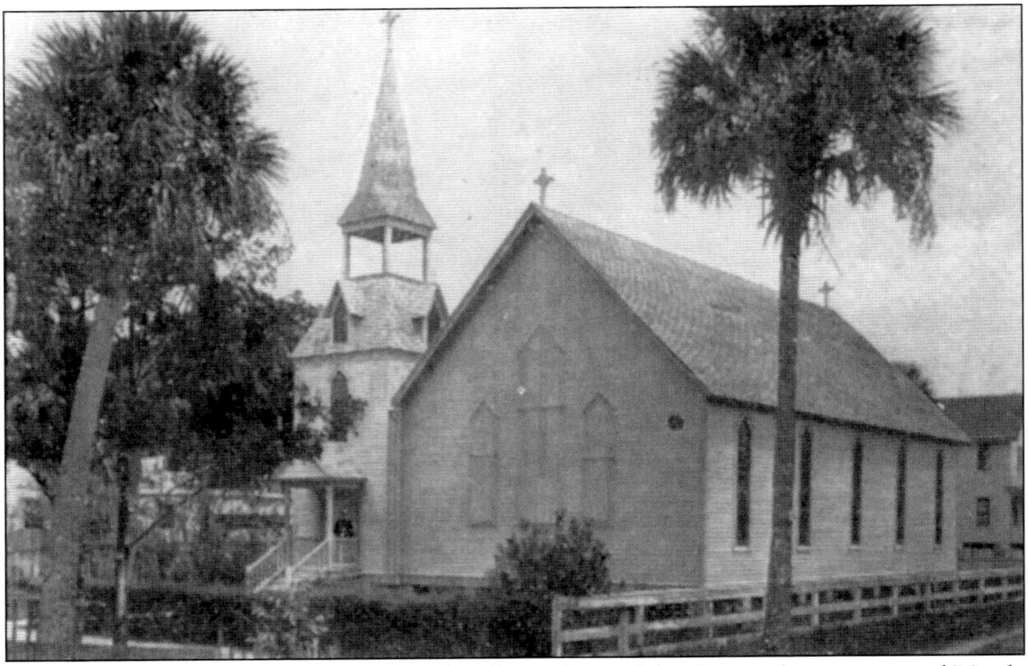

THE CATHOLIC CHURCH, 1900. This church was located on the northeast corner of Myrtle Lane and Palmetto Avenue. Father O'Boyle, a missionary priest, first held services in the old armory on the northeast corner of Palmetto and Volusia Avenues. When the church was built in 1900, he moved into this new sanctuary, where he held services for many years. When St. Paul's Catholic Church was built in 1927, the American Legion acquired the old building for their meeting hall. They used it until World War II. (Courtesy of Cardwell Family Collection.)

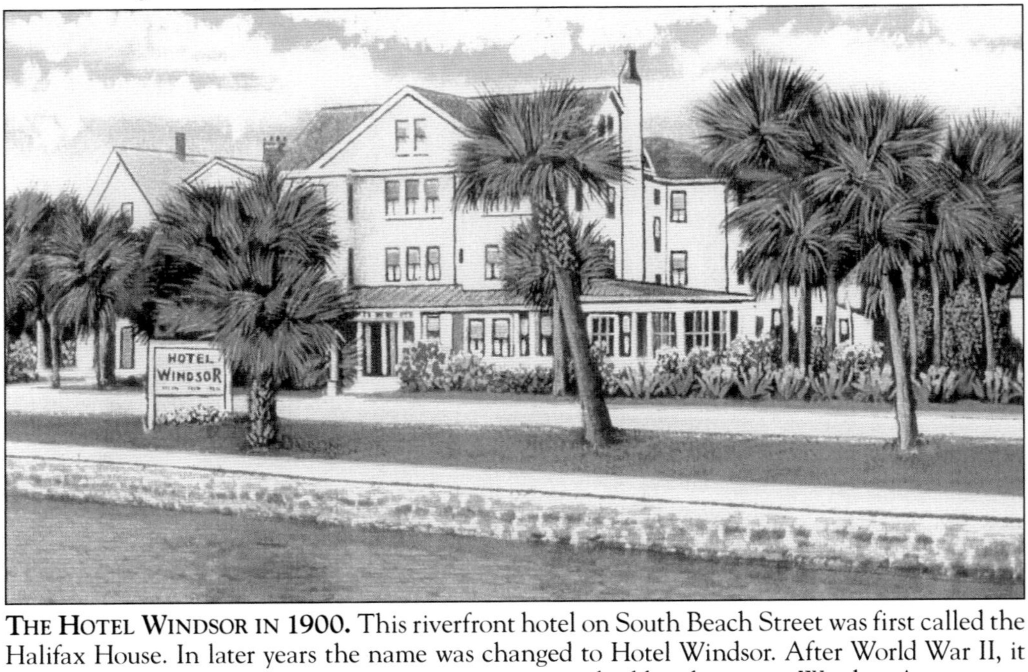

THE HOTEL WINDSOR IN 1900. This riverfront hotel on South Beach Street was first called the Halifax House. In later years the name was changed to Hotel Windsor. After World War II, it was demolished, and a retired senior-citizens apartment building known as Windsor Apartments stands there today. (Courtesy of Cardwell Family Collection.)

Three

TRANSPORTATION AND INDUSTRY 1901–1911

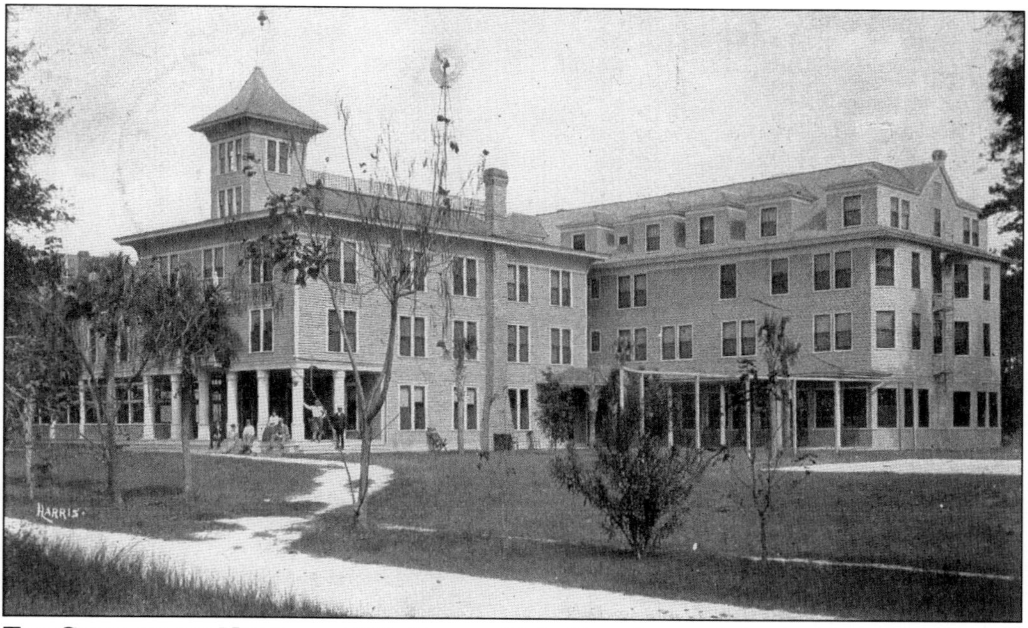

THE COLONNADES HOTEL IN 1901. Sumner Hale Gove designed this building, located near Seabreeze Boulevard and Halifax Drive. It had 125 rooms with steam heat and electricity. The proprietor was C.C. Post. This structure burned down in 1909. (Courtesy of Cardwell Family Collection.)

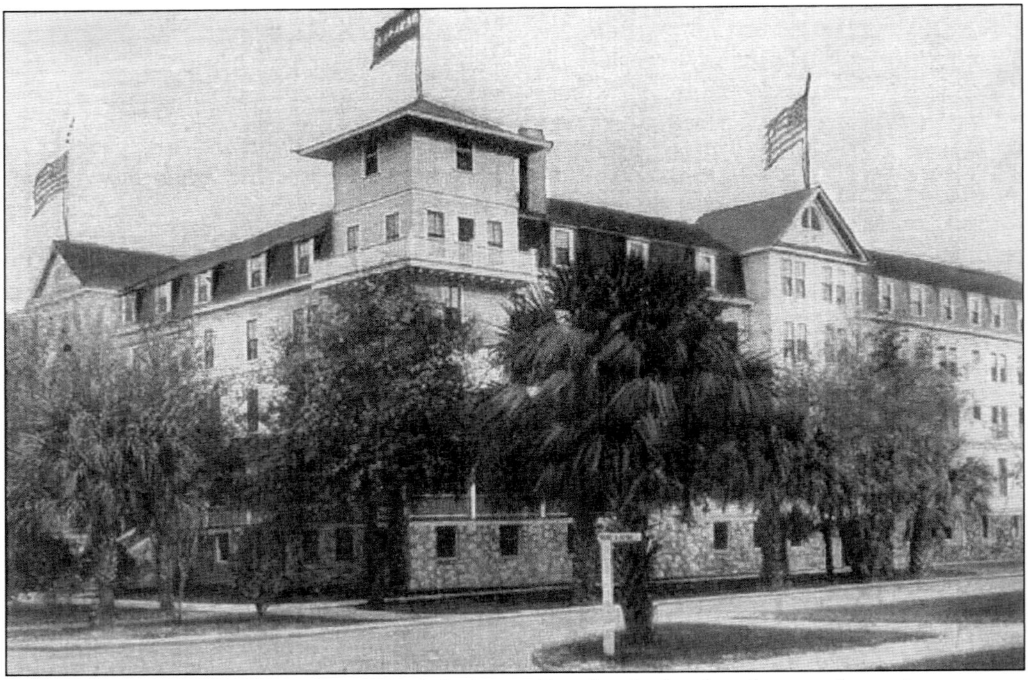

THE DESPLAND HOTEL IN 1901. Built by Leon Despland, this hotel catered to winter guests and stood on the southeast corner of Palmetto and Magnolia Avenues. In 1917 the hotel was sold and renamed the Williams Hotel. After expansion, the Williams Hotel had 250 rooms, a family restaurant, and shops located at street level. It was demolished in 1968 and is now a vacant lot. (Courtesy of Midkiff Family Collection.)

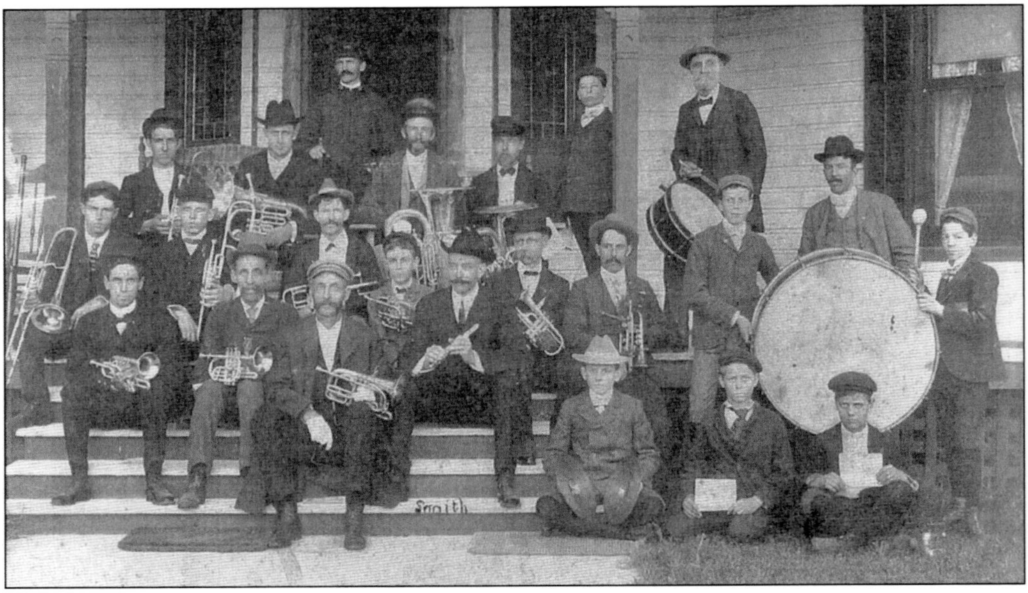

THE DAYTONA BAND C. 1902. Band members are pictured in front of the Goodall Home on the peninsula. Through the years Daytona has always had a band representing the city. After 1937 the City Band played in the band shell on the boardwalk at special summer concerts, the Fourth of July, and Labor Day. The author Harold Cardwell played trombone from 1943 to 1944 in the City Band. (Courtesy of the Halifax Historical Society.)

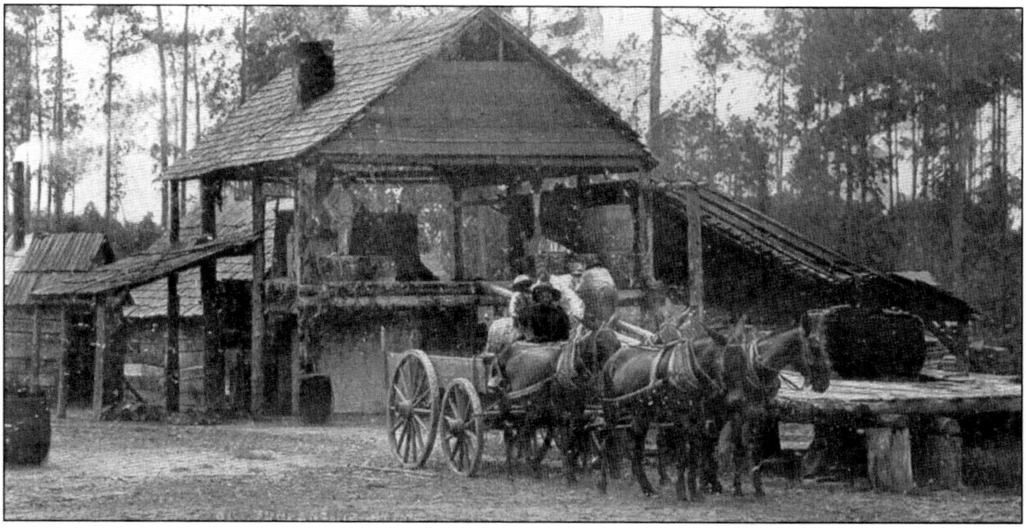

NAVAL STORES OPERATION NEAR DAYTONA C. 1902. A large turpentine still operated west of Daytona at the turn of the century. The still produced turpentine and rosin, which were shipped to Savannah, Georgia, for distribution. Forest products were an important industry for the economic growth of the area. The team of horses that pulled the "gum" wagon can be seen near the ramp at the still. The workers are unidentified. (Courtesy of Florida State Archives.)

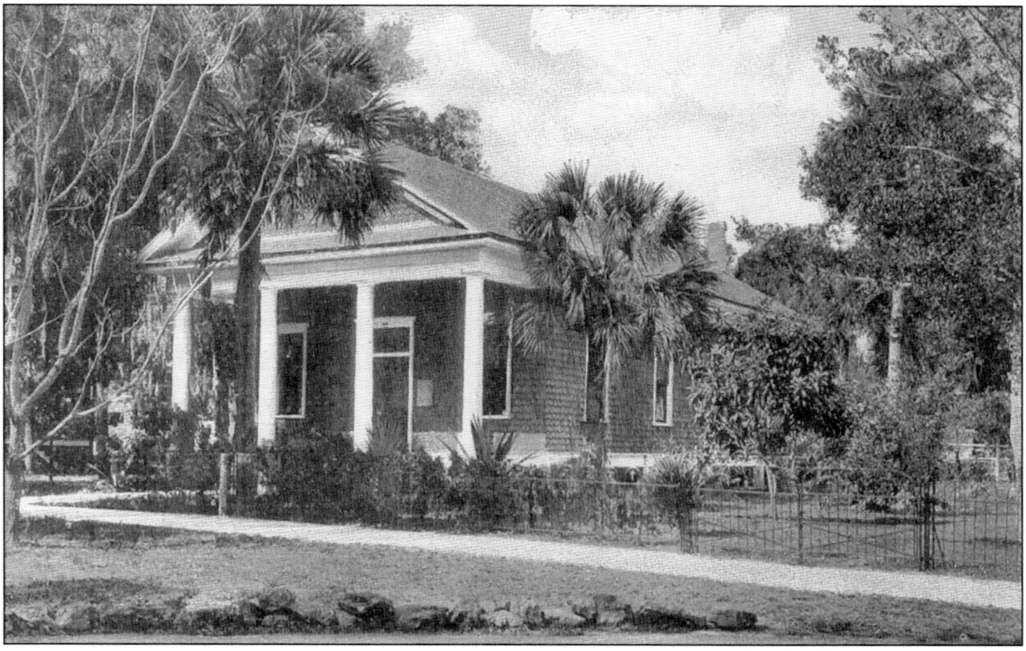

THE FIRST PALMETTO CLUB C. 1903. This clubhouse was built by L.Z. Burdick, an outstanding builder, who also constructed the First Church of Christ Scientist and other fine buildings. The club stood behind St. Mary's Episcopal Church at 210 Orange Avenue. The first meeting of the Palmetto Club was held in the home of Jane Weeks on Ridgewood Avenue in 1894. (Courtesy of Cardwell Family Collection.)

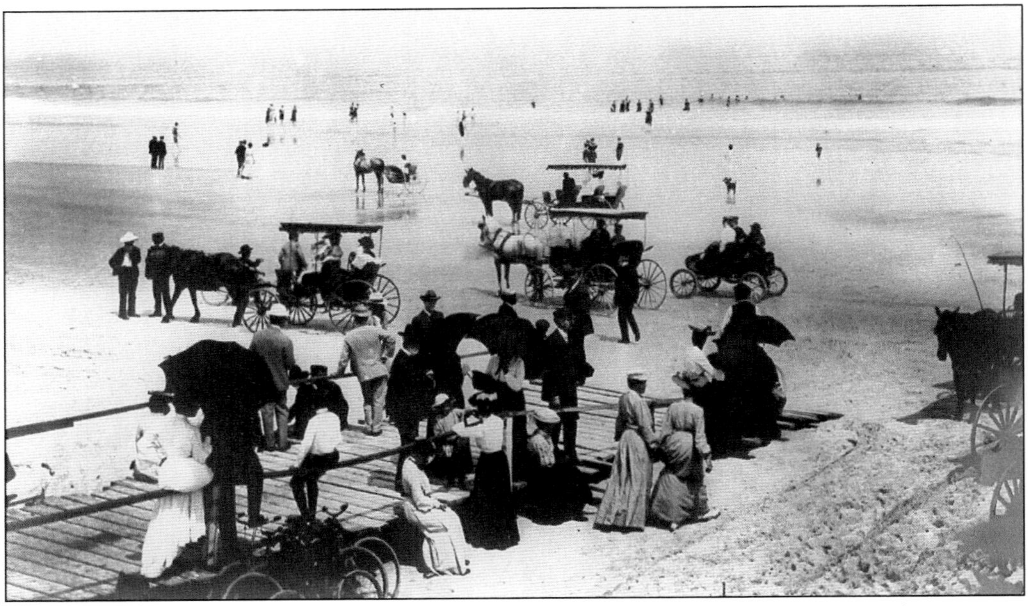

OLD BUGGIES AND PEOPLE ON THE BEACH IN 1903. Everybody liked to pose for pictures. Notice the period dress of the men and women, the horses and carriages, the bicycles, and the one "horseless carriage." Many were curious about this new machine, while others were afraid to get close. (Courtesy of John Gontner.)

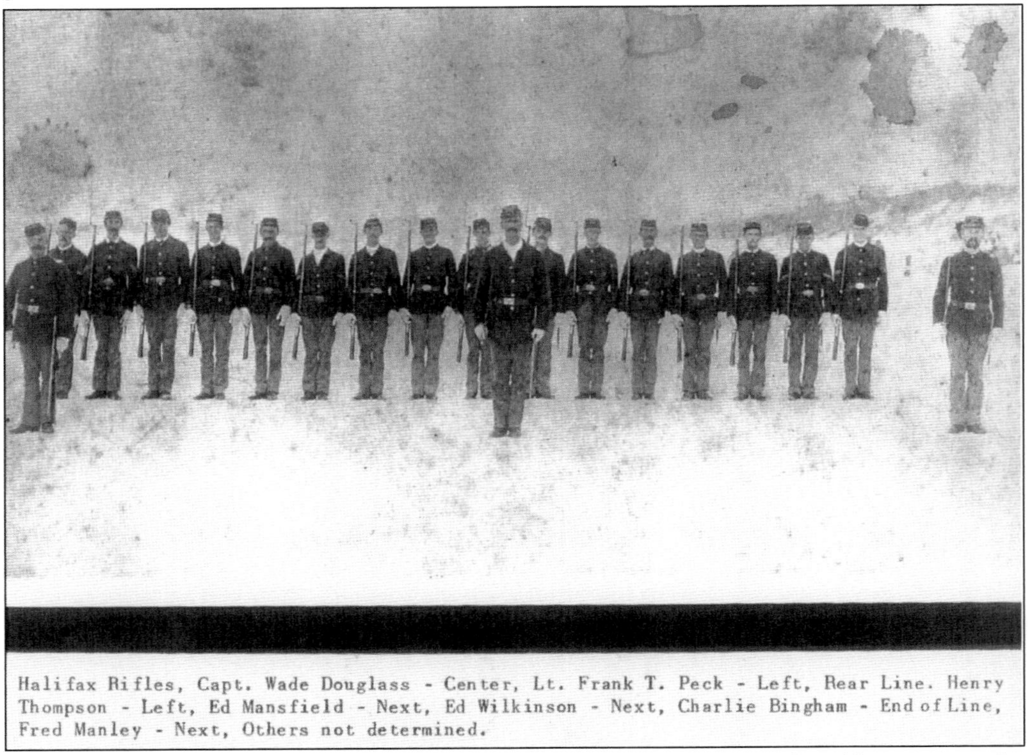

HALIFAX RIFLES C. 1904. This local militia unit was headquartered at the old armory on the northeast corner of Palmetto and Volusia Avenue. The Halifax Rifles were called to service during the Spanish-American War in 1898. (Courtesy of Halifax Historical Society.)

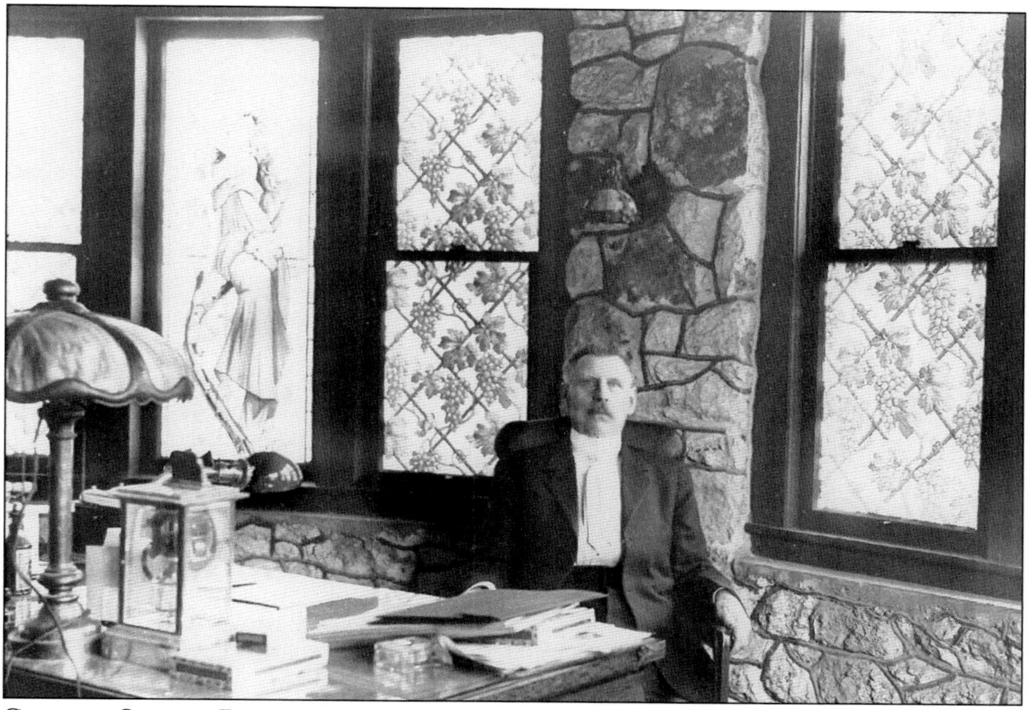

CHARLES GROVER BURGOYNE C. 1904. Mr. Burgoyne, a wealthy New York printer, is seen here seated at his desk in his North Beach Street home. Mr. Burgoyne spent his own money to promote Daytona. He made many improvements on Beach Street, including the Burgoyne Casino and the Esplanade promenade. He sponsored band concerts during the winter season each year and was president of the Florida East Coast Automobile Association, mayor of Daytona, and commodore of the Halifax Yacht Club. (Courtesy of John Gontner.)

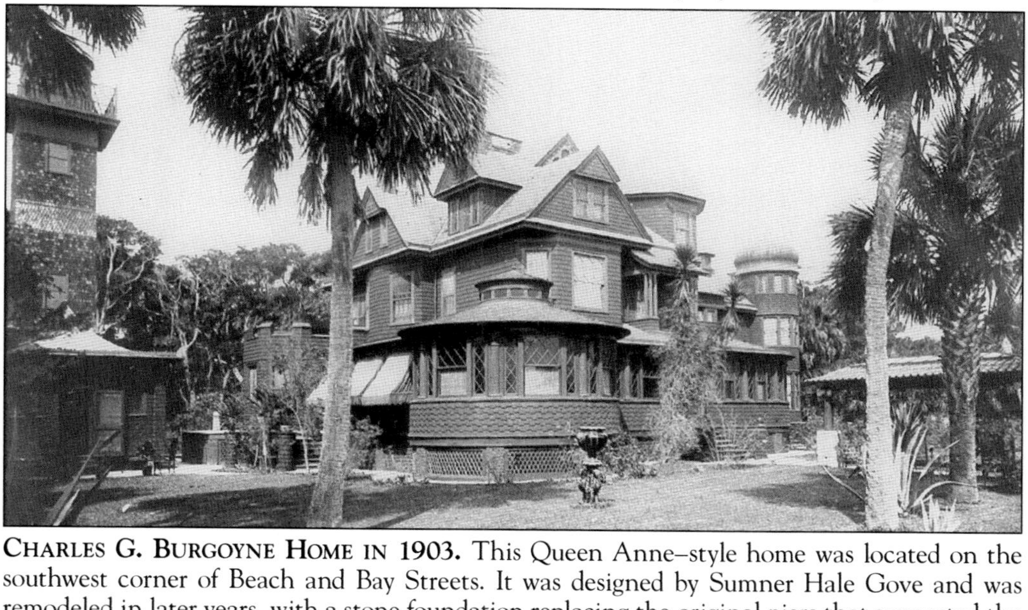

CHARLES G. BURGOYNE HOME IN 1903. This Queen Anne–style home was located on the southwest corner of Beach and Bay Streets. It was designed by Sumner Hale Gove and was remodeled in later years, with a stone foundation replacing the original piers that supported the structure. This expansive manor house and estate was demolished in 1941 to make way for new stores, forming a large shopping area along Beach Street. (Courtesy of John Gontner.)

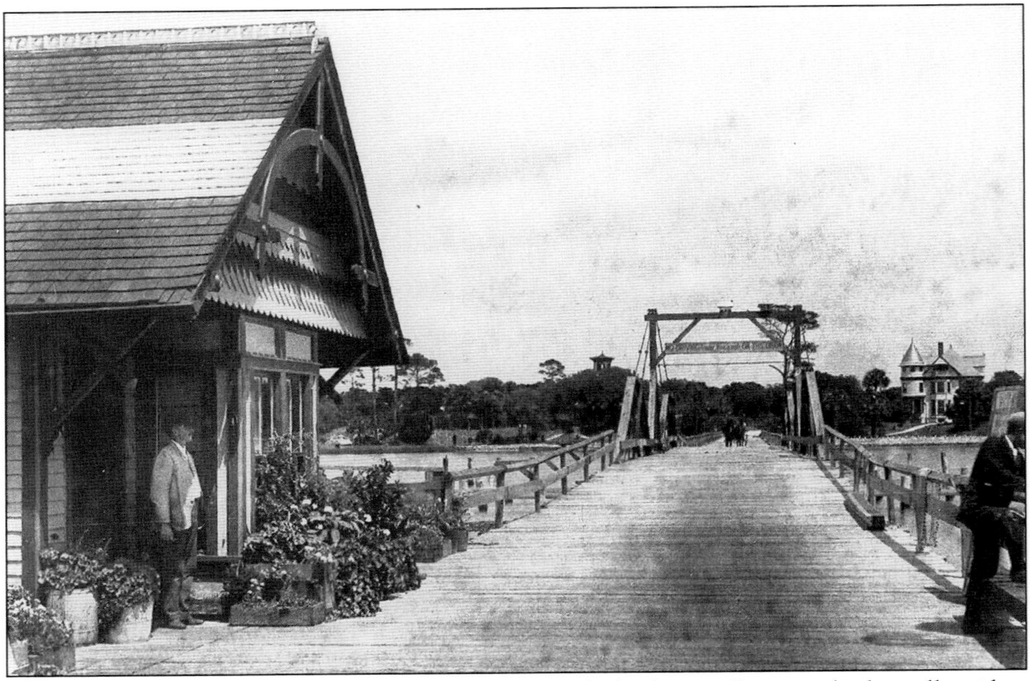

SOUTH DRAWBRIDGE LOOKING EAST IN 1904. Early bridges at Daytona had a toll paid at the bridge house. The Gamble Mansion stands on the right at the river shore. Barely visible to the north is Lilian Place. Notice the horse-drawn wagon and the fisherman on the bridge. (Courtesy of John Gontner.)

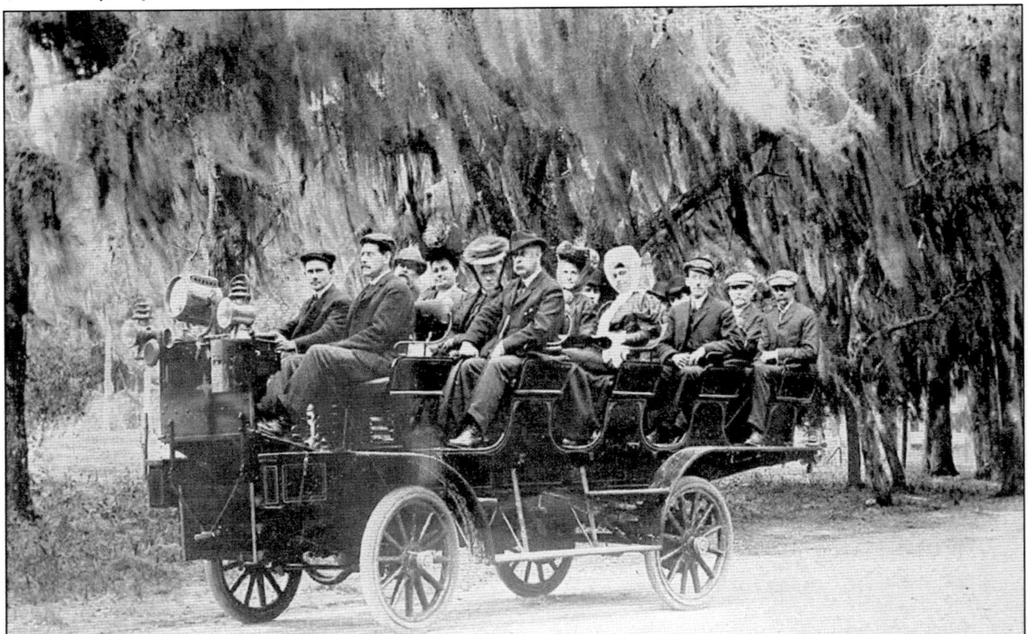

AN OMNIBUS WITH PASSENGERS C. 1905. This unique man-made machine caused quite a stir at Daytona. This was a jitney service to the depot and from the depot to hotels. This type of service was the forerunner of the city bus service. Later canvas tops were added to prevent riders from getting wet from a sudden downpour. (Courtesy of Florida State Archives.)

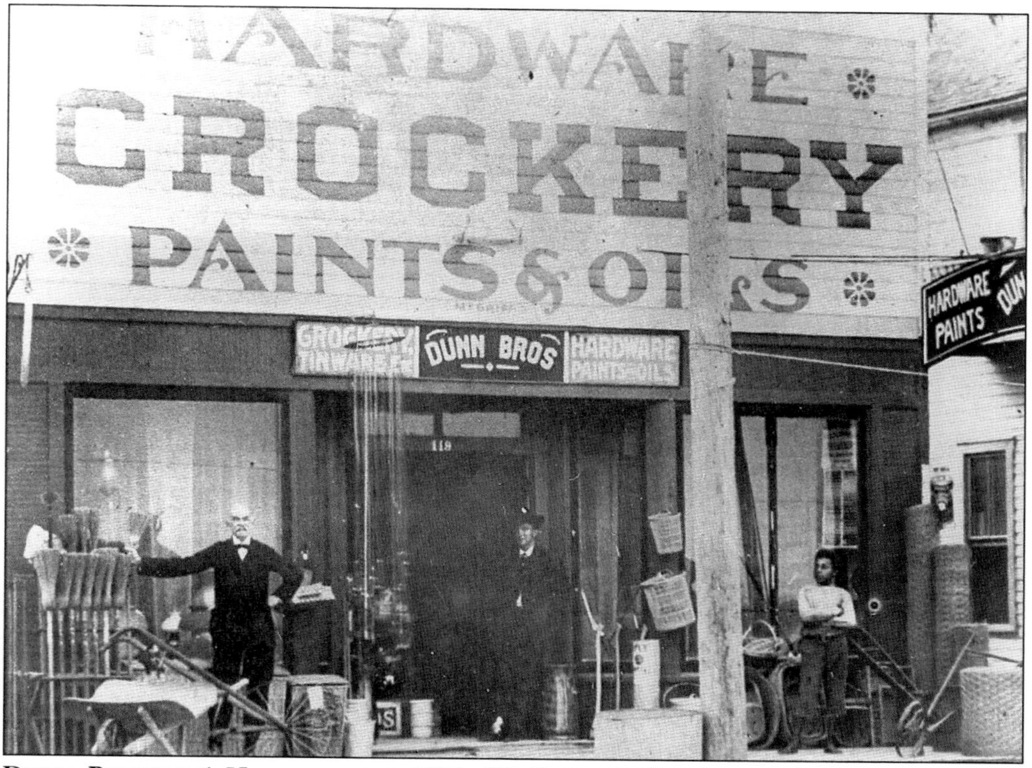

DUNN BROTHERS' HARDWARE IN 1905. J.T. Dunn Sr. bought out the Mason and Wall Hardware Store just north of Bay Street near where the post office is today and operated there for three years. In 1908 they needed a larger store, so they moved to 154 South Beach Street, where they had a blacksmith shop in the rear. After Dunn Brothers closed, the building was sold to Angell and Phelps Candy and Gifts. They combined with another store and today operate as a café and candy shop. (Courtesy of John Gontner.)

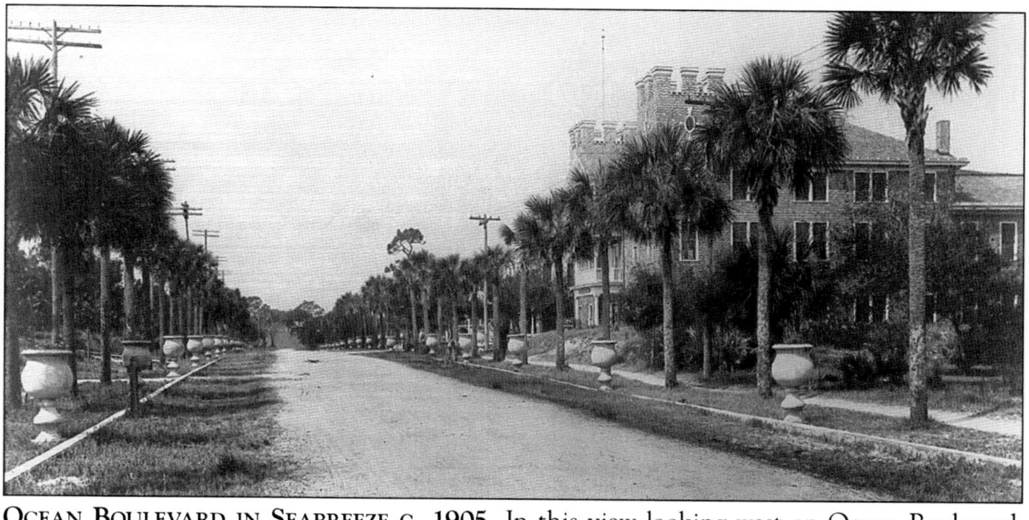

OCEAN BOULEVARD IN SEABREEZE C. 1905. In this view looking west on Ocean Boulevard, later renamed Seabreeze Boulevard, large flower urns and palm trees line the boulevard. On the north side at Peninsula Drive and Ocean Boulevard stood the Wilmans Opera House. Mrs. Helen Wilmans Post is credited with founding the town of Seabreeze. (Courtesy of John Gontner.)

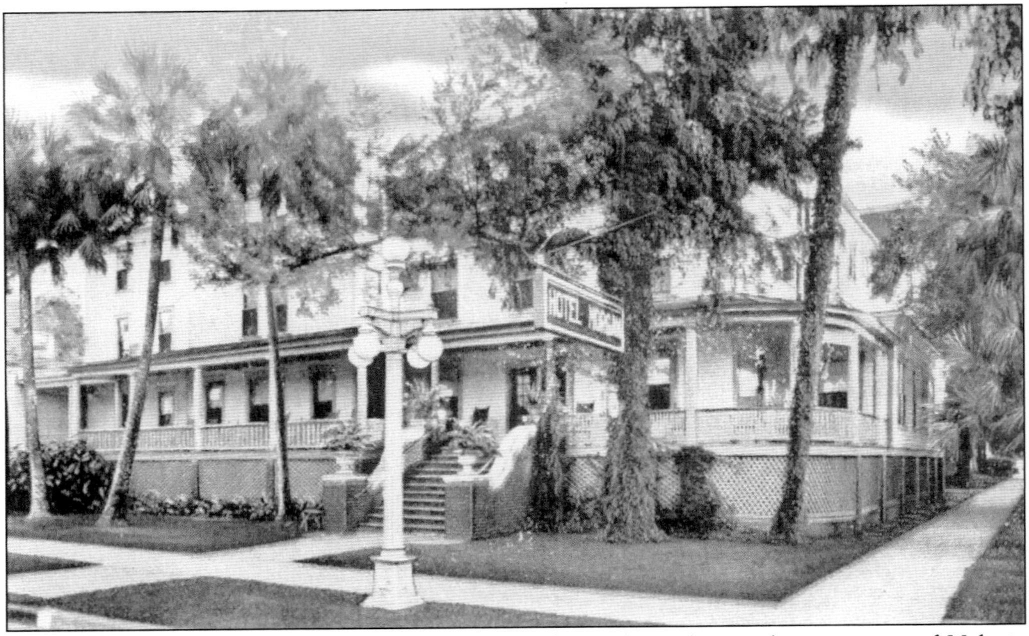

The Morgan Hotel in 1906. This hotel was located on the southeast corner of Volusia and Palmetto Avenues. The hotel advertised luxurious accommodations, including elevators, innerspring mattresses, and steam heat. In earlier years it featured a popular, family-style restaurant. The structure was demolished in 1947. (Courtesy of Cardwell Family Collection.)

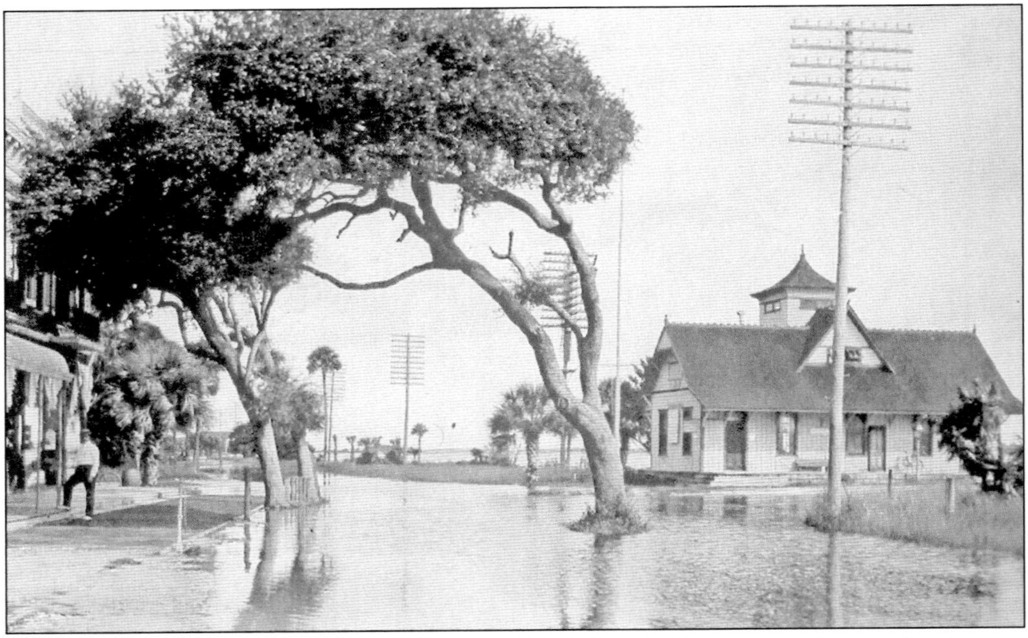

A Tropical Storm Causes Flooding c. 1906. Beach Street and Orange Avenue are under water from high tides caused by a tropical disturbance. Often northeasters caused minor flooding along Beach Street. More recently, in 1950 Hurricane King lightly flooded Beach Street. In 1960 Hurricane Donna caused shallow flooding again on Beach Street. The building on the right is the first depot, which was converted into the City Hall. (Courtesy of Halifax Historical Society.)

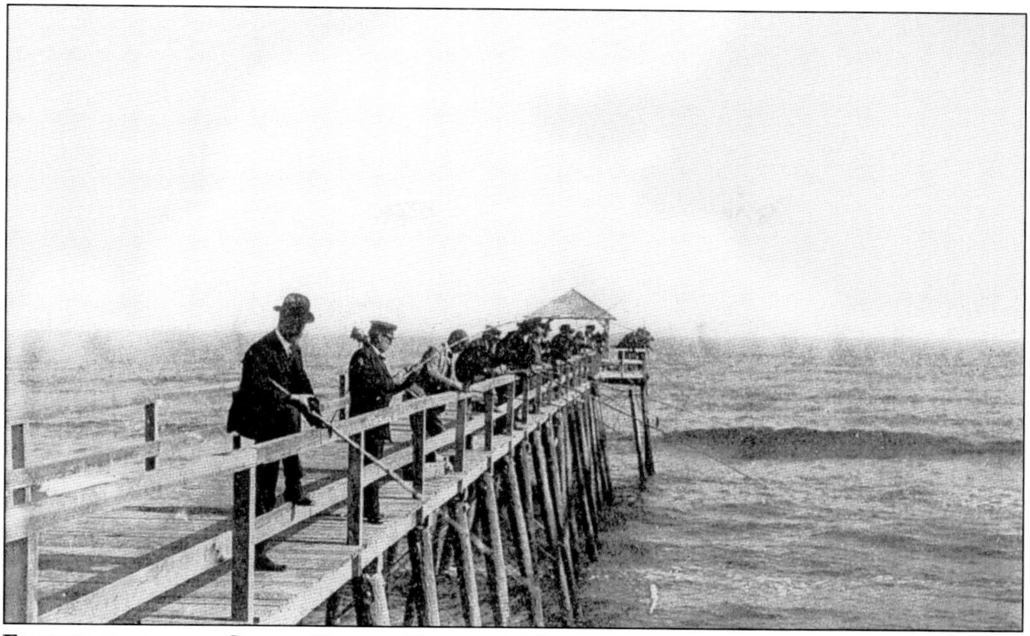

FISHING FROM THE OCEAN PIER, A TOURIST'S DELIGHT, 1906. Daytona's greatest attraction was the ocean and the Ocean Pier. Notice the angler who has hooked a fish. The thrill of catching a "big one" can be told over and over to friends in the North. The Ocean Pier was a place to see and be seen. (Courtesy of Cardwell Family Collection.)

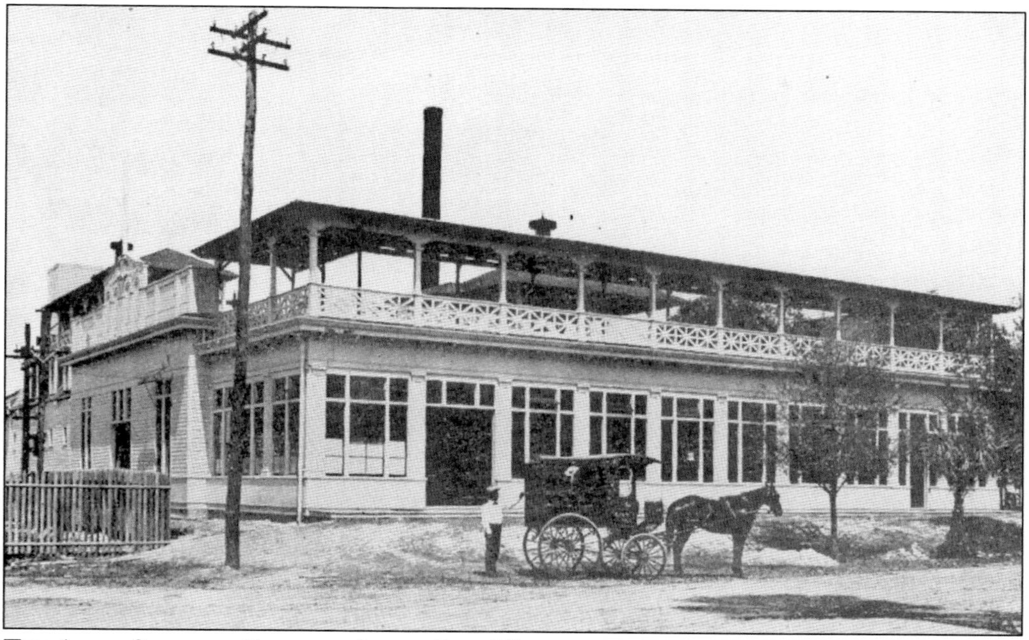

THE ADAM SCHANTZ ELECTRIC LIGHT, LILY WATER, AND ICE PLANT IN 1906. This company operated the first electric plant and also provided home delivery of ice and water. The iceman would place a block of ice in the home box and leave a water jug alongside. Electricity had to be purchased and used before 8:00 p.m., as it was turned off each night and came back on at 6:00 a.m. The plant was originally located on the northwest corner of Segrave Avenue and Volusia Avenue, now International Speedway Boulevard. (Courtesy of Cardwell Family Collection.)

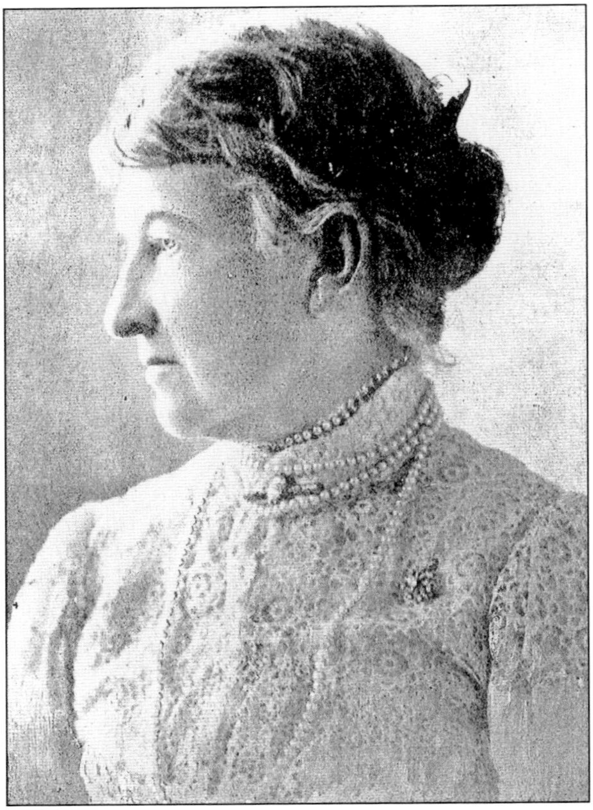

HELEN WILMANS POST, 1831–1907. An eminent writer and teacher, Helen Wilmans Post came to Seabreeze in 1892 to expound the principles of mental science. Mrs. Post was highly educated and, along with her husband, Charles Cyril Post, helped establish Seabreeze. Together they brought the finer arts to the town. People opposed her teachings, and soon persecution and lawsuits took place. They both died in 1907 from the apparent stress of opposition to their mental science beliefs. (Courtesy of Cardwell Family Collection.)

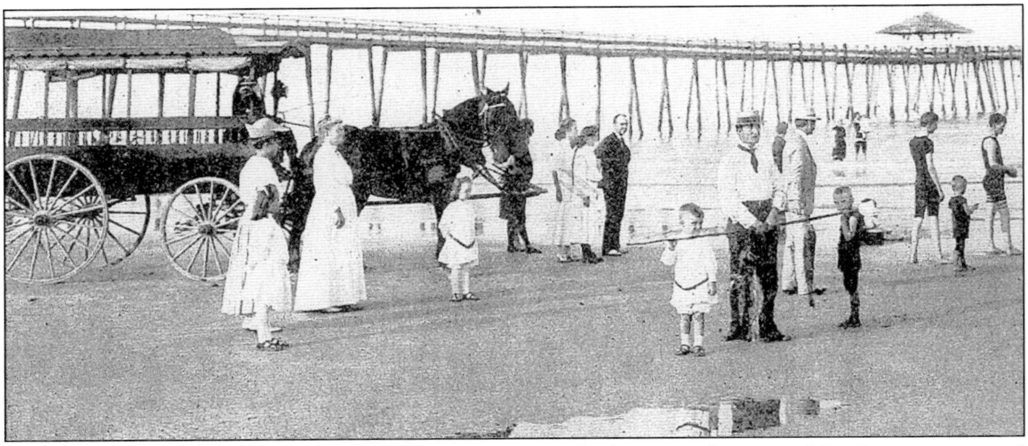

DAYTONA BEACH IN 1907. The first Ocean Pier, bathers in their wool bathing suits, and onlookers in their finest attire show a picture of dreams come true for those from the cold North. The horse-drawn wagon offers rides to and from the beach for added pleasure. (Courtesy of Cardwell Family Collection.)

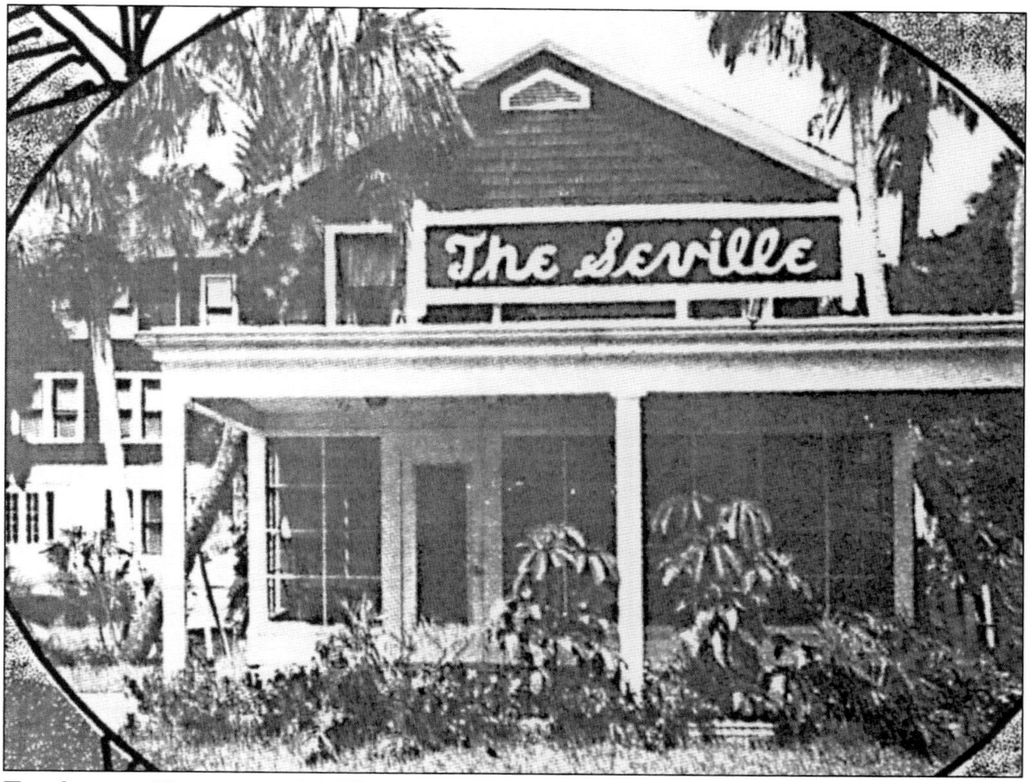

THE SEVILLE HOTEL IN 1907. This unusual distinguished building was constructed by E.H. Purdy. Each winter season many of the same familiar faces met in the lobby in flight from the cold North. The "Purdy Plantation Shortcake," a delicacy made of ham, turkey, and cornbread, was a featured food in their dining room for many years. The Seville Hotel was located at 211 South Street, on the southeast corner of South Street and Ridgewood Avenue. (Courtesy of Halifax Historical Society.)

A CITY DIRECTORY FOR DAYTONA FROM 1907. Cities commonly used advertising like this to inform the public what services and businesses they had to offer, especially for tourists who came each winter to enjoy the warm climate. This information was printed in the *Daytona Gazette News*. (Courtesy of Cardwell Family Collection.)

DAYTONA HAS

One bank.
No saloon.
One florist.
A city hall.
Six churches.
Five dentists.
A yacht club.
A high school.
A piano store.
Four Lawyers.
Three garages.
Twenty hotels.
Three jewelers.
Several dairies.
Two tin shops.
Three bakeries.
One fruit store.
Three groceries.
Board of Trade.
One ice factory.
A bowling alley.
Eight physicians.
A base ball park.
One green-house.
One opera house.
Two book stores.
Three restaurants.
One public library.
Three drug stores.
Two lumber yards.
Electric light plant.
Four barber shops.
One steam laundry.
A Chinese laundry.
Several wood yards.
One wagon factory.
Two novelty works.
An automobile club.
A Lily Water plant.
Three bicycle shops.
Two bottling works.
Four photographers.
Four meat markets.
A military company.
Three livery stables.
A telephone system.
A cold storage plant.
Two millinery stores.
Three haberdasheries.
An ice cream factory.
Two blacksmith shops.
Three hardware stores.
Three furniture stores.
Three dry goods stores.
Eight benevolent orders.
Two weekly newspapers.
Five real estate agencies.
A palmetto brush factory.
Hundreds of automobiles.
Two kindergarten schools.
An excellent water supply.
A number of curio stores.
One ladies' furnishing store.
Four fire insurance agencies.
Two plumbing establishments.
Boarding houses by the dozen.
One undertaking establishment.
One colored Industrial Training School.
Three draw bridges spanning the Halifax.
More fine residences than any other resort in Florida.
The finest paved streets of any city in Florida of its size.
Carpenters, masons, plasterers, painters and laboring men galore.

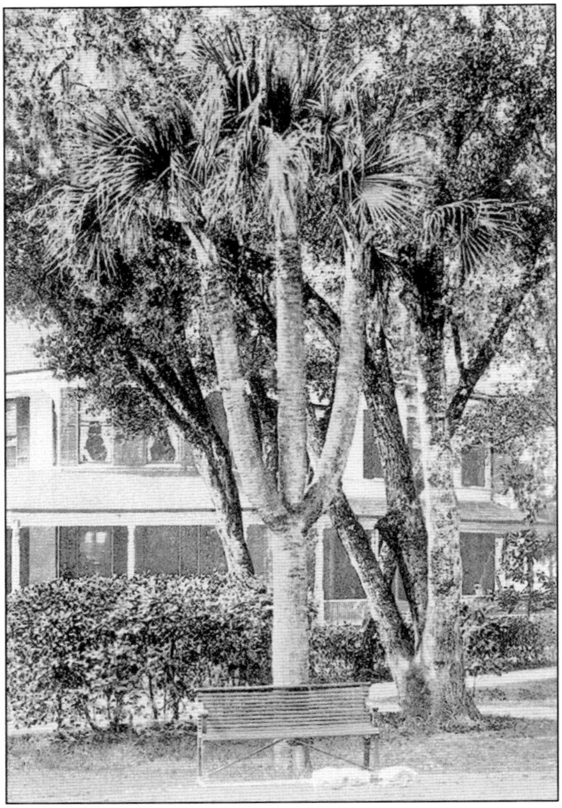

THREE-LIMBED SABLE PALM IN 1908. This unique palm stood for many years on Volusia Avenue. After the widening of U.S. Highway 1 in 1960, the palm was moved to the median of the highway for parkway beautification. It did not survive, however, and this unusual species was a big loss for the community. The house in the background is the former home of George H. Foote. (Courtesy of Cardwell Family Collection.)

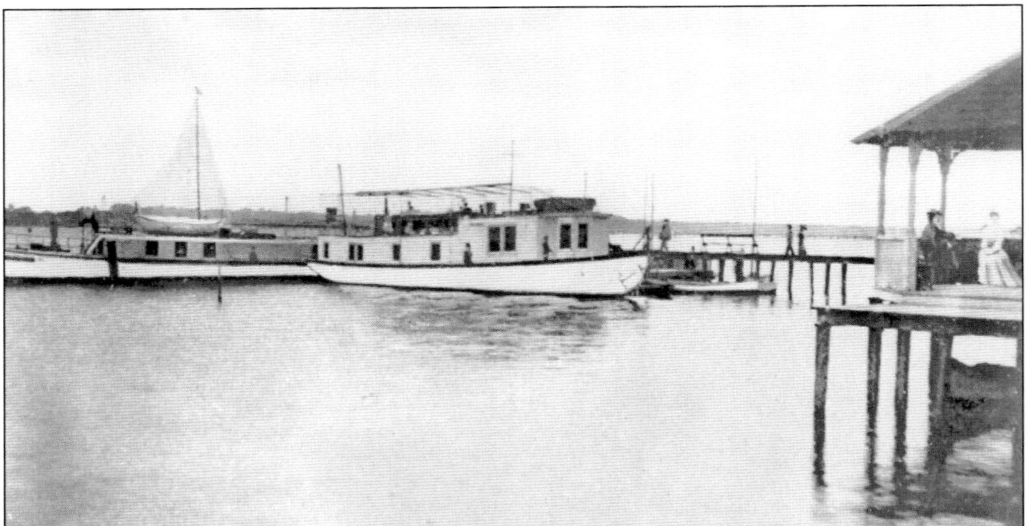

GILLES DOCK IN DAYTONA BEACH C. 1908. Daytona's Beach Street waterfront had a number of docks that reached into the deep water to accommodate the steamboats bringing supplies from Jacksonville and Savannah. When the railroad started bringing freight supplies, the river traffic slowed. The largest amount of freight, citrus, and produce was shipped North during the winter season. (Courtesy of Florida Sate Archives.)

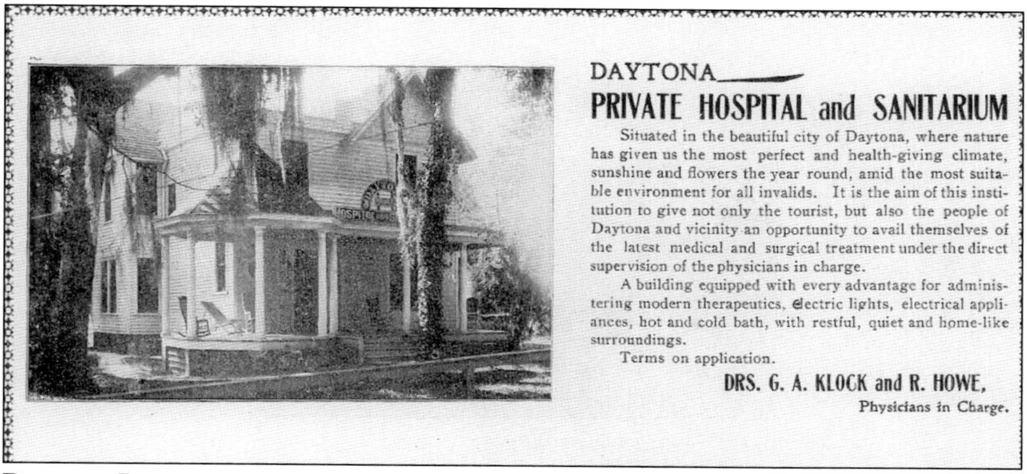

DAYTONA PRIVATE HOSPITAL AND SANITARIUM IN 1908. This hospital operated at 532 South Beach Street for many years. Drs. G.A. Klock and R. Howe were respected physicians in the Daytona area. Dr. Klock's wife was a registered nurse who worked in this facility alongside her husband. (Courtesy of Cardwell Family Collection.)

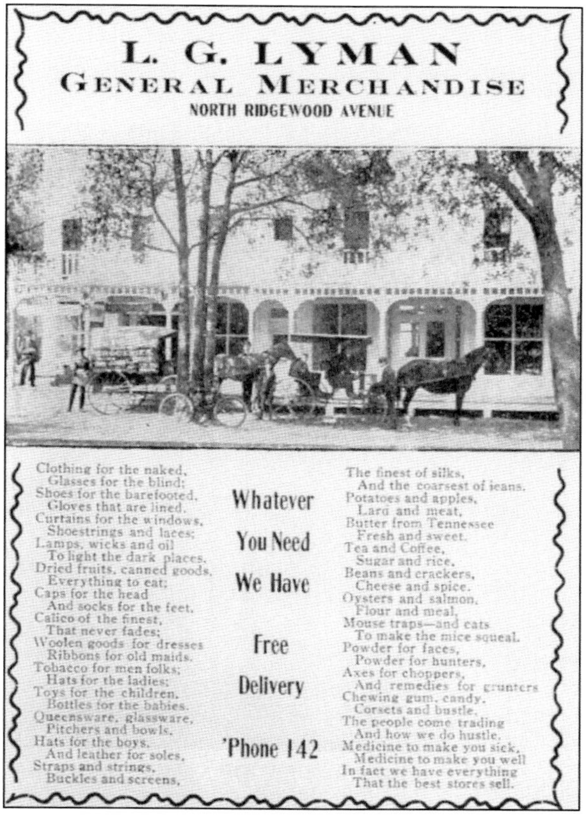

L.G. LYMAN'S GENERAL STORE ADVERTISEMENT FROM 1908. The proprietor of this store was very innovative; he listed his hundreds of items in a poetic column. This was his way of telling customers that whatever they needed, he had in the store. (Courtesy of Cardwell Family Collection.)

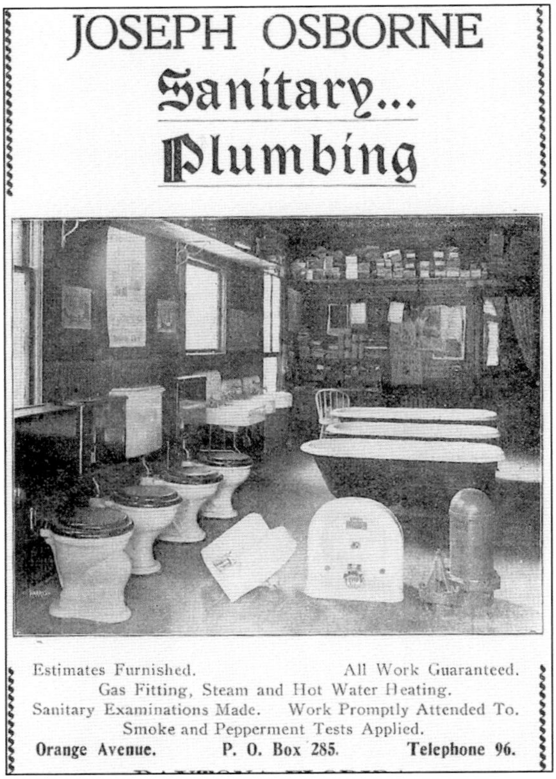

A PLUMBING CONTRACTOR'S ADVERTISEMENT FROM 1908. The modern bathroom fixtures offered in 1908 were designed to meet the needs of proper hygiene and grooming. The lion-footed bathtub was common in the bathroom for years. Today this tub is an antique and has a place in a restored historical home. (Courtesy of Cardwell Family Collection.)

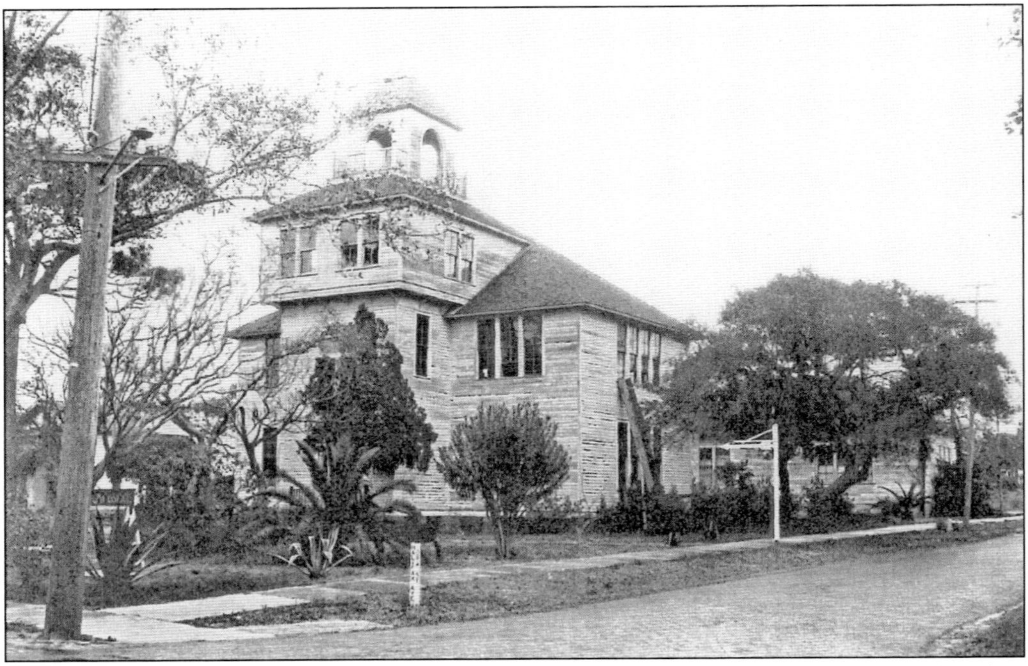

FIRST SEABREEZE HIGH SCHOOL BEACHSIDE, 1908. Seabreeze High School graduated its first class of three students in 1908. This school building was used until 1918 as a high school and then demolished in 1931. Most of the wooden schools were demolished by the 1920s as new masonry schools were constructed in Volusia County. (Courtesy of Halifax Historical Society.)

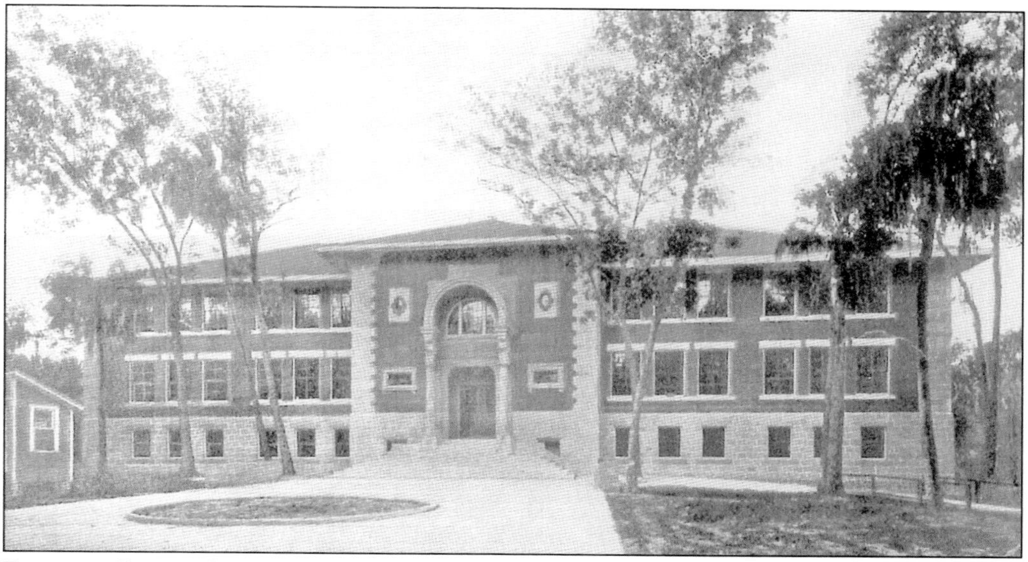

DAYTONA PUBLIC SCHOOL IN 1909. This school building, designed by Sumner Hale Gove, was located at 118 Bay Street. The masonry building was originally designed to reflect the identity and culture of Daytona. Prior to the old school's demolition in 1985, it operated as a seventh-grade center. (Courtesy of Cardwell Family Collection.)

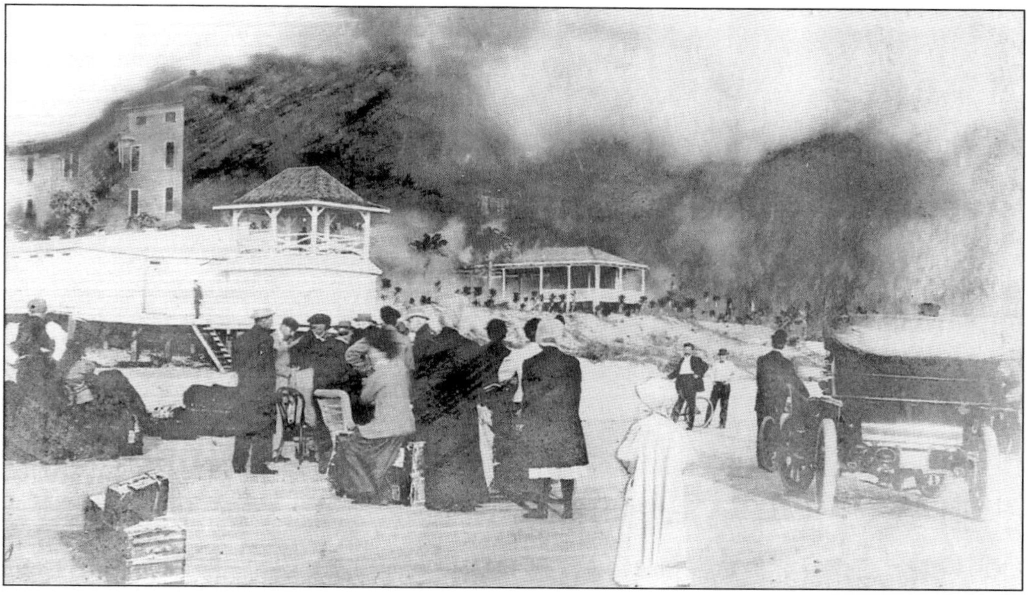

CLARENDON HOTEL ON FIRE IN 1909. This luxury hotel was designed by Sumner Hale Gove. The guests had to evacuate the hotel on quick notice in 1909. Hotel workers helped the guests move their luggage and belongings onto the sandy beach. Strong winds fanned the flames and carried the thick, black smoke away from the hotel. Many guests were still dressed in their nightclothes and robes as they stood in small groups on the beach. Old timers said it was an orderly evacuation of the hotel. (Courtesy of Cardwell Family Collection.)

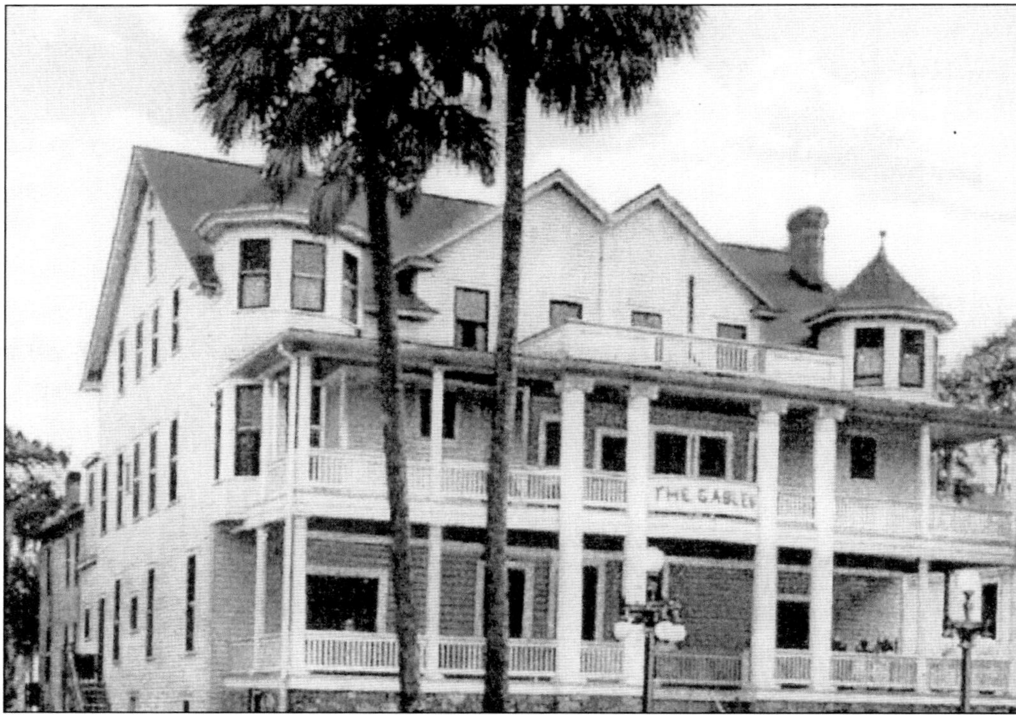

The Gables Hotel in 1909. This fashionable hotel was popular with tourists and traveling salesmen. In the beginning there were 50 rooms let for $1.50 a day. Around 1917, a fire partially destroyed the upper floors. The hotel was rebuilt and called the New Gables Hotel, with the east end renovated to accommodate Florida Motor Lines, later Greyhound Lines. The restaurant was segregated, with whites served on the north side and blacks on the south with separate restrooms. A ticket counter adorned the east wall of the restaurant. This hotel was on the south side of Volusia Avenue near Beach Street. In 1960 the building was torn down to make way for a parking lot. (Courtesy of Midkiff Family Collection.)

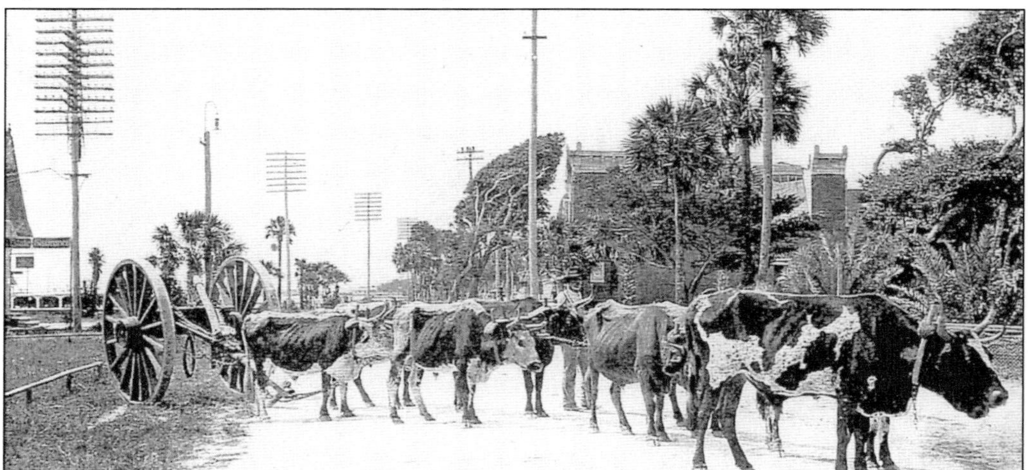

A Logging Cart Pulled by Oxen c. 1909. Logs were hauled from the nearby forest by teams of oxen. As late as the early 1930s oxen were used to remove hardwood from the hammocks near Canal Road, today's Nova Road, west of Daytona. (Courtesy of Halifax Historical Society.)

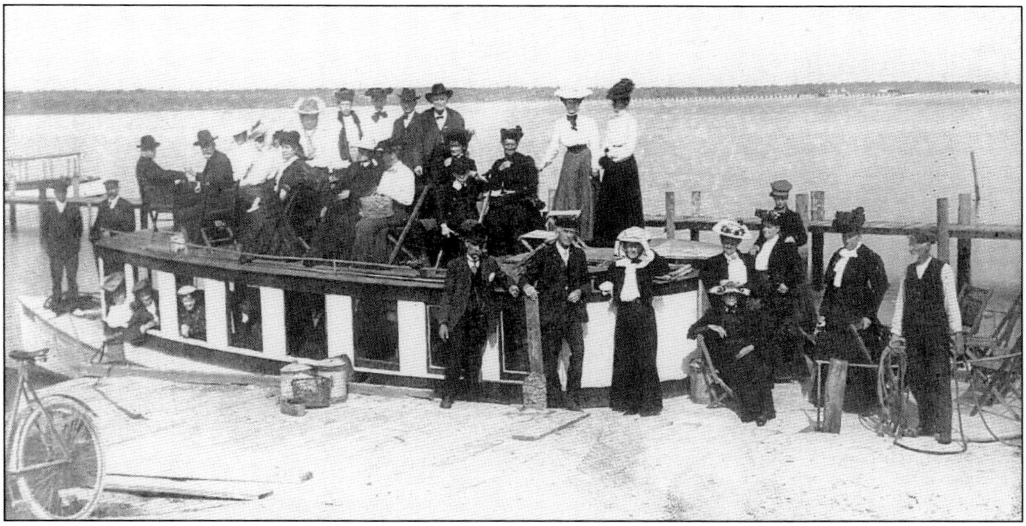

BOARDING THE EXCURSION BOAT *MAXINE* AT PONCE INLET C. 1909. After a long day's outing, unidentified passengers begin boarding for their return trip to Daytona. Oyster roasts and fish fries were very popular among visitors from the North. Note the attire worn for this occasion. (Courtesy of Cardwell Family Collection.)

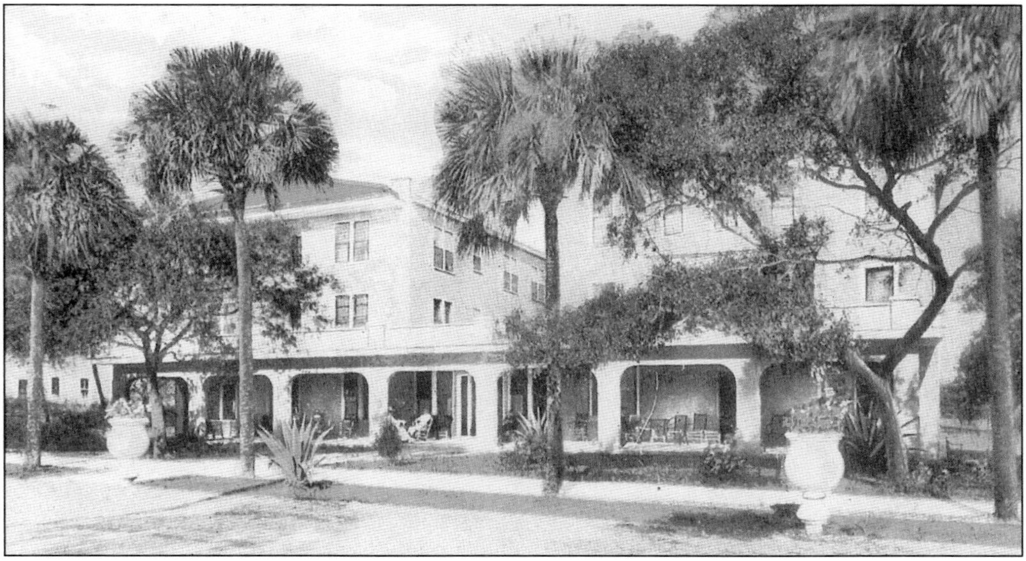

THE GENEVA HOTEL AT 319 SEABREEZE BOULEVARD IN 1910. On cool evenings, guests often gathered and visited by the fireplace in the lobby of this popular hotel. Guests could have drinks in the lounge and walk out the back door and across the street to the Princess Issena Cocktail Lounge. The hotel, with its adjoining restaurant and cocktail lounge named The Silver Bucket, was demolished in the 1980s. (Courtesy of Cardwell Family Collection.)

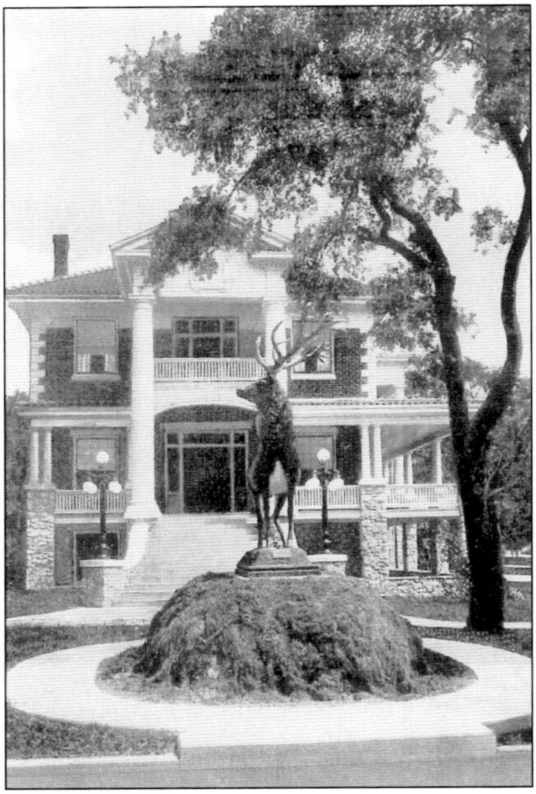

ELKS B.P.O.E. HOME IN 1911. This masonry building at 200 Volusia Avenue was designed by Sumner Hale Gove. In the 1960s it was demolished to make way for a modern appliance store and the widening of Volusia Avenue. The Elk statue that stood in front of this building was damaged by a young naval officer's car during World War II. The restored Elk stands today at the new clubhouse located at 700 South Ridgewood Avenue. (Courtesy of Cardwell Family Collection.)

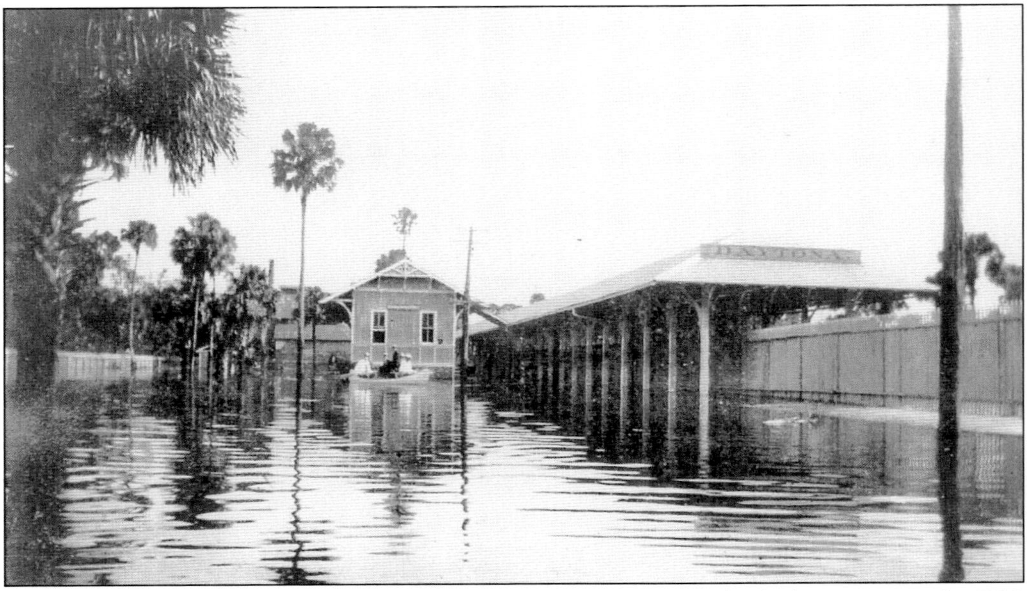

DAYTONA STREETS FLOODED IN SEPTEMBER 1911. A northeaster backed water up to the FEC Railroad Depot. This was the second depot, located between Magnolia Avenue and Volusia Avenue, now International Speedway Boulevard. Proper street drainage was lacking, and canals overflowed because of high water in the Halifax River. Most folks chose to ride in wagons rather than wade in the water and wet their shoes and clothes. This situation did occur from time to time until adequate drainage of low areas was provided. (Courtesy of Halifax Historical Society.)

Four

Growth and Development 1912–1920

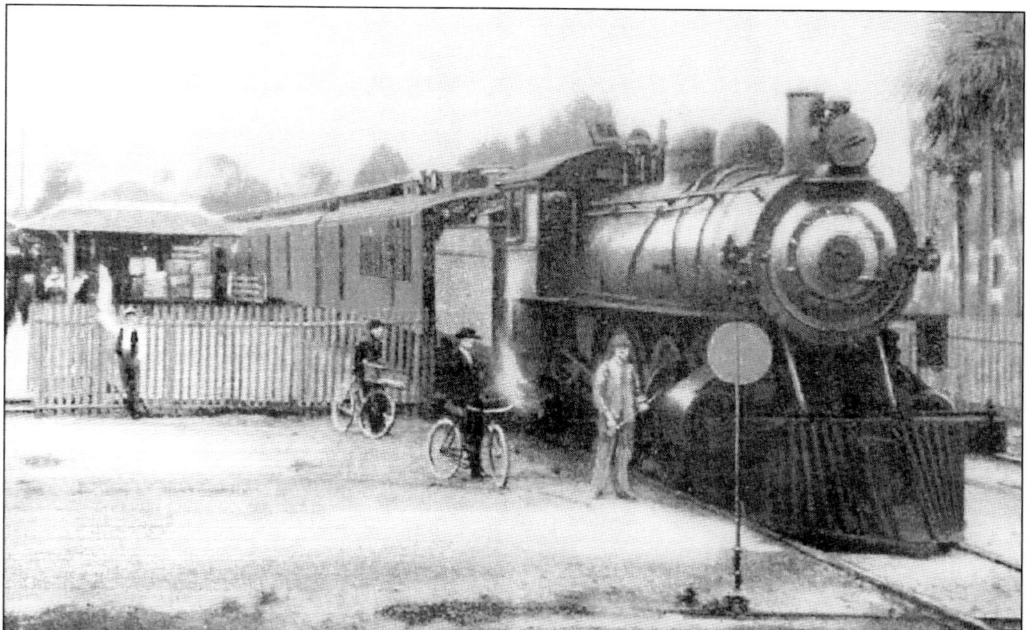

FEC Railroad c. 1912. A steam-locomotive passenger train stops between Volusia Avenue and Magnolia Avenue for unloading and loading of passengers. The winter season was a very busy time for the FEC. Passengers arrived for their winter stay in Daytona and left for the North in the early spring. The depot can be seen in the distance. (Courtesy of Cardwell Family Collection.)

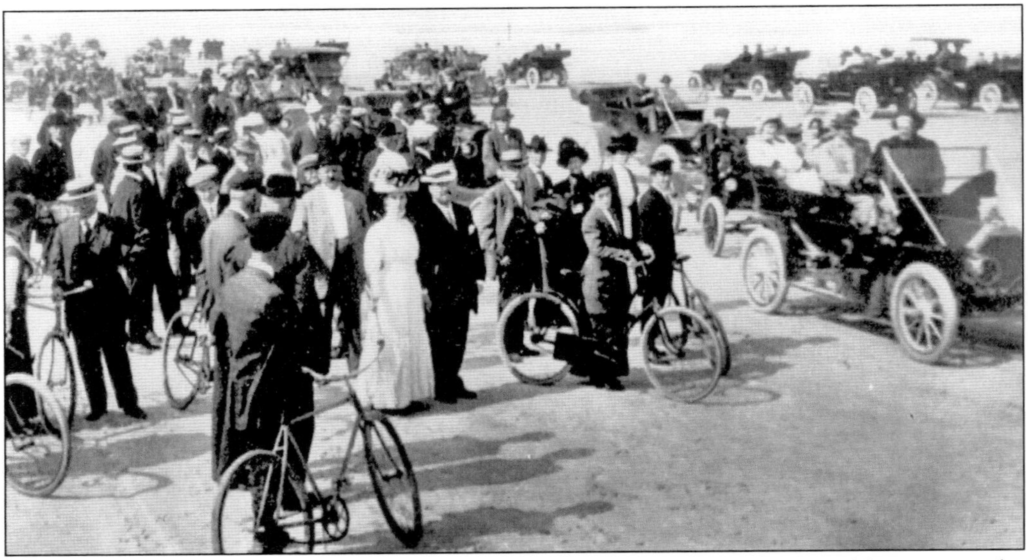

AUTOMOBILES, BICYCLES, AND TOURISTS C. 1912. This was a time to see and be seen on the beach with the horseless carriages, bicycles, and tourists in their best-dressed finery. Notice the women's hats with flowers and their long dresses, as well as the men's dark wool suits, their black felt hats, Palm Beach straws, and riding caps. (Courtesy of John Gontner.)

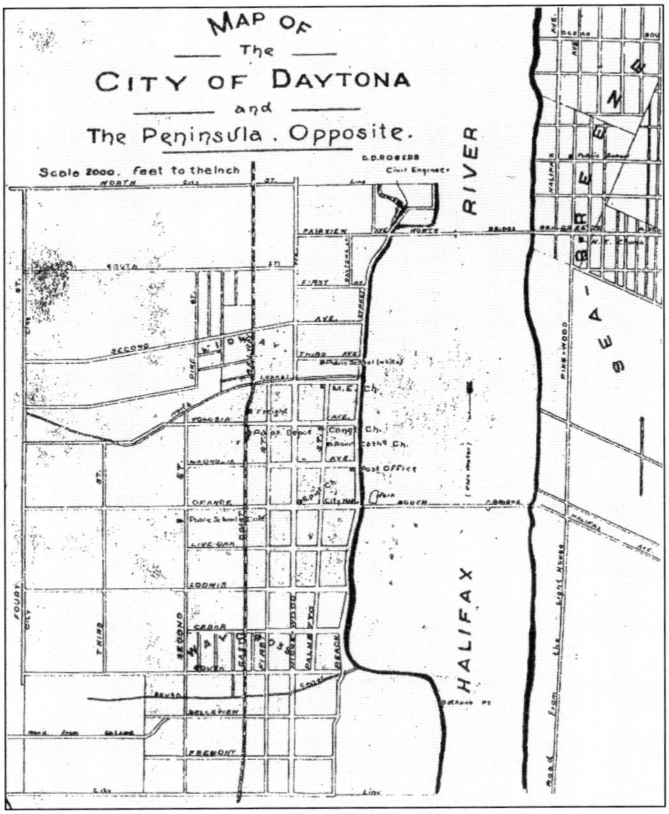

MAP OF DAYTONA AREA IN 1912. D.D. Rogers, a civil engineer, prepared this map. He was one of the founders of Daytona and surveyed many land areas in Volusia County. His home on North Beach Street had a dock that extended into the Halifax River. (Courtesy of Halifax Historical Society.)

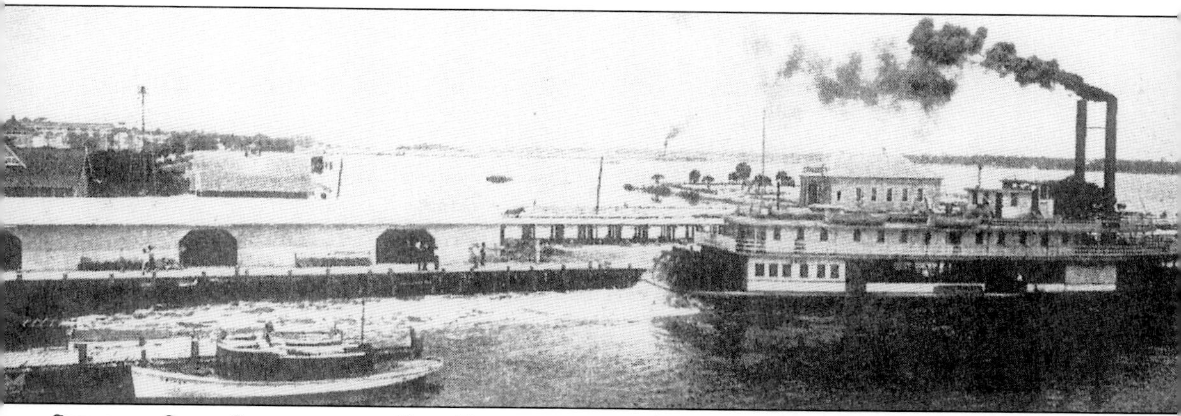

Steamer Swan Leaving the City Dock c. 1913. The *Swan* carried passengers and cargo. Boats took the Halifax River south to the ocean inlet. To the north on the left is the city hall and old railroad depot building. The emergency bell can be seen in the background. The city jail was near the waterfront. (Courtesy Cardwell Family Collection.)

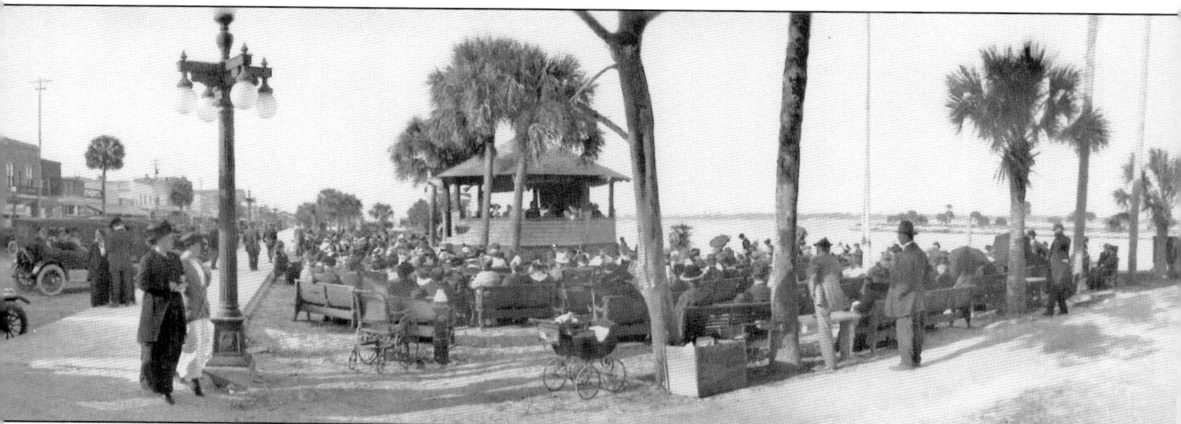

Band Concert at Beach Street and Orange Avenue c. 1914. During the winter season, concerts were held daily at this pavilion. One of the featured bands was Rocco Saracina's Italian Orchestral Band. Notice the baby carriage and wheelchair sitting empty behind the benches. The Anthony Building can be seen midway up the block. (Courtesy of John Gontner.)

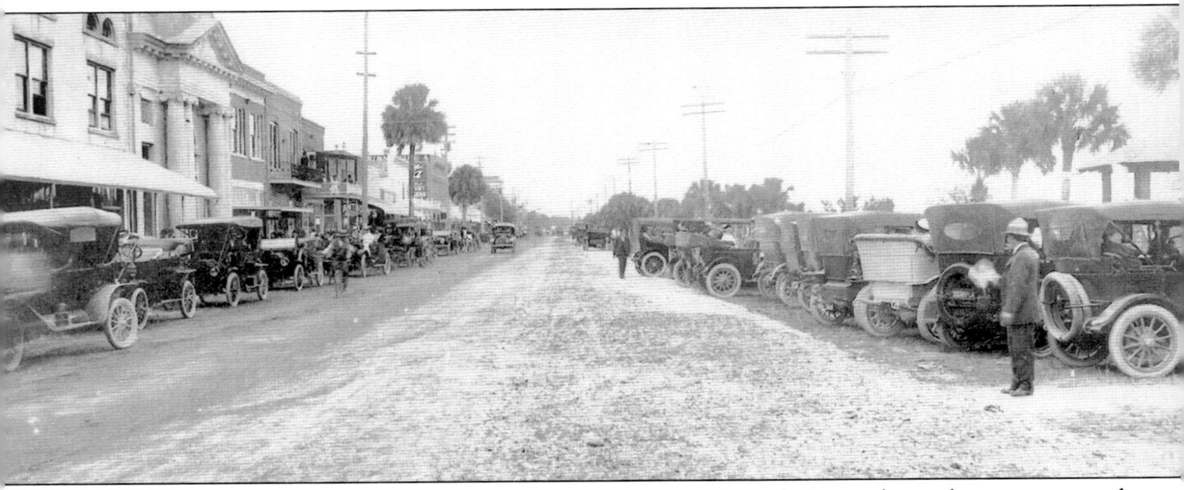

Beach Street Looking North in 1914. This image of Beach Street shows that it is unpaved, with a base of white marl and crushed shell topping. Later improvements would include sidewalks, the Burgoyne Esplanade and Casino, and eventually the concrete bridge and trolley service. On the right is the upper portion of the gazebo where Rocco Saracina's Italian Orchestral Band played during the winter season, and the second building on the left is Merchants Bank. (Courtesy of John Gontner.)

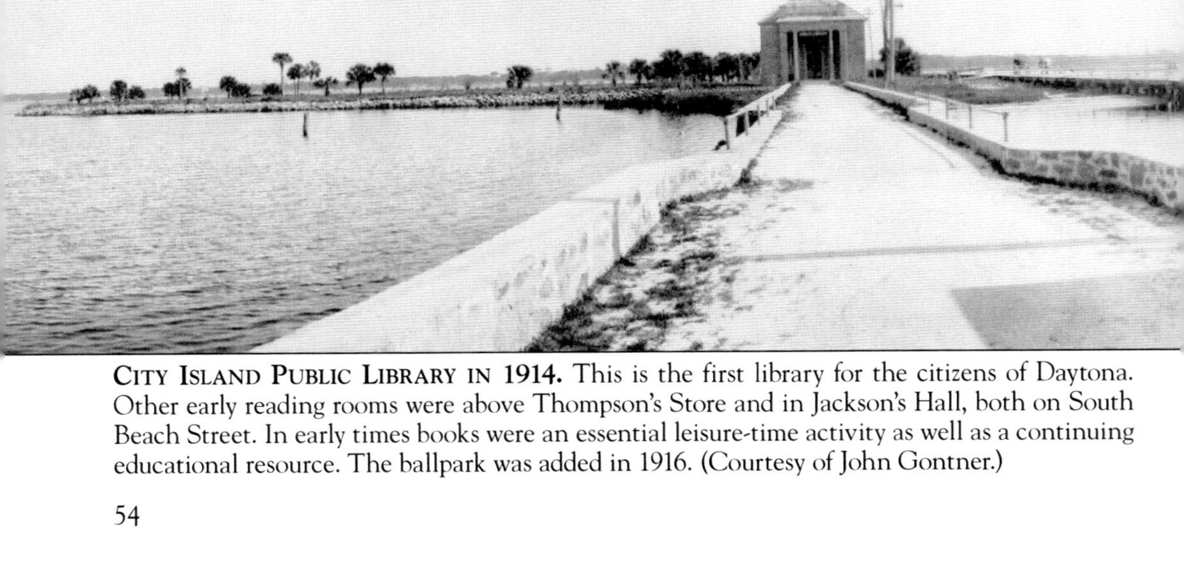

City Island Public Library in 1914. This is the first library for the citizens of Daytona. Other early reading rooms were above Thompson's Store and in Jackson's Hall, both on South Beach Street. In early times books were an essential leisure-time activity as well as a continuing educational resource. The ballpark was added in 1916. (Courtesy of John Gontner.)

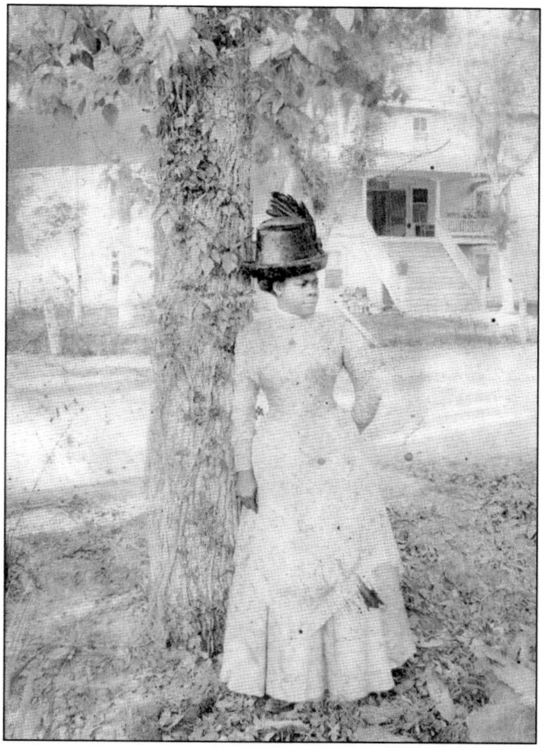

Dr. Mary McLeod Bethune, 1875–1955. Mary McLeod Bethune established a school for children of FEC railroad workers in 1904. She started with five African-American girls, using wooden boxes as desks and chairs. From this humble beginning the school grew into the Daytona Normal and Industrial Institute. In 1923 they became affiliated with the Methodist Church, which merged the school with the Cookman Institute of Jacksonville and created Bethune-Cookman College. (Courtesy of Bethune-Cookman College.)

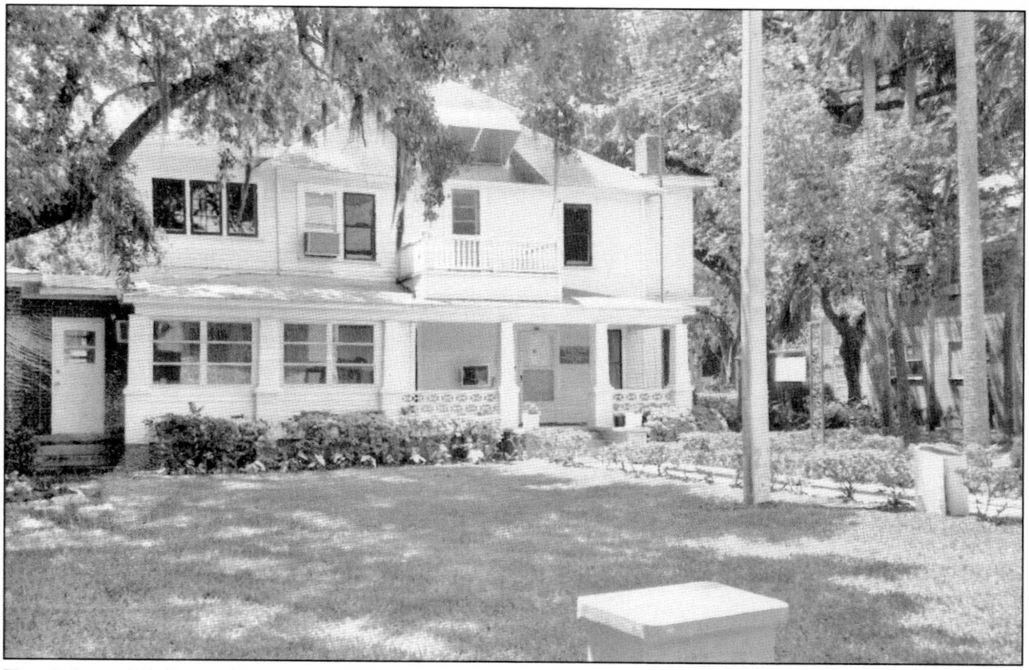

Dr. Mary McLeod Bethune Home in 1996. The Bethune Home, built in 1915, is situated on the Bethune-Cookman College Campus. Today it is a museum with period furnishings and artifacts. Bethune's grave and memorial are located just west of the home on the campus. This property was once the site of the Heriot Plantation during the Territorial Period in Florida. (Courtesy of Cardwell Family Collection.)

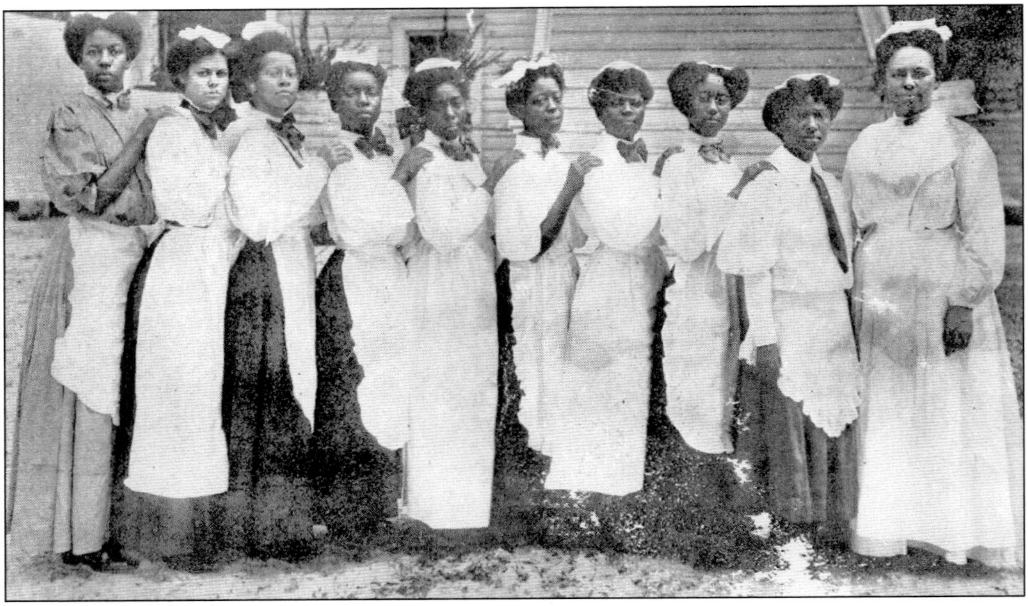

DAYTONA EDUCATIONAL AND INDUSTRIAL TRAINING SCHOOL FOR NEGRO GIRLS C. 1915. This school was established by Mary McLeod Bethune in 1904. It is alleged that to raise money to keep the school operating, she sold sweet-potato pies. Later she was able to convince wealthy industrialists who wintered in Daytona to help her fund this educational institution. (Courtesy of Florida State Archives.)

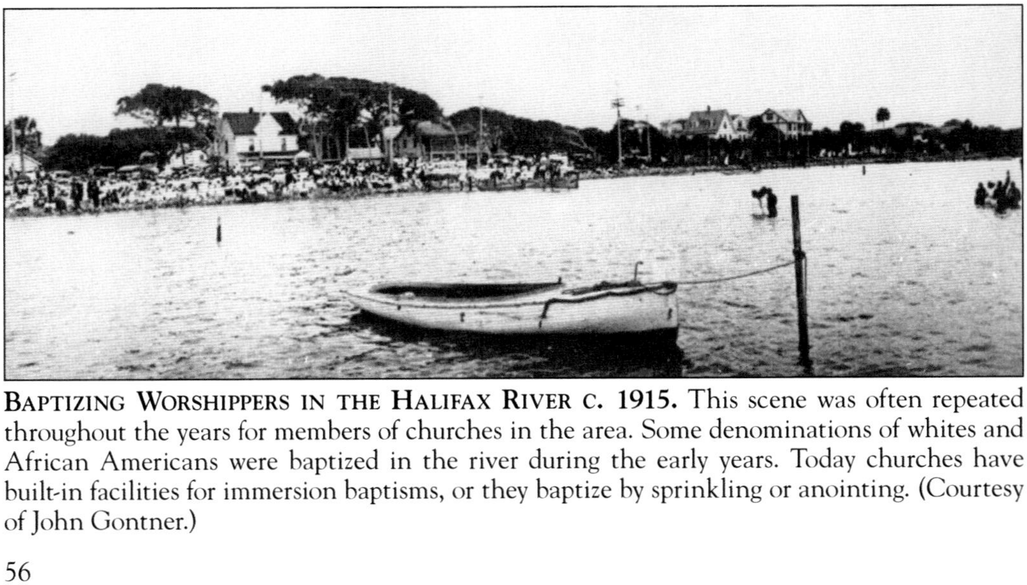

BAPTIZING WORSHIPPERS IN THE HALIFAX RIVER C. 1915. This scene was often repeated throughout the years for members of churches in the area. Some denominations of whites and African Americans were baptized in the river during the early years. Today churches have built-in facilities for immersion baptisms, or they baptize by sprinkling or anointing. (Courtesy of John Gontner.)

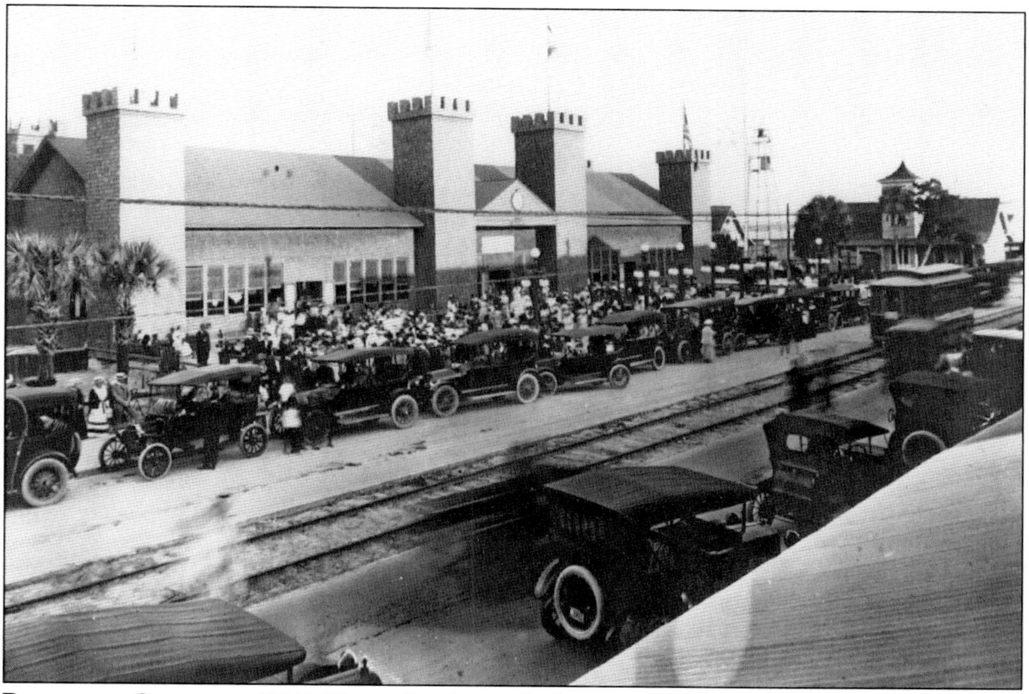

BURGOYNE CASINO C. 1915. The trolley line, which ran down the middle of Beach Street and Orange Avenue, also ran north and east over the concrete bridge to a point near Seabreeze. Notice the canvas-covered vintage automobiles parked on the street and the trolley in transit. The Burgoyne Casino had special programs for visitors, and Charles Burgoyne sponsored band concerts for winter guests. (Courtesy of John Gontner.)

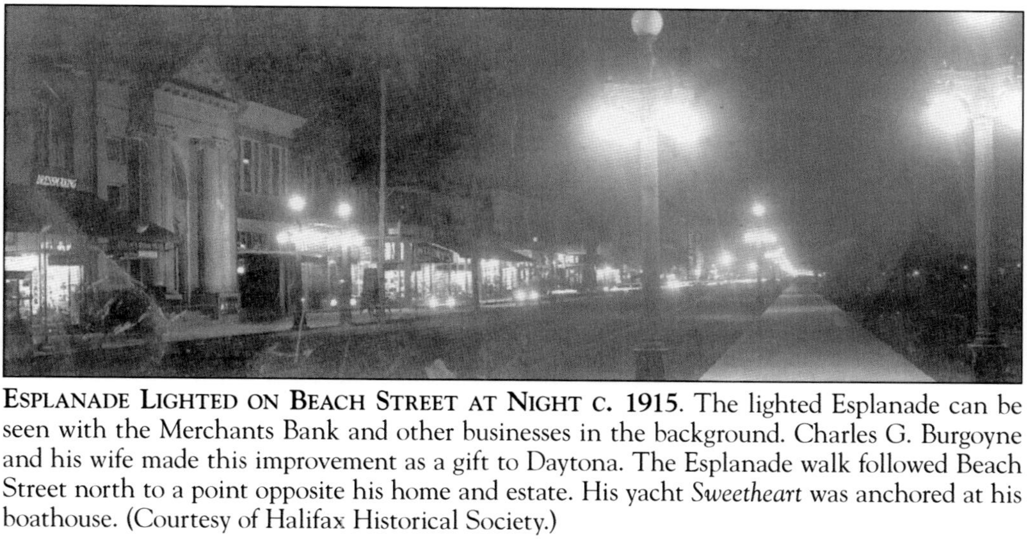

ESPLANADE LIGHTED ON BEACH STREET AT NIGHT C. 1915. The lighted Esplanade can be seen with the Merchants Bank and other businesses in the background. Charles G. Burgoyne and his wife made this improvement as a gift to Daytona. The Esplanade walk followed Beach Street north to a point opposite his home and estate. His yacht *Sweetheart* was anchored at his boathouse. (Courtesy of Halifax Historical Society.)

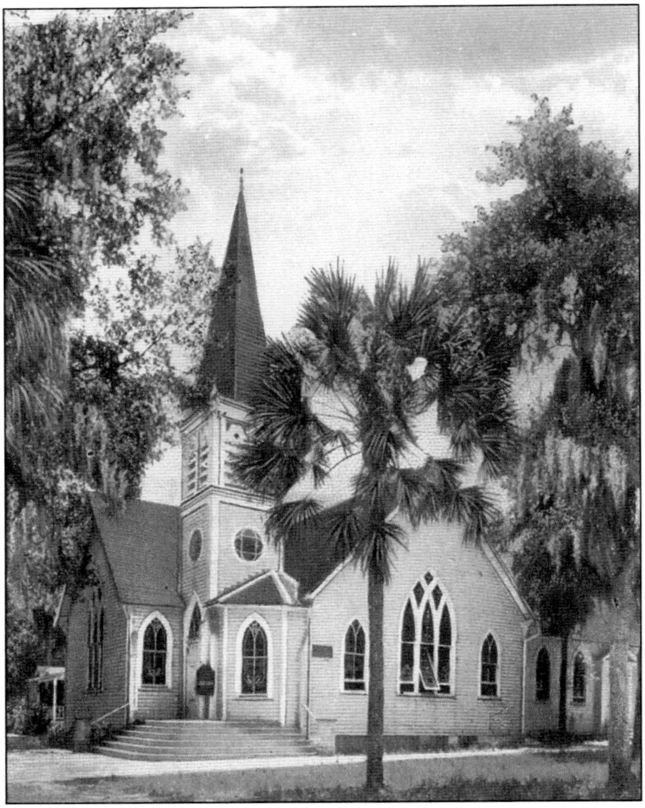

FIRST METHODIST CHURCH C. 1915. First Methodist Church was organized at W.F. Stewart's Hall on Beach Street in 1889 and moved into a small structure at the southwest corner of Bay Street and Palmetto Avenue in 1892. Many improvements were made, and in 1906 Dr. D.H. Rutter was appointed pastor. The congregation was dissolved in 2001, and the sanctuary was listed for sale. (Courtesy of Cardwell Family Collection.)

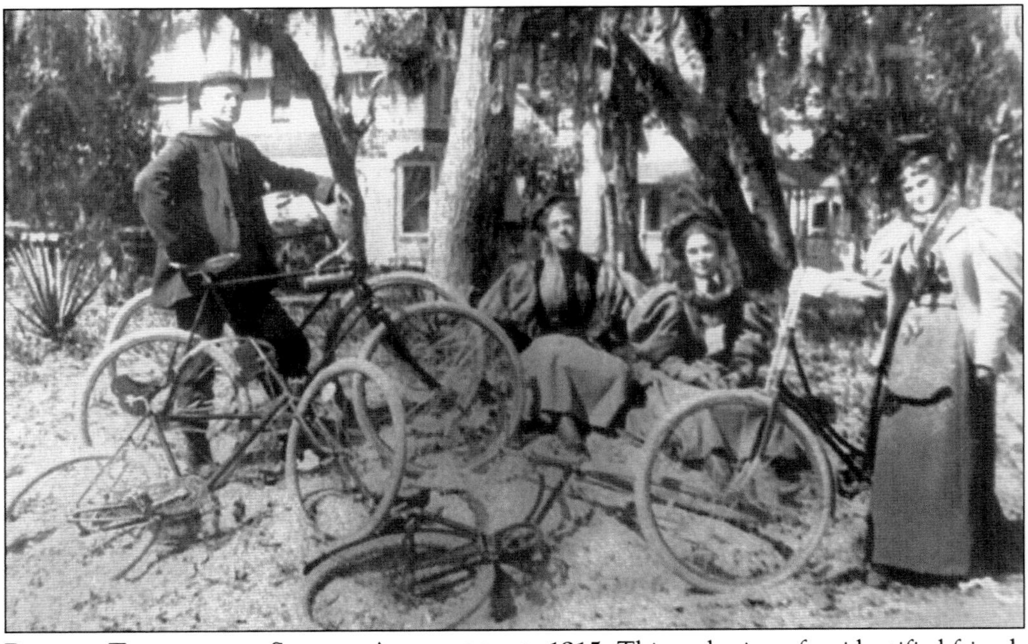

PICTURE-TAKING ON A SUNDAY AFTERNOON C. 1915. This gathering of unidentified friends poses for the hooded camera. Notice the period clothing with the women's hats, the gentleman with a riding cap, and bicycles, which were popular sights on Daytona's downtown streets. (Courtesy of John Gontner.)

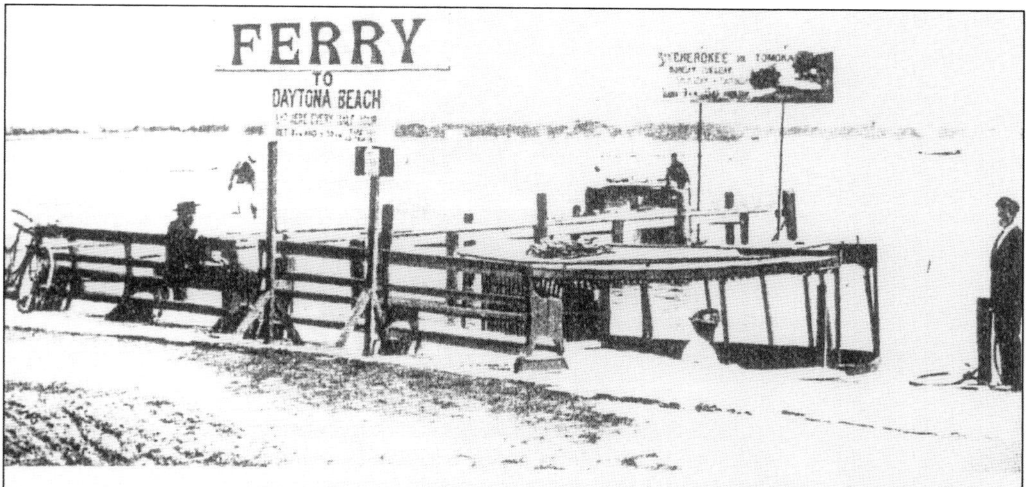

The ferry landing at the foot of Volusia Avenue, Daytona, circa 1915. For 10 cents you could cross the Halifax River from Daytona to Daytona Beach.

THE HALIFAX RIVER FERRY C. 1915. Regular service was offered from mainland Daytona to peninsular Daytona Beach, and the departure dock was near today's Bay Street. The riverboat *Cherokee* can be seen at the dock in the background. Eventually enough bridges were built to make the ferry service obsolete. (Courtesy of Florida State Archives.)

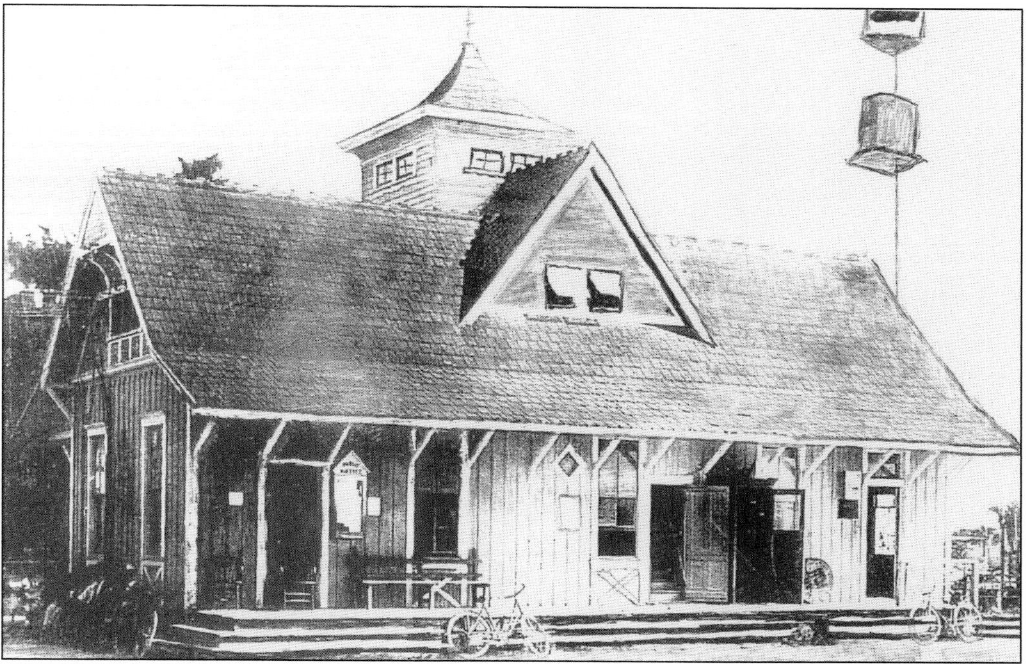

DAYTONA'S FIRST CITY HALL C. 1916. This former depot was converted into Daytona's first city hall and fire station. Notice the bell that warns citizens of a fire or other local emergency. The fire station was moved to a new site across the street *c.* 1926. The city hall was moved into a new building in 1920 on the southwest corner of Orange Avenue and Palmetto Avenue. (Courtesy of Cardwell Family Collection.)

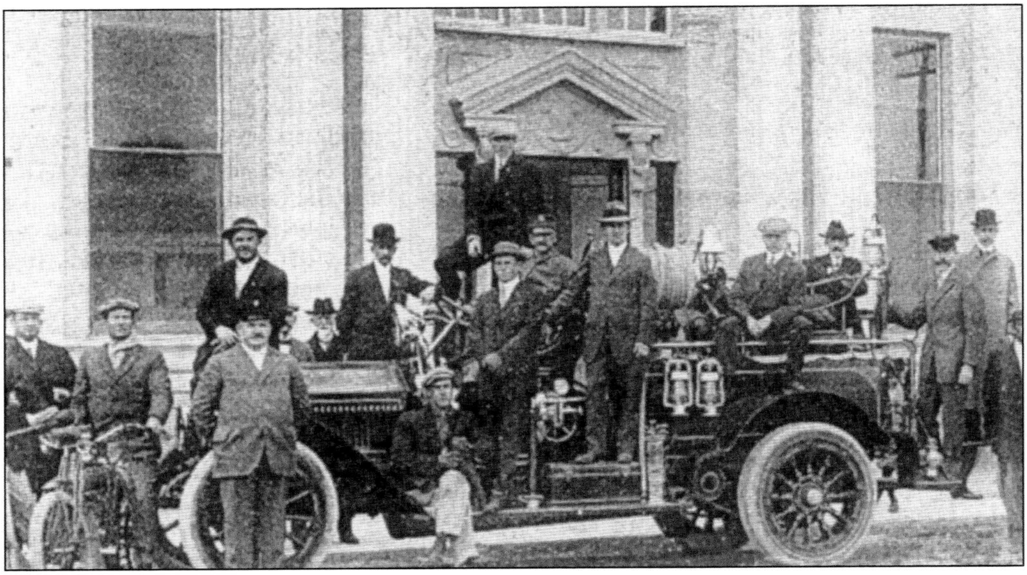

DAYTONA FIRE TRUCK AND FIREMEN C. 1916. Pictured together are the volunteers and paid firemen with the new fire equipment in front of the Merchants Bank on South Beach Street. The city had to depend on volunteers to take care of any emergency that arose and required human rescue. (Courtesy of Halifax Historical Society.)

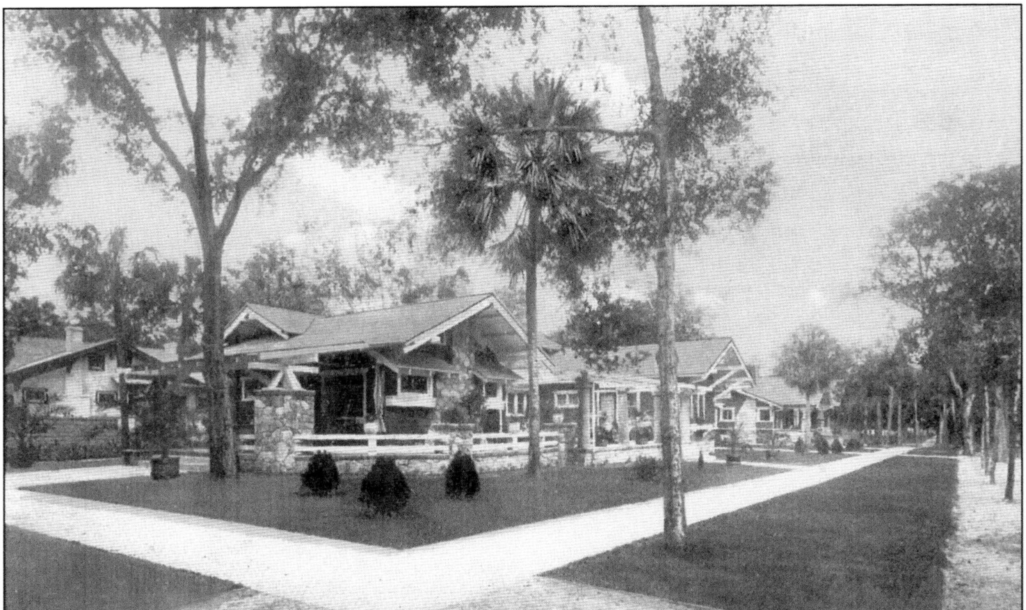

THE THREE BUNGALOWS C. 1916. This property is listed on the National Register of Historic Places and is located in the National Historic District at the northeast corner of South Street and Ridgewood Avenue. These structures were built for T.A. Snider, a famous ketchup maker. Reportedly the structures were designed by Green and Green, who specialized in bungalow-style architecture. S.H. Gove oversaw the construction of these unique winter homes. (Courtesy of Cardwell Family Collection.)

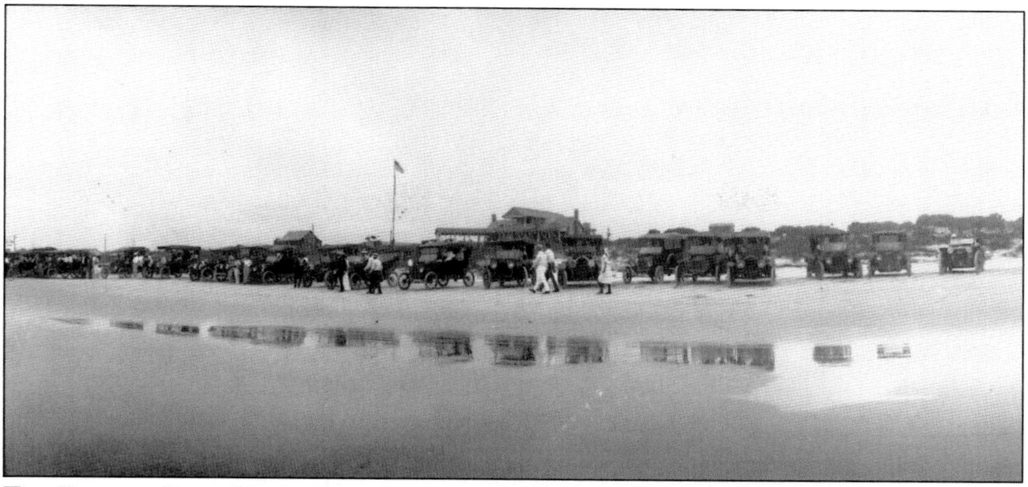

THE FLORIDA EAST COAST AUTOMOBILE ASSOCIATION CLUBHOUSE IN 1916. The club was organized by over 200 members in 1903. A few of the more prominent wealthy members were W.K. Vanderbilt, Henry M. Flagler, Howard Gould, and John Jacob Astor. The clubhouse was originally located near the Silver Beach approach. (Courtesy of John Gontner.)

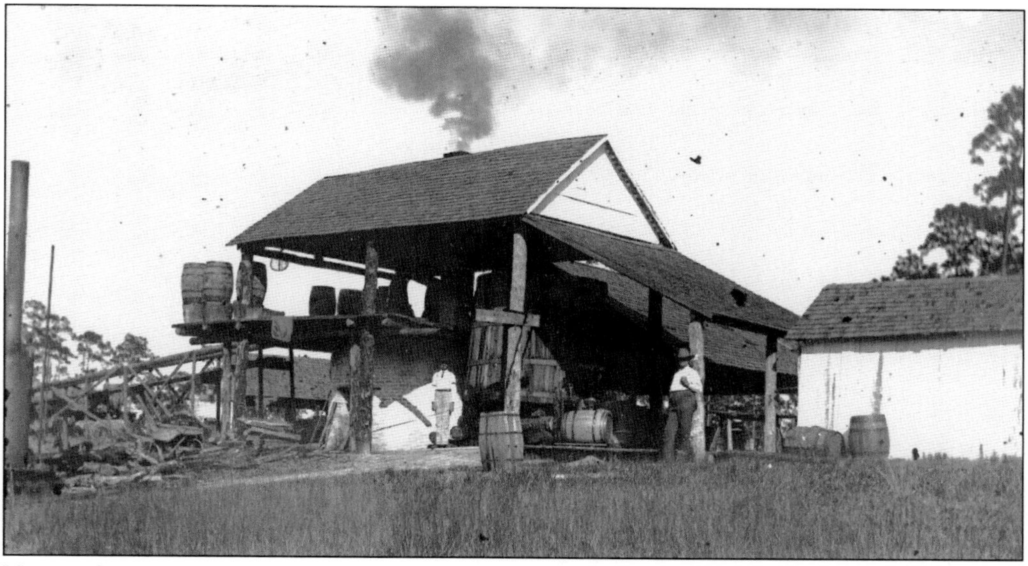

NAVAL STORES OPERATION ON OLD DAYTONA-DELAND ROAD C. 1916. Mr. Paxton, at right, the supervisor of this turpentine distillery near Daytona, stands near the barrels used to hold turpentine and rosin. The ramps on the left side were used to roll the barrels up and down for shipment to the market. The distillery worker at left is unidentified. (Courtesy of Florida State Archives.)

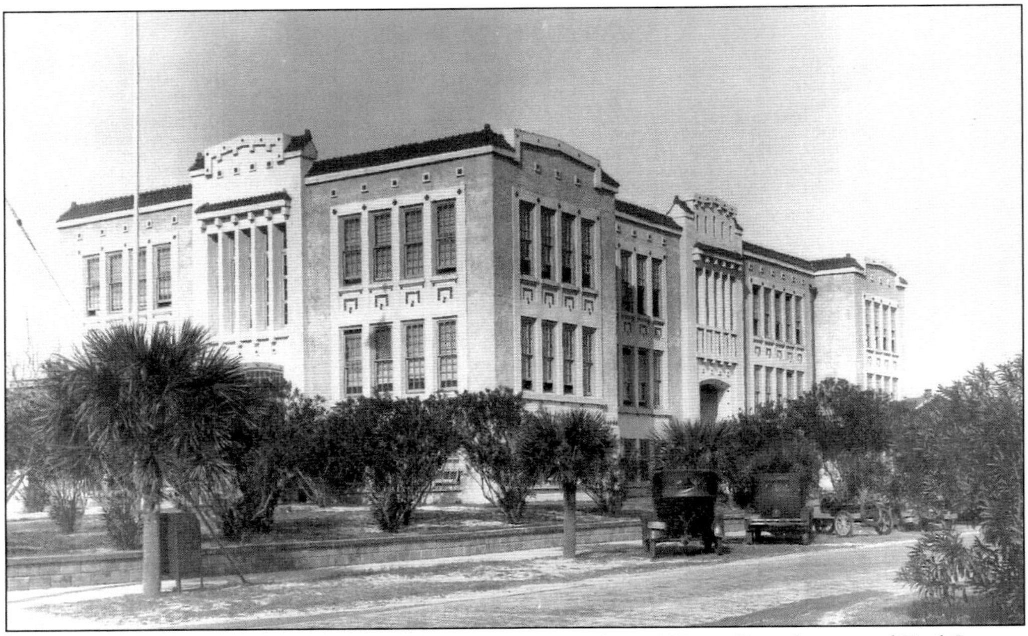

SEABREEZE HIGH SCHOOL. This school was constructed in 1917 on Grandview and Earl Streets at a cost of $58,484.09. A new high school was built in 1962 at 270 North Oleander Street for a cost of $1,257,000. The first school on the peninsula was Momento, built in 1886 at Halifax and Ora Streets. In its growth, two other frame additions were made. The last was on Peninsula and Ora Streets. In 1917 grades 1 through 12 were moved to the new facility. Through the years many changes had to be made because of the growing population on the peninsula. The 1917 Seabreeze High School was demolished in 1985–1986 to make way for the new Volusia County Ocean Center. There is a historic marker near the site commemorating the old school. (Courtesy of Halifax Historical Society.)

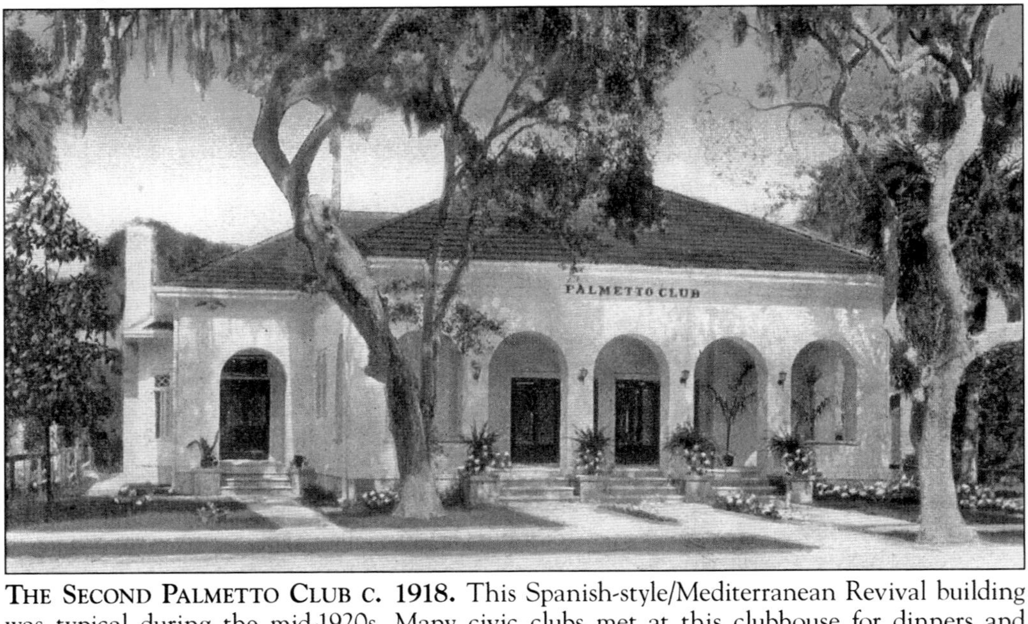

THE SECOND PALMETTO CLUB C. 1918. This Spanish-style/Mediterranean Revival building was typical during the mid-1920s. Many civic clubs met at this clubhouse for dinners and banquets. (Courtesy of Cardwell Family Collection.)

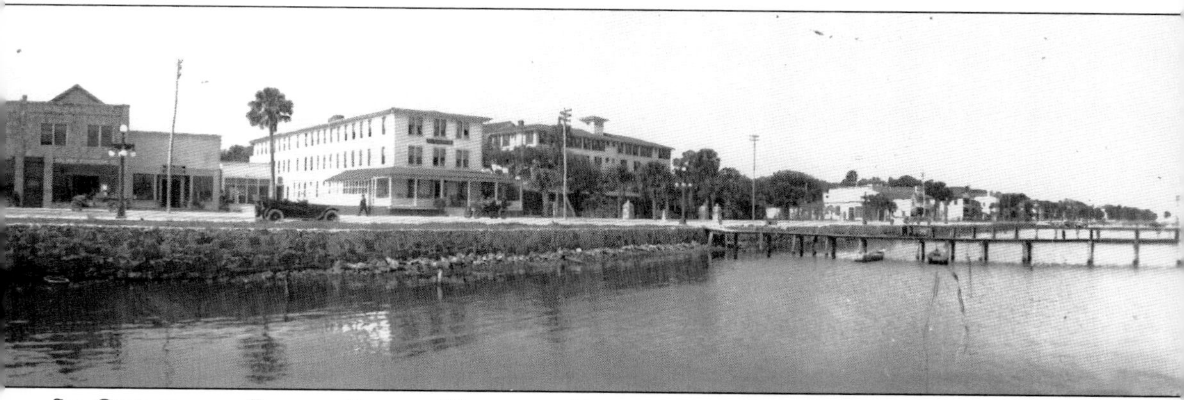

St. George and Prince George Hotels in Daytona c. 1918. These two hotels, located on North Beach Street facing the Halifax River, were very popular. Nearby was the Halifax Furniture Company building. (Courtesy of John Gontner.)

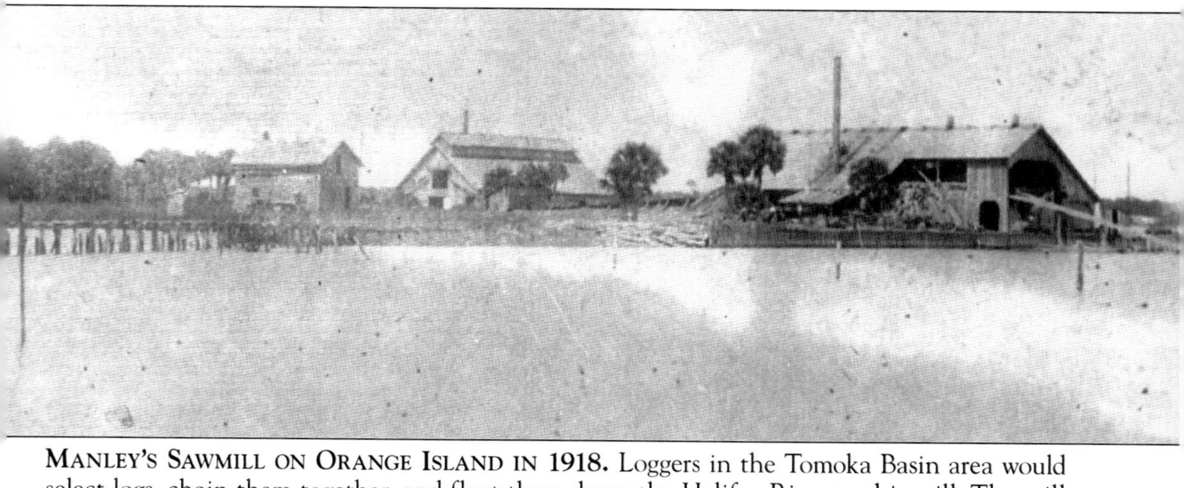

Manley's Sawmill on Orange Island in 1918. Loggers in the Tomoka Basin area would select logs, chain them together, and float them down the Halifax River to this mill. The mill was operated by steam and had a cable-grab that would catch the logs in the river. The lumber company, located just off of North Beach Street on the river, sold many large timbers for bridges and all types of construction. (Courtesy of John Gontner).

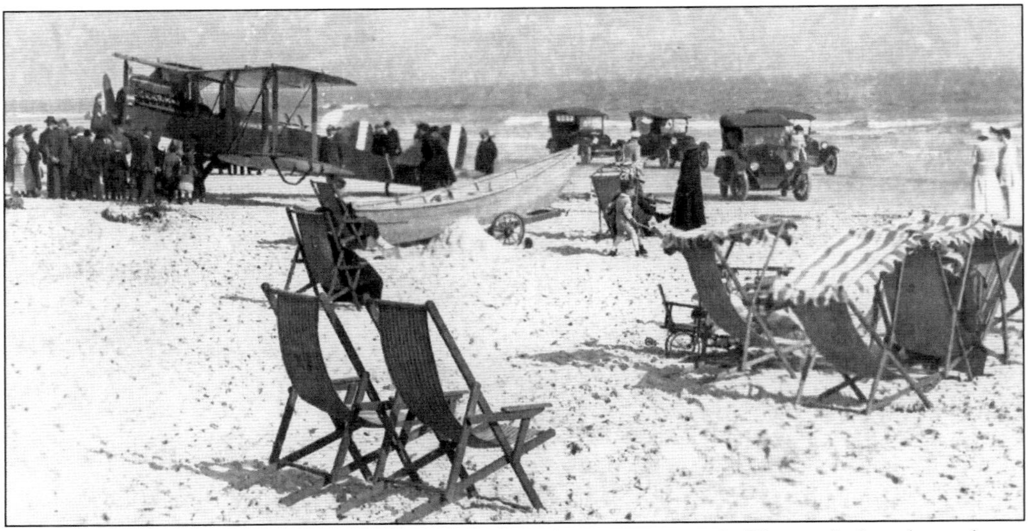

AIRCRAFT, AUTOMOBILES, AND PEOPLE ON THE BEACH IN 1919. The wide beach made an excellent landing strip for aircraft. Later, when the beach became more congested, a commercial airport was constructed on South Beach Street near Wilder's Cut. Automobile owners liked to drive their car at high speeds on the beach because of the smooth, hard-packed sand. The beach was a place for people to gather for leisure time activities. (Courtesy of John Gontner.)

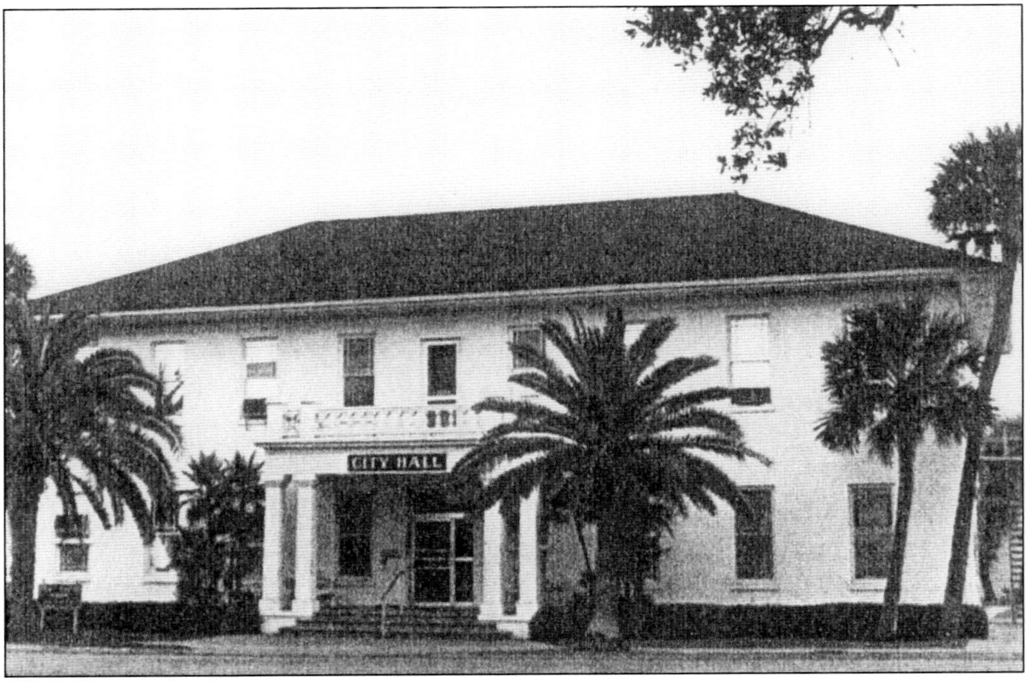

OLD DAYTONA CITY HALL C. 1920. The second city hall was constructed for $20,000 on the corner of Orange Avenue and Palmetto Avenue in 1919. It was here that the Mayor Edward Armstrong Government Feud took place in 1937 (see page 90). City government meetings were held in Jackson's store, the Palmetto House, above the Thompson Brothers' store, and Jackson Hall until 1898. (Courtesy of City of Daytona Beach.)

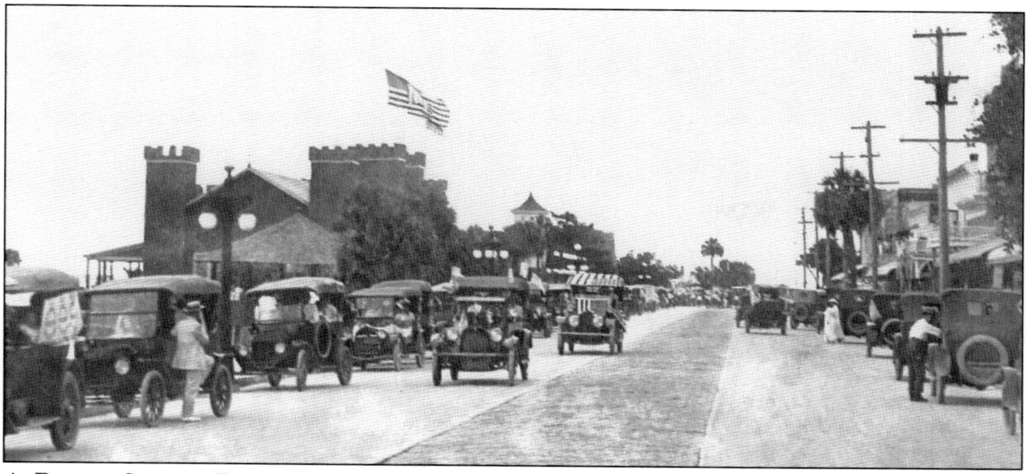

A Beach Street Parade in 1920. Citizens celebrate the Fourth of July on South Beach Street near the Burgoyne Casino, seen in the left background. People demonstrated patriotism after World War I in Daytona; the main holidays were the Fourth of July, Armistice Day, and Memorial Day. (Courtesy of John Gontner.)

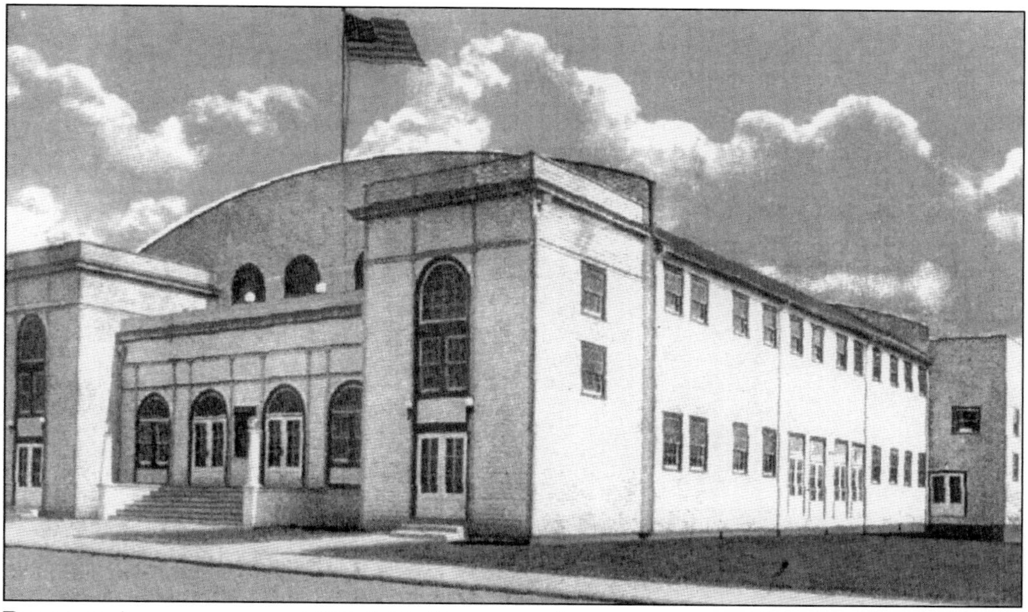

Peabody Auditorium in 1920. This Daytona auditorium was named for Simon J. Peabody, a timber baron residing on North Halifax Drive who donated funds to build the structure. Many nationally known orchestras and bands gave concerts at this auditorium, including John Philip Sousa. It burned c. 1948 and was rebuilt by 1950. Peabody Auditorium continues to provide a tradition of fine entertainment for the public. (Courtesy of City of Daytona Beach.)

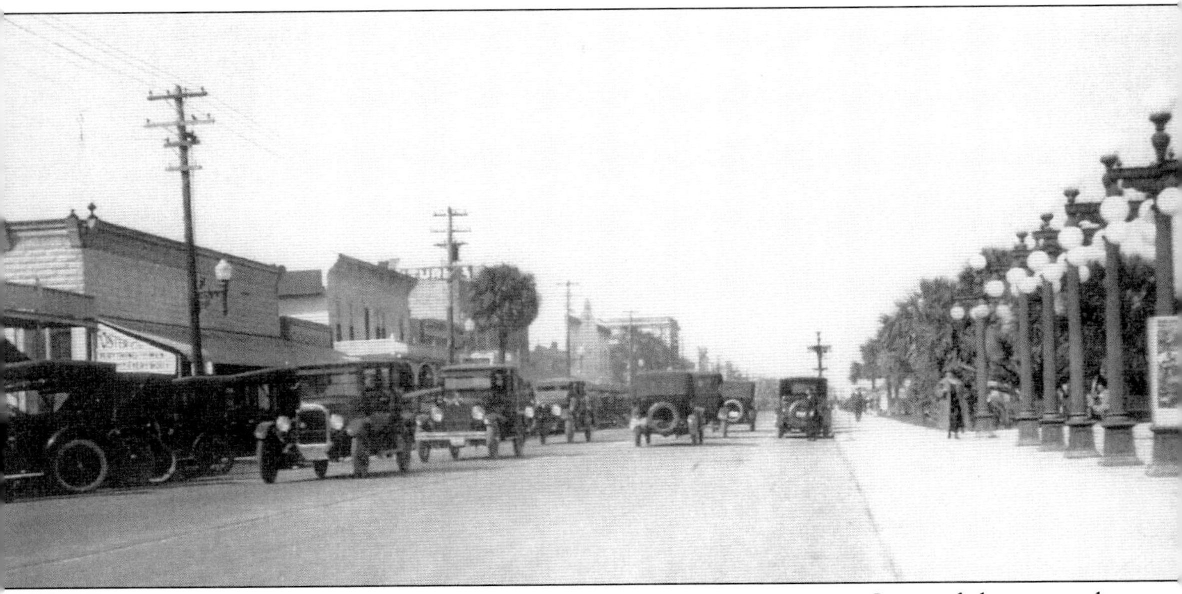

BEACH STREET LOOKING NORTH FROM IVY LANE IN THE 1920S. Some of the stores that can be seen are Foster's, Bingham and Maley, and the Anthony Brothers', which later became Yowell-Drew Ivey's Store. (Courtesy of Halifax Historical Society.)

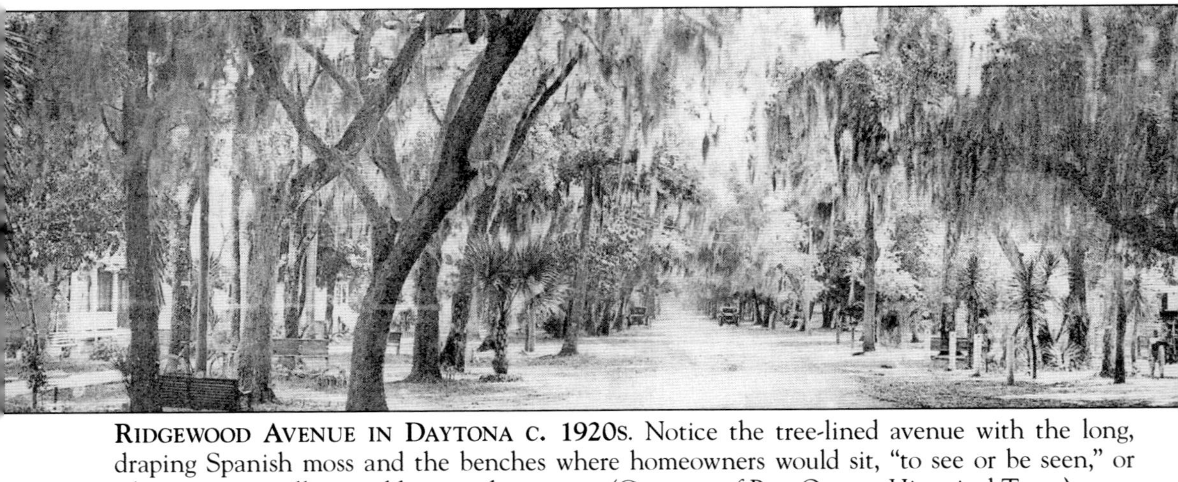

RIDGEWOOD AVENUE IN DAYTONA C. 1920S. Notice the tree-lined avenue with the long, draping Spanish moss and the benches where homeowners would sit, "to see or be seen," or where weary strollers could rest and converse. (Courtesy of Port Orange Historical Trust.)

Five

Real Estate Boom 1921–1930

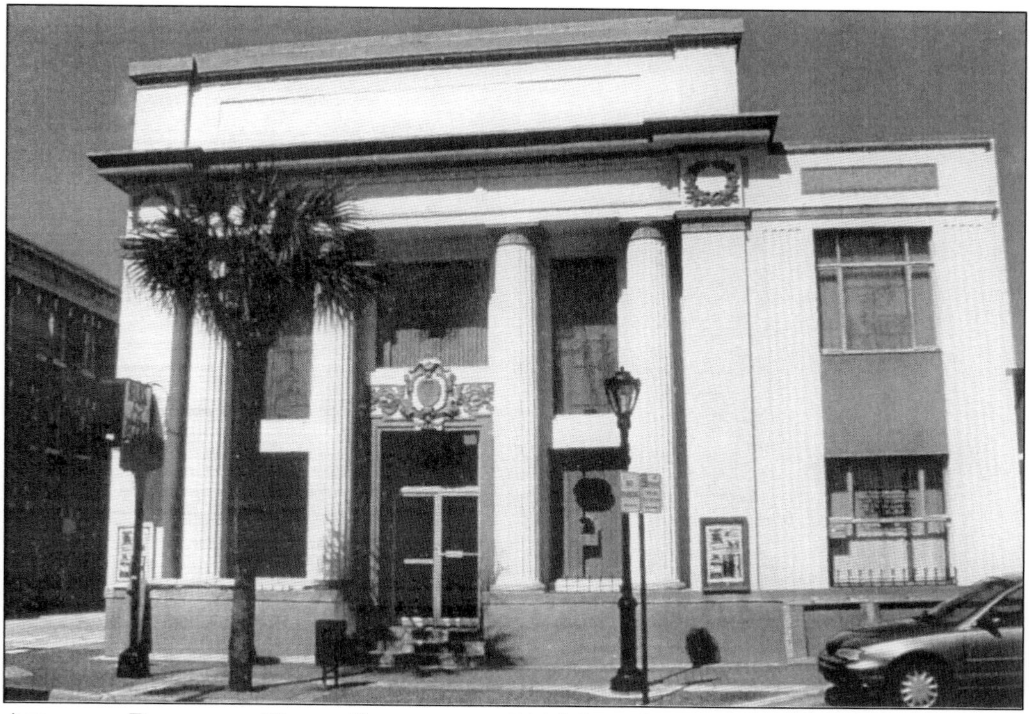

Atlantic Bank and Trust Company at 701 Main Street in 1921. F.N. Conrad was president, and C.A. Randall was cashier. The bank closed on July 11, 1929, after panic-stricken depositors withdrew their money prior to the stock market crash, and in 1934 it became the First Federal Savings and Loan Association. Today this building is a nightclub called The Bank and Blues Club. The original boardroom furniture is currently being utilized at the Halifax Historical Society Museum. (Courtesy of City of Daytona Beach.)

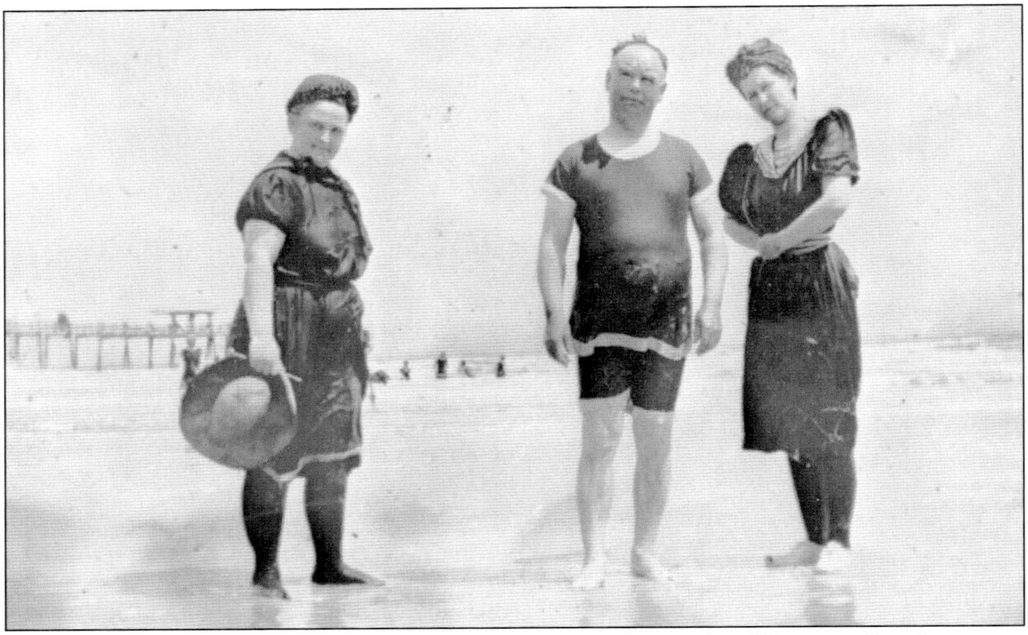

Bathers on the Beach c. 1921. These bathers on the sands of Daytona Beach pose in their latest-fashion beachwear. Most bathing suits were made of wool and did not really fit the subtropical heat. The enjoyment of wading and swimming in the surf took away the thought of the hot and itchy woolen suits. (Courtesy of Florida State Archives.)

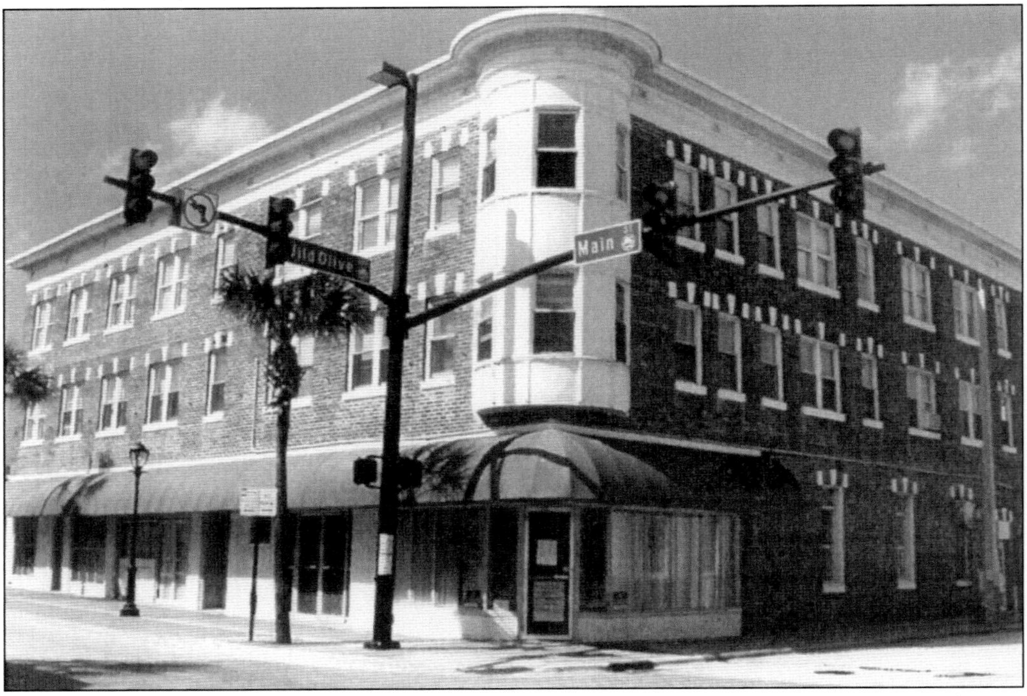

The Fernwood Hotel c. 1922. Winter visitors came back to this popular hotel each year to see and meet each other. Mrs. Bessie S. Crews was owner and manager for many years. Demolished in 2001, this landmark hotel was located at 615 Main Street near the beach, Ocean Pier, and the boardwalk. (Courtesy of City of Daytona Beach.)

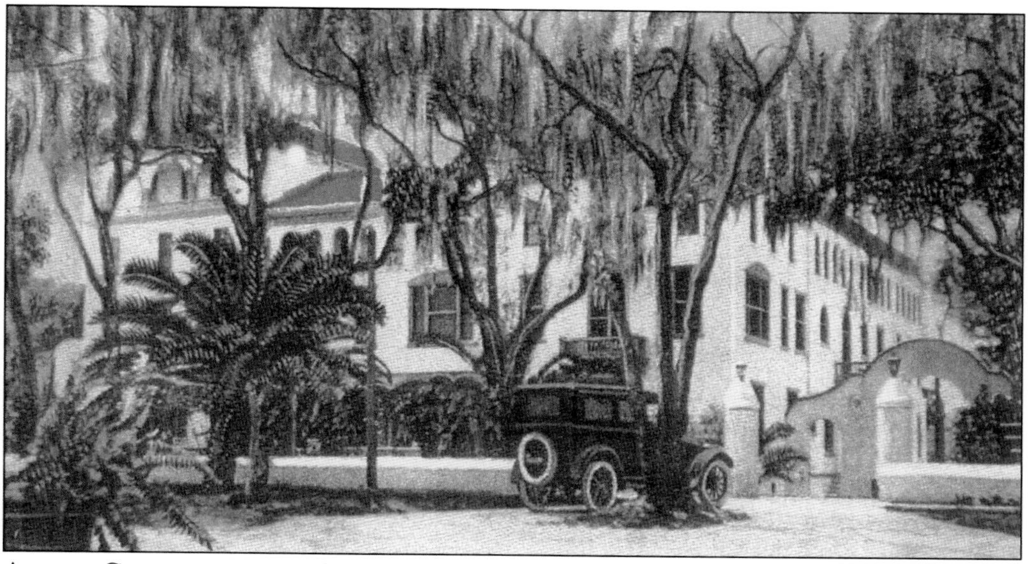

ARROYO GARDENS C. 1923. Originally built as a garden-apartment complex for winter visitors, this complex was purchased by R.E. Olds, an automobile manufacturer, as a home for retired ministers in 1940; he renamed it Olds Hall. Today this property is known as the Olds Hall Good Samaritan Center, a retirement assisted-living facility and nursing home located at 325 South Segrave Street. (Courtesy of Midkiff Family Collection.)

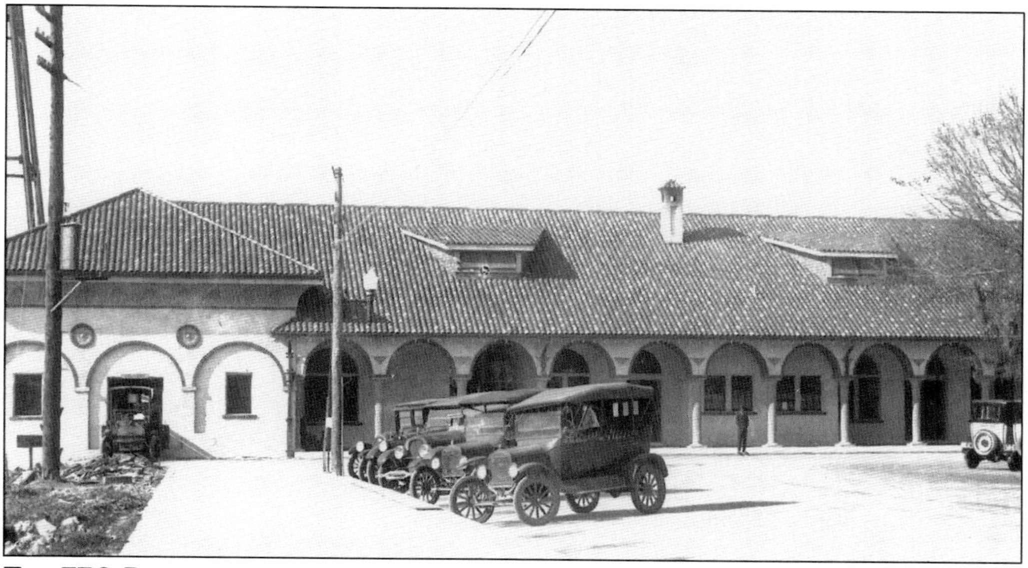

THE FEC PASSENGER DEPOT C. 1925. This beautiful Mediterranean-Revival depot had a red, barrel-tile roof, marble benches, and an ornate clock and ticket window. The depot was located at the foot of Magnolia Avenue at the railroad and was demolished in the 1980s by the FEC trustees. Today there is no longer passenger service out of Daytona Beach. (Courtesy of John Gontner.)

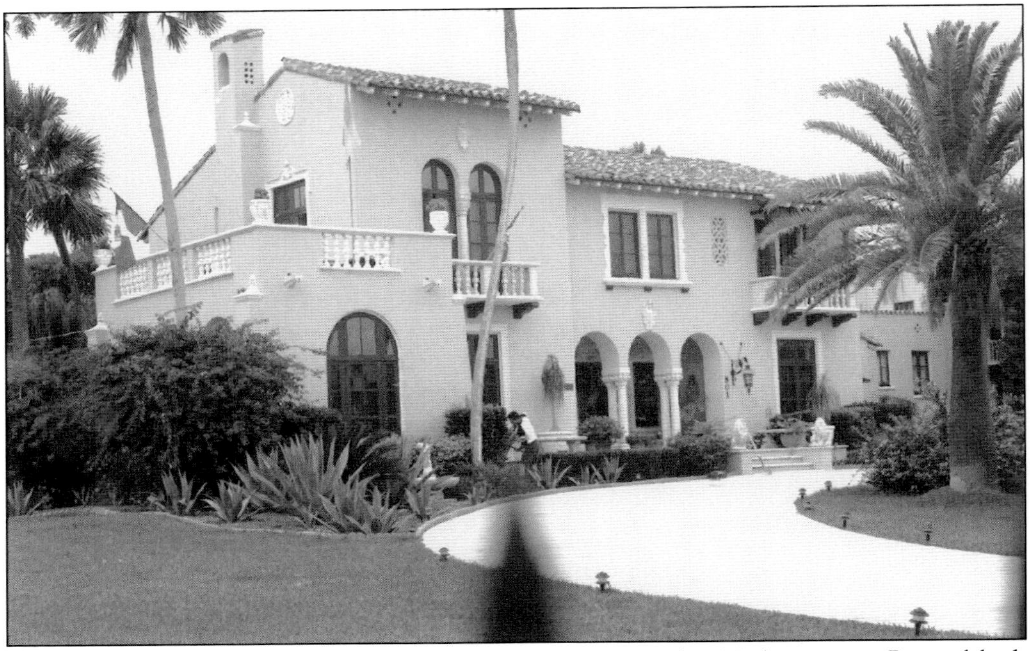

The Villa at 801 North Peninsula Drive in 1997. This Mediterranean-Revival bed-and-breakfast, the former Bartholomew Donnelly Home, was built *c.* 1926. This outstanding structure is one-and-a-half stories with a terra-cotta–tile roof and exterior stucco. The windows are embellished with terra-cotta surrounds and arched doorways. (Courtesy of Cardwell Family Collection.)

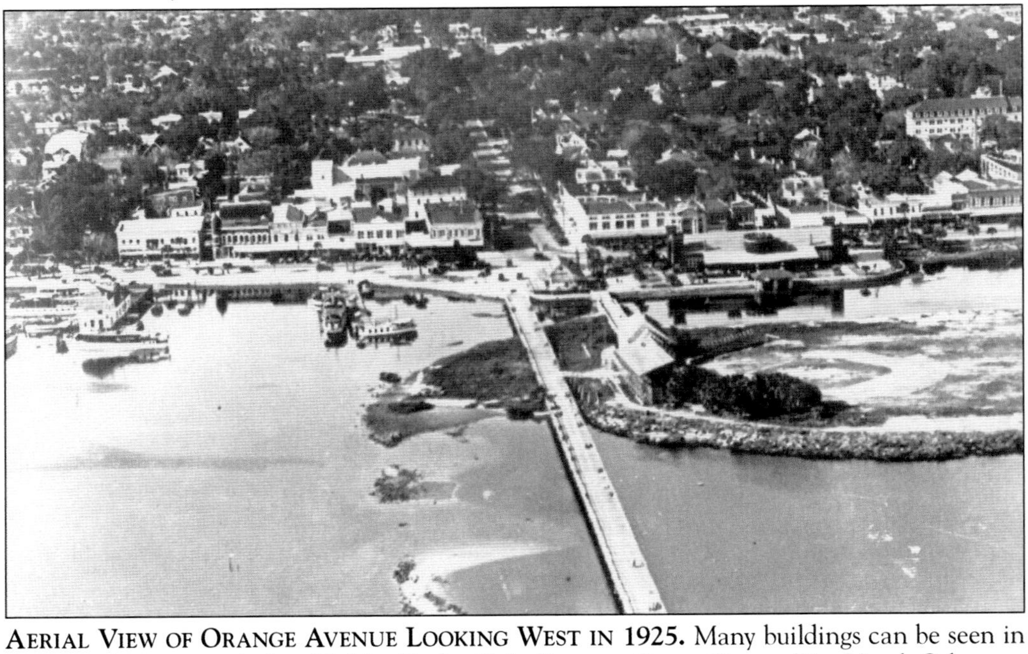

Aerial View of Orange Avenue Looking West in 1925. Many buildings can be seen in the near distance, including Halifax Yacht Club, Daytona Opera House, City Hotel, Osbourne Hotel, Conrad Building, Merchants Bank, the Williams Hotel (in the right background), and the Burgoyne Casino. Other buildings are unidentified. The ballpark is in the right front of the picture. (Courtesy of John Gontner.)

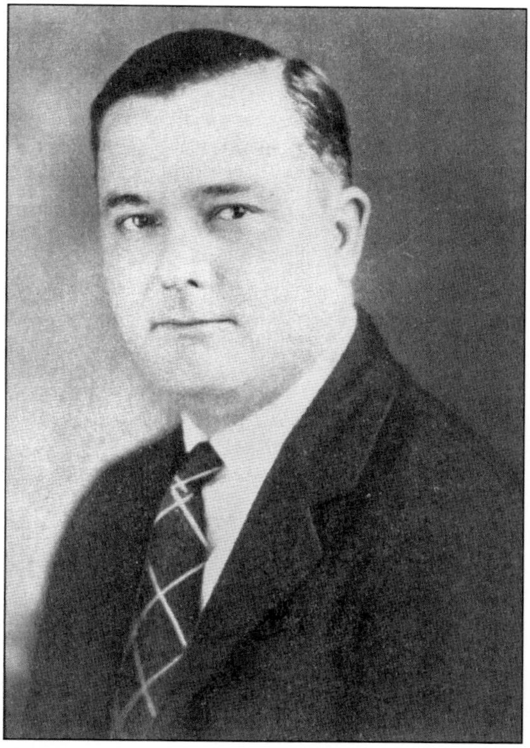

BASIL F. BRASS IN 1926. Basil Brass was an attorney who graduated from Stetson University with a law degree in 1916. Through a lawsuit he was able to bring the privately owned bridges to county ownership. He was elected the first mayor of the consolidated cities of Daytona, Seabreeze, and Daytona Beach, which made the city of Daytona Beach, Florida, in 1926. After involving himself in politics, he returned to his law practice of Gardiner and Brass, specializing in corporate law, and he continued to be involved with civic affairs and organizations. (Courtesy of Cardwell Family Collection.)

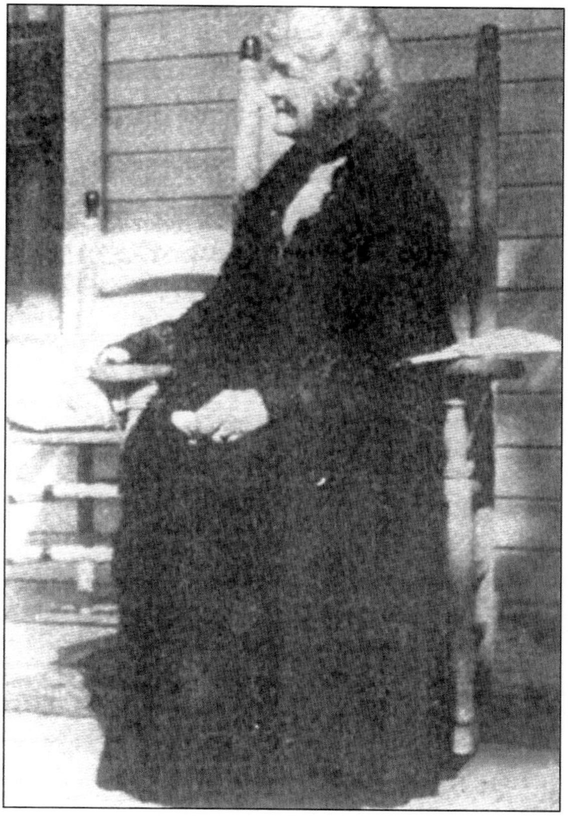

SARAH "SALLY" CUSTER C. 1926. Gen. George Armstrong Custer's widow sits in her favorite chair on the porch of the famous Seville Hotel at 211 South Street, where she wintered as a guest each year. Following her death c. 1930, she was laid to rest alongside her husband at the United States Military Academy in New York. (Courtesy of Halifax Historical Society.)

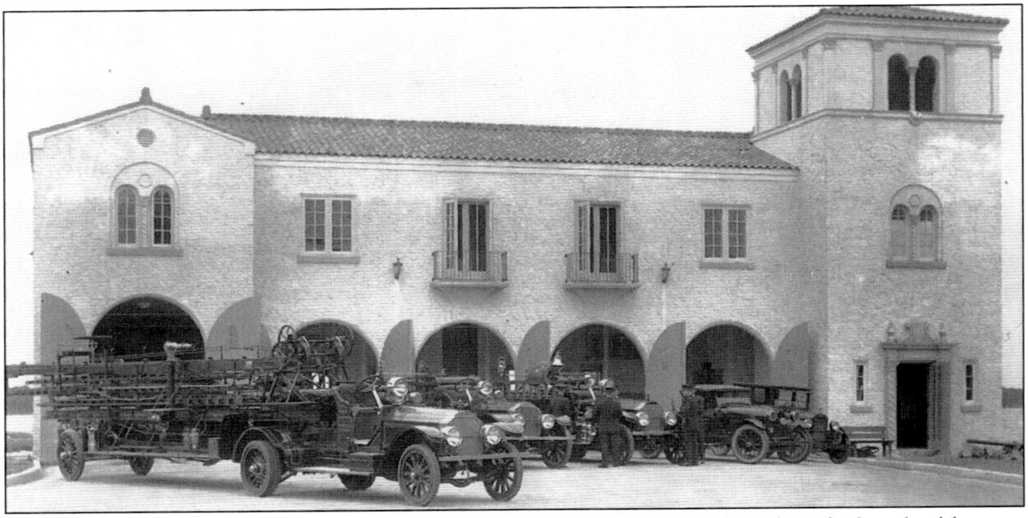

DAYTONA BEACH FIRE STATION C. 1926. The architectural style of this building is Mediterranean Revival. It is stucco on block with red, barrel-tile roofing. Notice the two French doors with balconies. The fire department was very proud of its ladder truck, parked in front of the main station on South Beach Street. (Courtesy of John Gontner.)

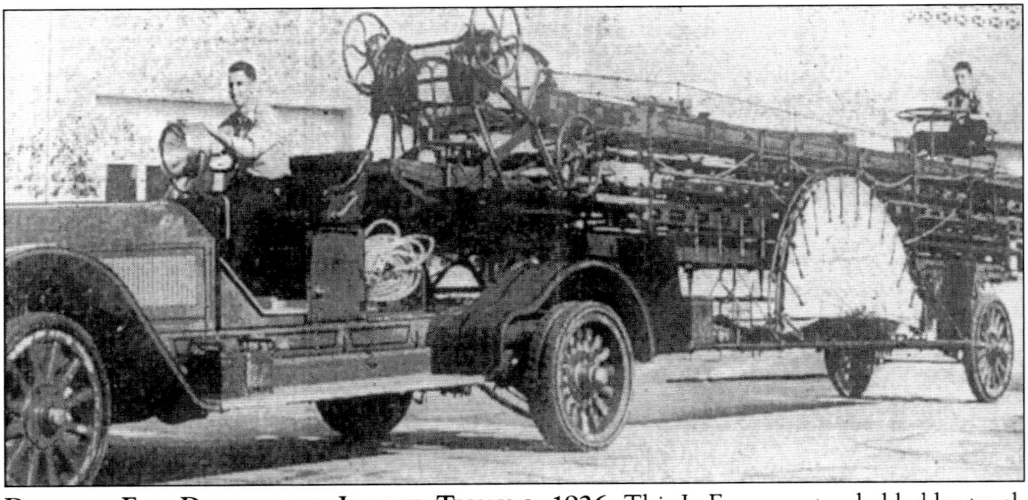

DAYTONA FIRE DEPARTMENT LADDER TRUCK C. 1926. This LaFrance extended-ladder truck required a fireman to guide the rear wheels when negotiating turns. The fireman had to develop steering skills to coordinate turns with the main truck. This was Daytona's first long-ladder rescue equipment with a chain-and-sprocket driven engine. The siren had to be hand-cranked by a passenger in the cab. (Courtesy of Halifax Historical Society.)

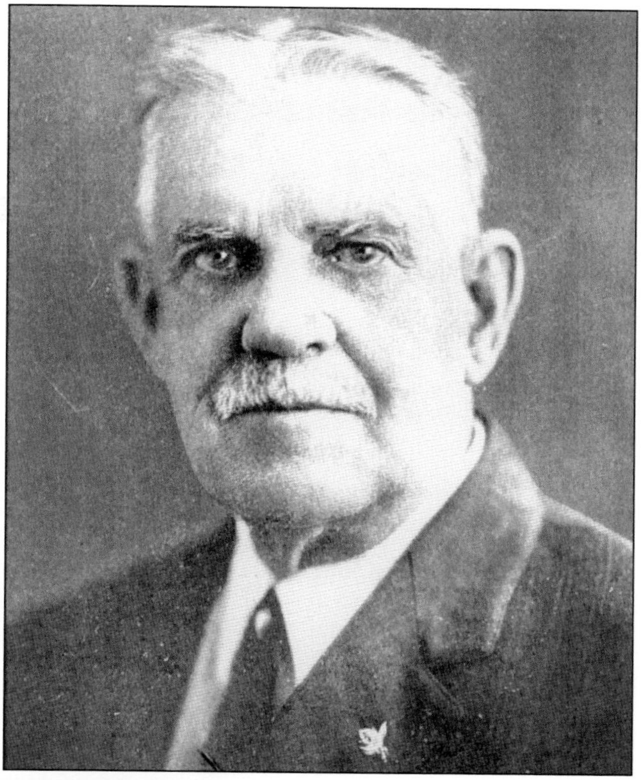

SUMNER HALE GOVE, 1853–1926. Gove was an architect and builder of many homes, businesses, and schools in the Daytona Beach area. He was a pioneer builder of many buildings, including the Rexall Drug Store, Daytona High School, the Anthony and Conrad Buildings, the Prince George Hotel, the first Clarendon Hotel, the old Colonnades Hotel, the Ormond Hotel addition, and the Port Orange and Seabreeze Bridges. His home on Anita Street still stands today. (Courtesy of Halifax Historical Society.)

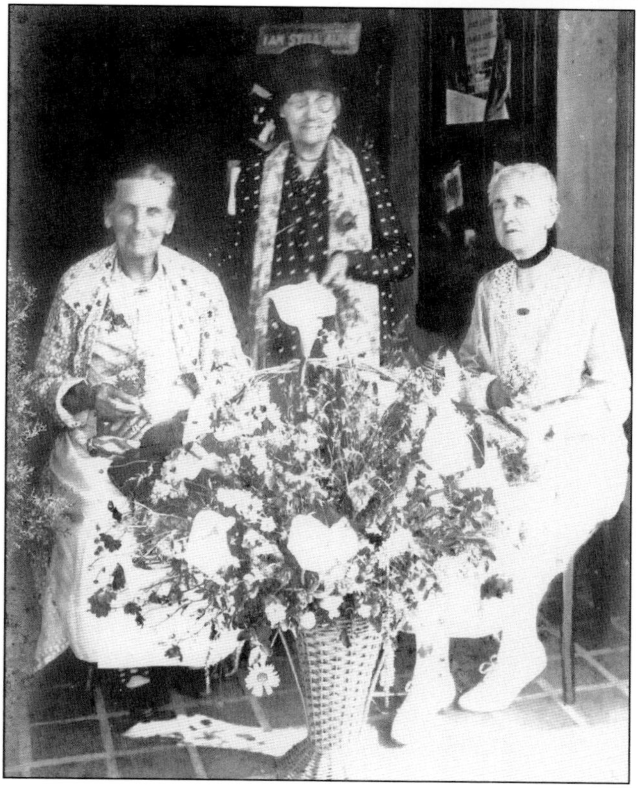

THE FLORIDA THEATRE AT 510 MAIN STREET C. 1926. A promotional feature to attract attention for the show *Three Moms* is shown here. These three local moms in costume dress are helping with the advertising of this great production. In early days, this was a way to draw attention to the theater. (Courtesy of Cardwell Family Collection.)

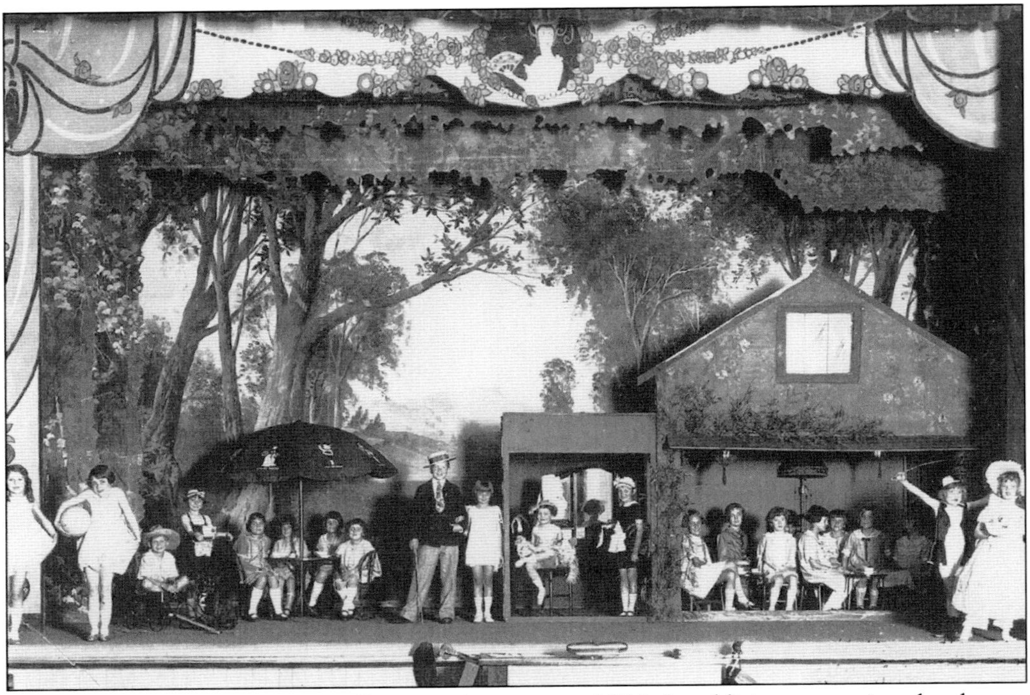

The Vivian Theatre at 129 Orange Avenue in 1926. In addition to movies, the theater management presented live stage productions. The featured show is a live children's fashion review that brings the whole family to the theater. Often local stage shows were featured to help increase attendance. (Courtesy of Cardwell Family Collection.)

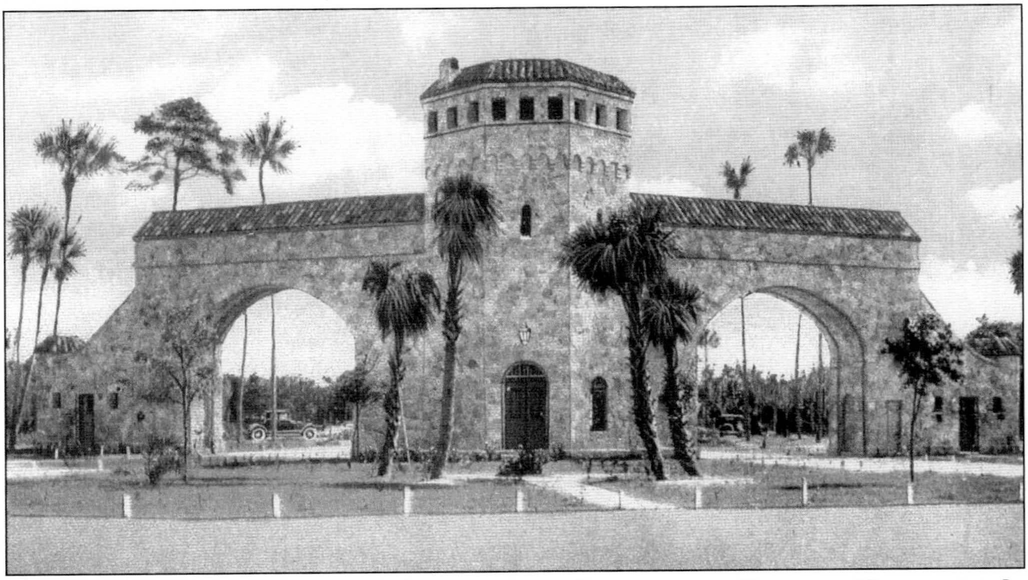

Tarragona Tower in 1926, the Medieval Arch Entrance to Daytona Highlands. In the 1920s Daytona Highlands was a suburb of small hills and lakes. Elias F. De La Haye designed this subdivision entrance, and the artwork was done by Don J. Emery. At the beginning of World War II the north gate was torn down to widen Volusia Avenue and facilitate the entrance to the Second WAC Training Center, where Daytona Beach Community College is located today. (Courtesy of Cardwell Family Collection.)

MAJ. HENRY O'NEILL DEHANE SEGRAVE C. 1927. Segrave received his knighthood when he returned to England after breaking the world ground speed record at Daytona Beach. One of Daytona's prominent streets bears his name, and many honors were given to him. He is credited with wearing the first safety helmet. (Courtesy of Halifax Historical Society.)

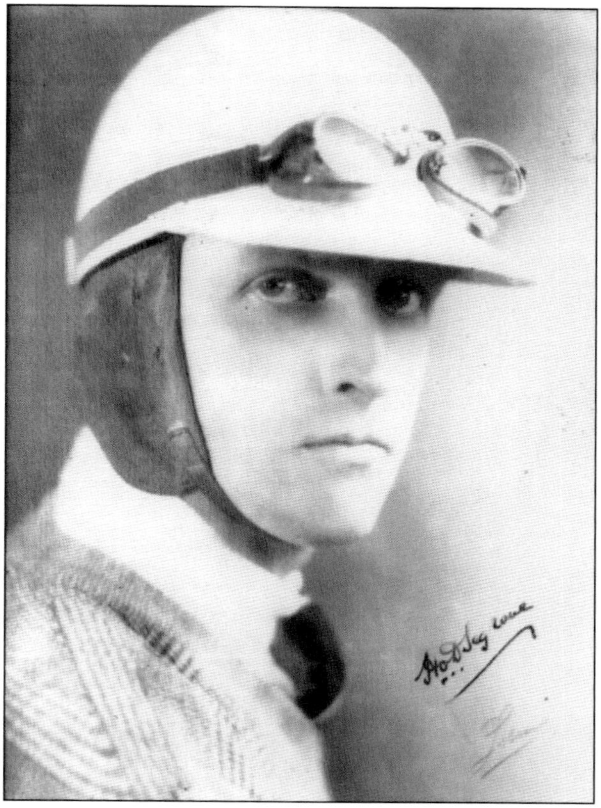

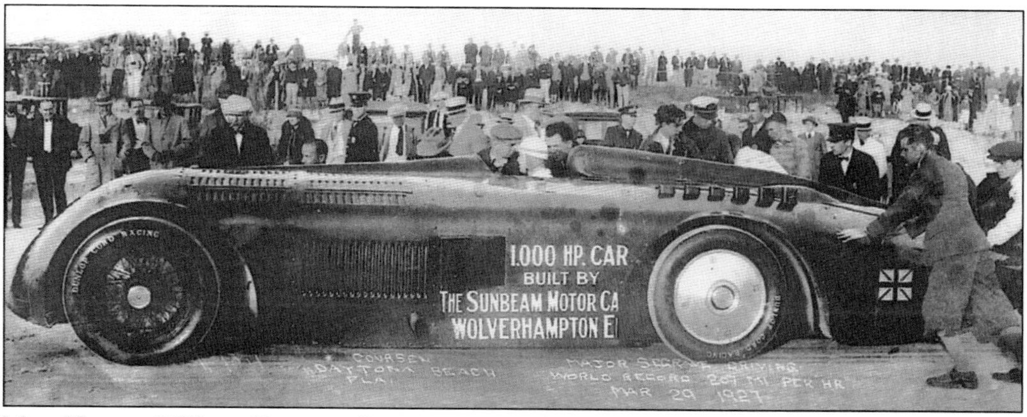

MAJ. HENRY O'NEILL DEHANE SEGRAVE IN HIS SUNBEAM MYSTERY-S ON MARCH 29, 1927. Segrave returned to Daytona Beach in 1929 and broke the world record through the Measured Mile at 231.36 miles per hour in his Golden Arrow. Segrave was killed in a speedboat accident in England in the summer of 1930. (Courtesy of Halifax Historical Society.)

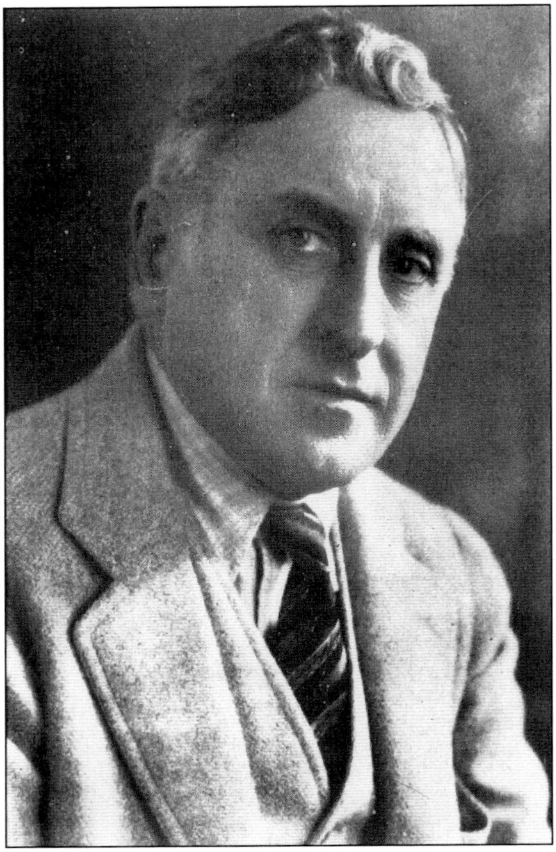

BANKER FREDERICK N. CONRAD IN 1927. Mr. Conrad began his career in DeLand, Florida, working as a lumber clerk for the Bond Lumber Company. The Volusia County Bank opened in 1896, and he started working as a bank clerk and cashier. Later that same year he was transferred to the Daytona branch and within five years became the most important banker on the east coast of Florida. Later he was president of the Merchants Bank and Trust Company, Florida Bank and Trust Company, Malby-Conrad Lumber Company, and other banking and lending corporations. A civic leader in Daytona and Volusia County, he was Daytona's most outstanding banker. (Courtesy of Cardwell Family Collection.)

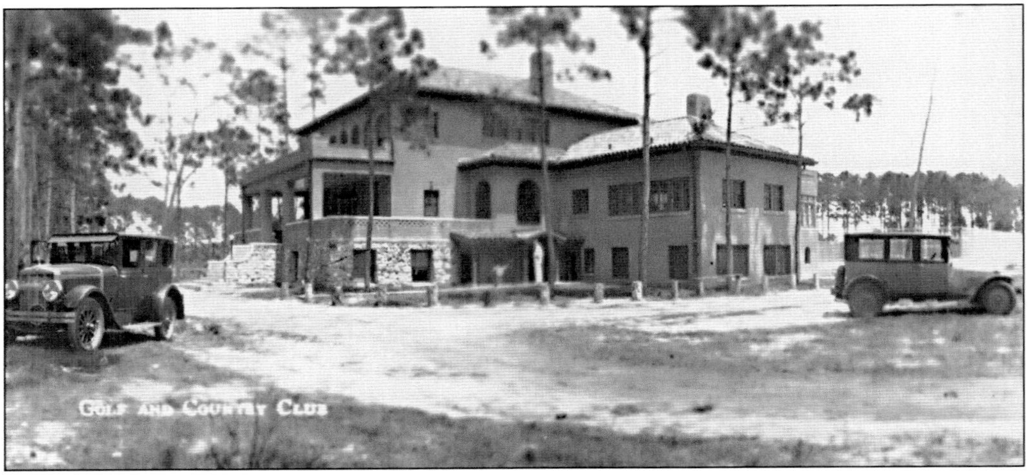

DAYTONA BEACH GOLF AND COUNTRY CLUB IN 1927. The clubhouse featured fine dining and also was a place for banquets, wedding receptions, and reunions. Dances were often held featuring local bands and other entertainment. (Courtesy of John Gontner.)

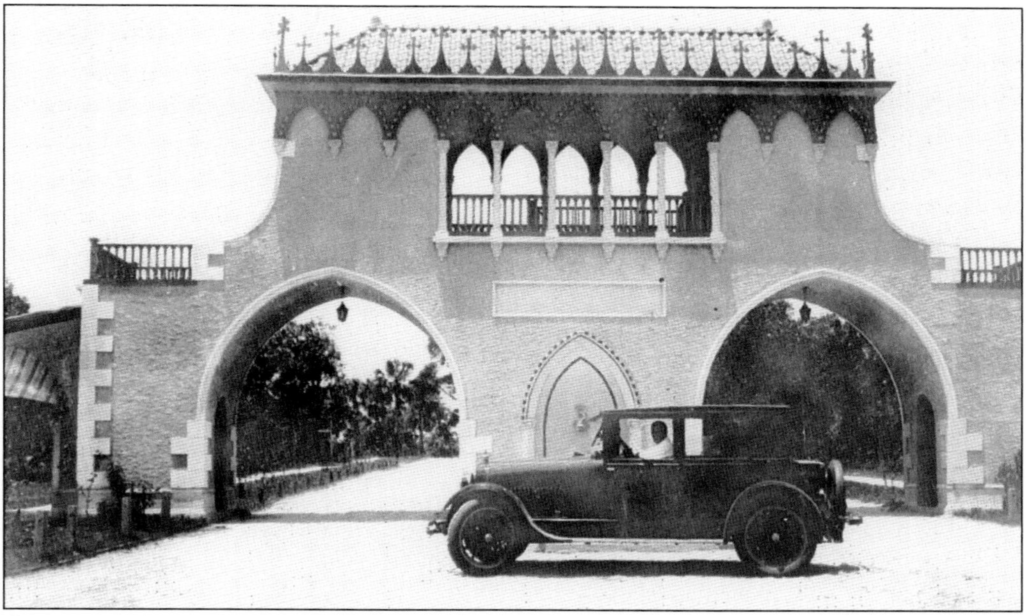

GANYMEDE ARCH C. 1927 IN SOUTH DAYTONA. Ridge Boulevard goes into this subdivision today. During the real estate boom, this subdivision had grandiose plans. The arch was completed along with seven model homes. All the main streets were laid out and the sidewalks were put in, but the streets were never paved. A large hotel and golf course were planned but never constructed. The old, Spanish-style model homes are all still standing amid a beautiful community of modern residences. Unfortunately this magnificent arch was demolished in the 1950s to accommodate the widening of U.S. Highway 1. Notice the vintage car parked in front of the archway. (Courtesy of Cardwell Family Collection.)

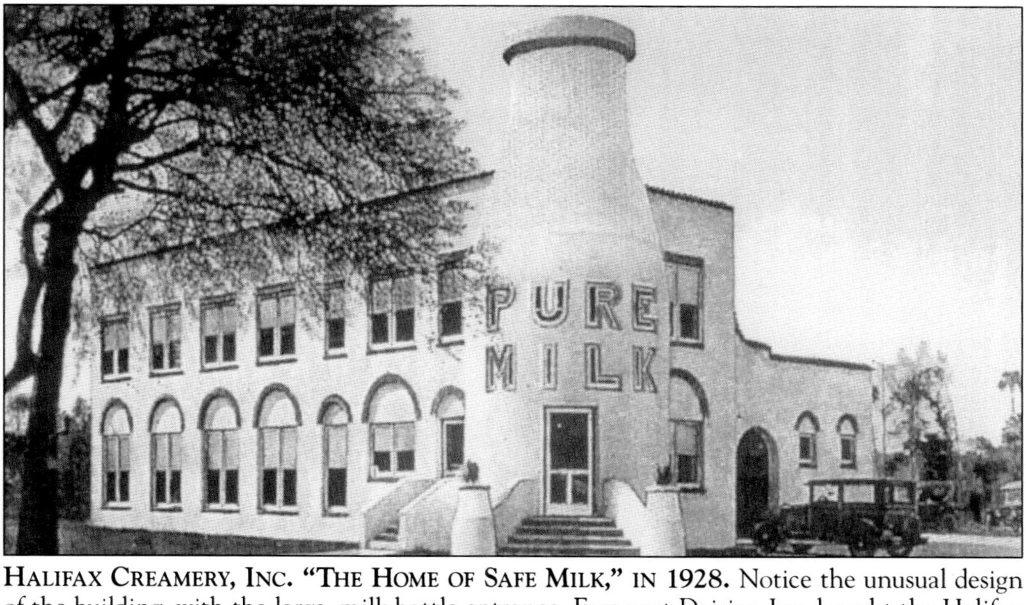

HALIFAX CREAMERY, INC. "THE HOME OF SAFE MILK," IN 1928. Notice the unusual design of the building, with the large, milk-bottle entrance. Foremost Dairies, Inc. bought the Halifax Creamery in the mid-1930s. They advertised "Golden Guernsey Milk," and in the 1950s they sold to Borden Dairies, Inc. The original site was located at present-day 950 West International Speedway Boulevard. (Courtesy of D. Spencer.)

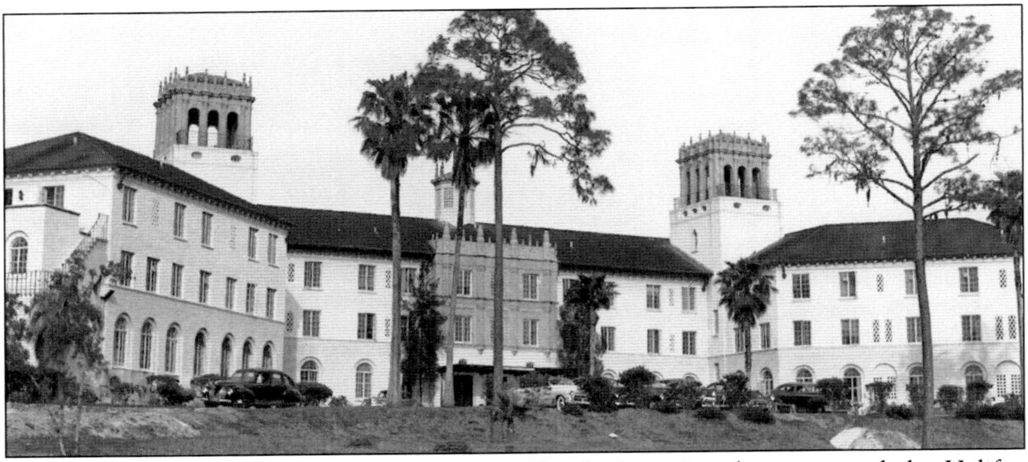

HALIFAX DISTRICT HOSPITAL IN 1950. The Florida State Legislature created the Halifax District Hospital by a special act and issued $750,000 in bonds in 1925. This three-story Mediterranean-Revival hospital was completed in 1928 with 125 beds. The county leased the hospital to the U.S. Army from 1942 to 1947. Halifax Hospital was moved to 624 South Atlantic Avenue and moved back to its present location in January 1947, when the army released their contract. The first expansion program started in 1953 at a cost of $300,000. Many more expansion projects have been added over the years as the district has grown. (Courtesy of Cardwell Family Collection.)

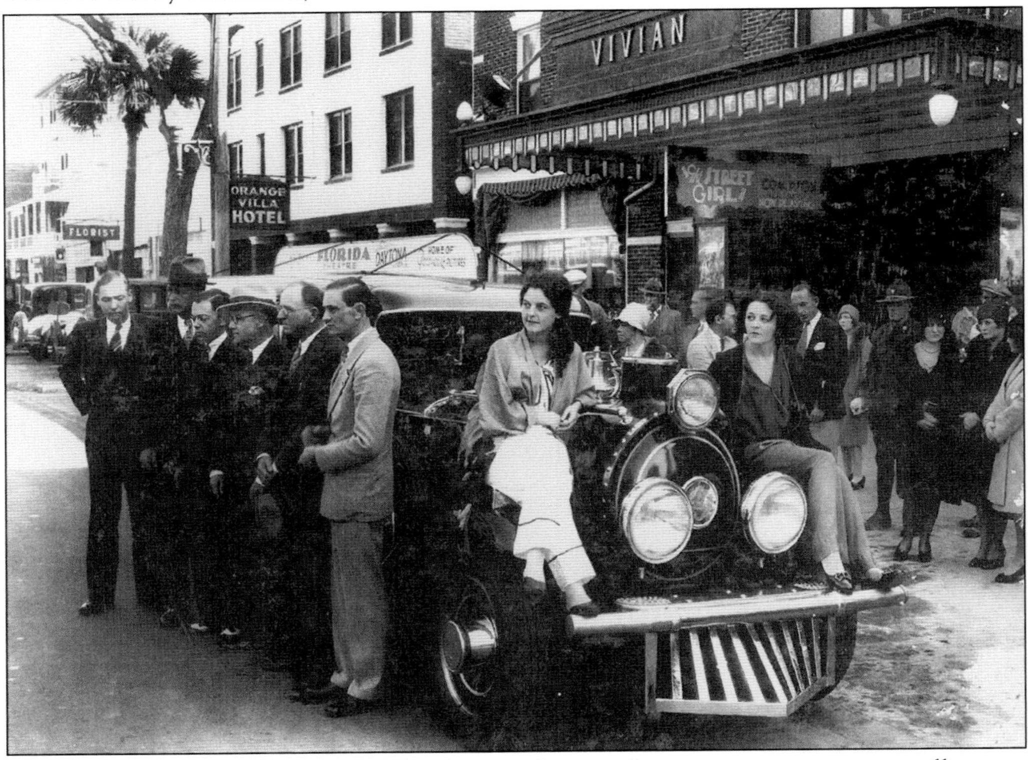

THE VIVIAN THEATRE C. 1929. The Orange Avenue theater management went all out to promote the different shows. This particular promotion featured *The Street Girl*. These two beauties were dressed for the occasion and posed on the luxurious limousine. (Courtesy of Cardwell Family Collection.)

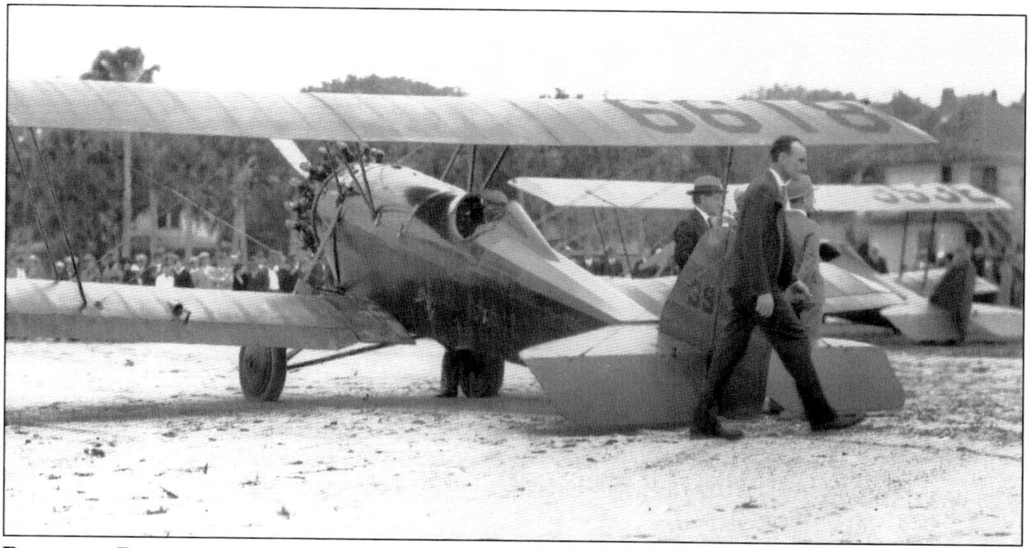

Bethune Point Airport on March 1, 1929. An air-mail plane sits at the end of the runway prior to take-off; the pilot can be seen in the cockpit. Shortly after becoming airborne, this plane crashed in the Halifax River. In 1925 this airstrip was graded for a runway, funded by local aircraft enthusiasts. (Courtesy of John Gontner.)

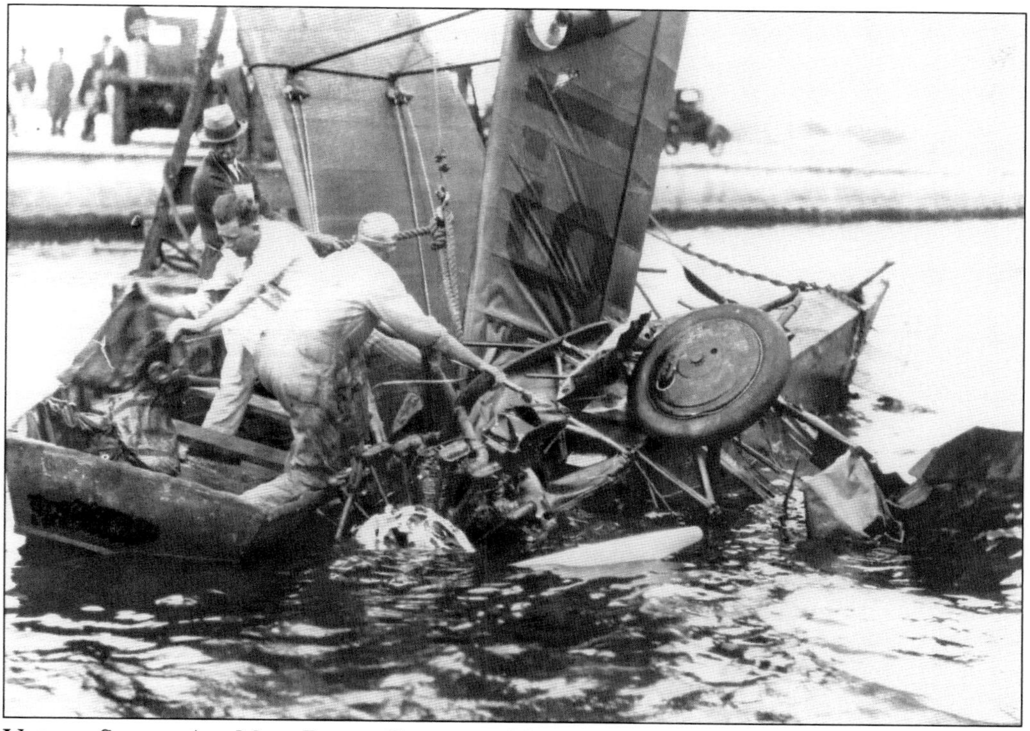

United States Air Mail Plane Crash on March 1, 1929. This plane crashed on take-off from the Bethune Point Airport on South Beach Street on its maiden flight. Airport workers and volunteers gathered to salvage the mail from the wreckage in the Halifax River. Pilot C.J. Faulkner survived with only a cut nose. Bethune Point was the first airport for Daytona Beach. (Courtesy of John Gontner.)

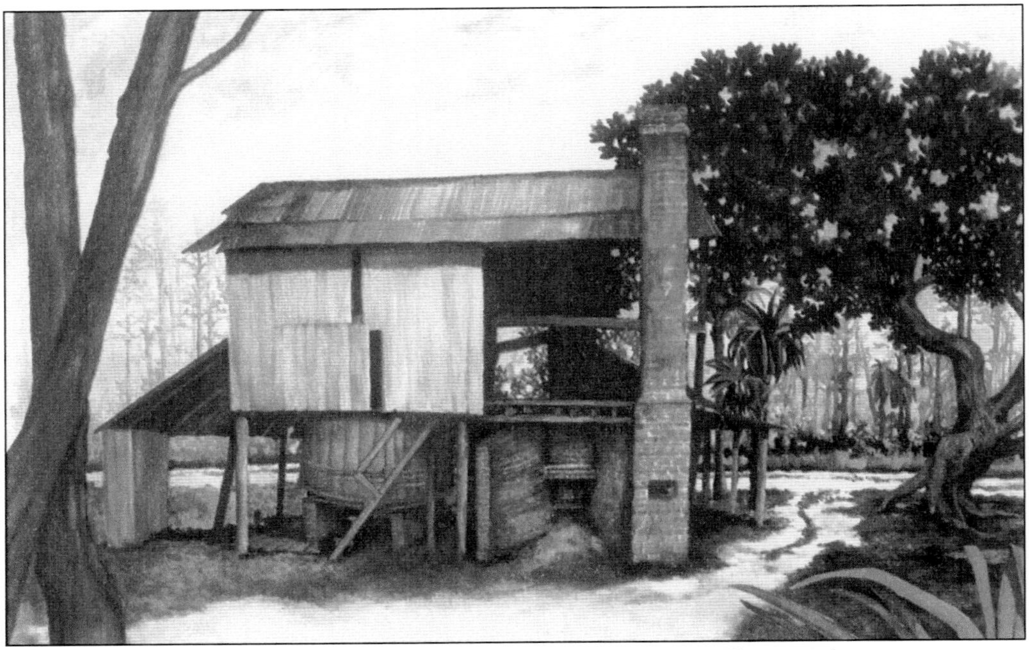

OLD TOMOKA LAND COMPANY TURPENTINE STILL C. 1929. This naval stores operation stood just outside Daytona Beach off old DeLand Road, today U.S. Highway 92. The camp consisted of a turpentine still, gum platform, spirits shed, cooperage house, and commissary. The living quarters consisted of a church, school, and cabins for the laborers. During production 50 to 75 men were employed to process rosin and turpentine. (Courtesy of Consolidated-Tomoka Land Co.)

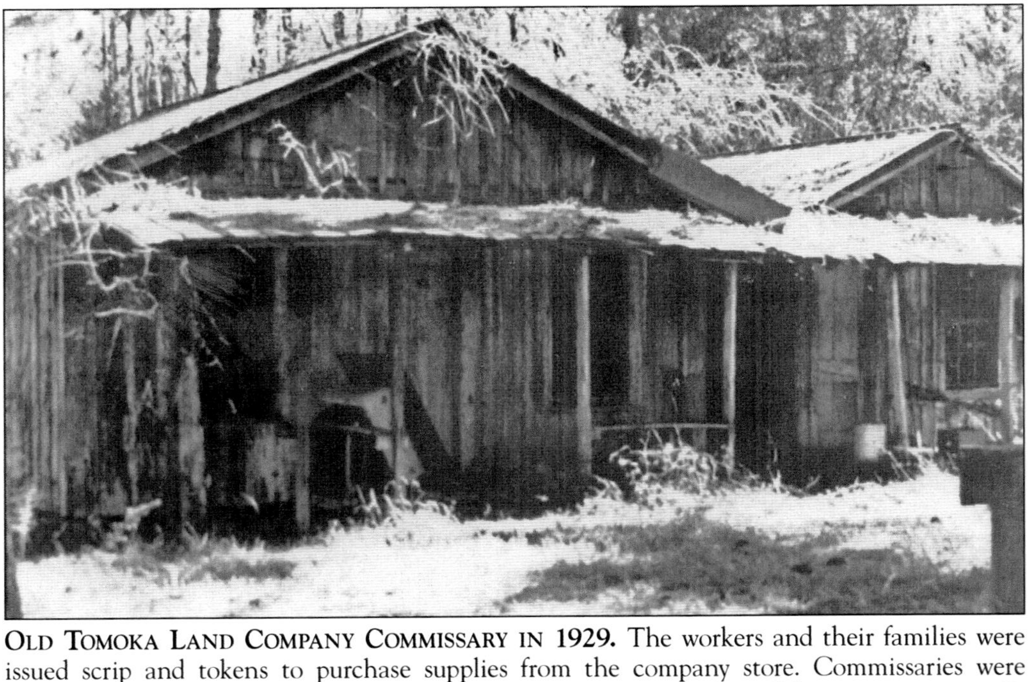

OLD TOMOKA LAND COMPANY COMMISSARY IN 1929. The workers and their families were issued scrip and tokens to purchase supplies from the company store. Commissaries were beneficial for both the worker and the employer and were located at all large turpentine stills and sawmills. This photo was taken in 1987. (Courtesy of Cardwell Family Collection.)

RAY KEECH IN 1929. Keech was a famed Indianapolis racer. He was hired by J.M. White to drive the massive Triplex at Daytona Beach in 1928. He suffered serious burns while behind the wheel, but he did push the car through a measured mile at a speed of 207.552 miles per hour, breaking the record for America. Keech refused to drive the Triplex in 1929, and White was forced to find a new driver. Daytona Beach honored Keech by naming a street after him. (Courtesy of Halifax Historical Society.)

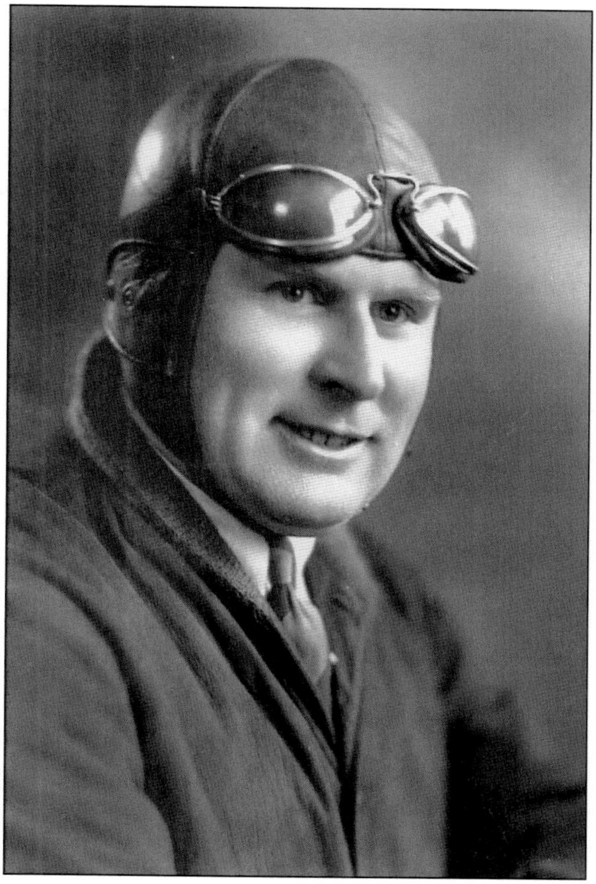

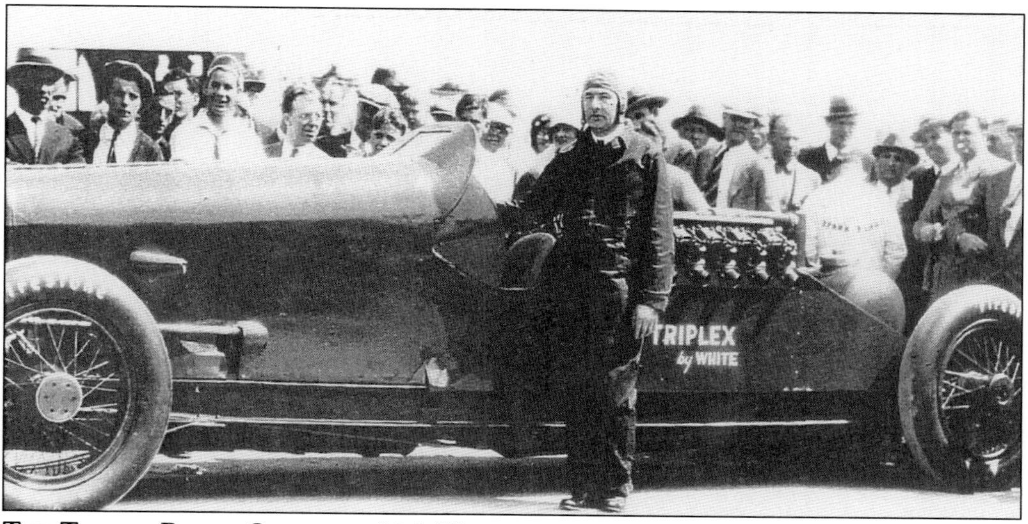

THE TRIPLEX RACER OWNED BY J.M. WHITE IN 1929. Ray Keech broke the world ground speed record in this car in 1928. His high speed was 207.552 miles per hour. The next year, Lee Bible, seen here standing next to the Triplex, was killed in an attempt to break the speed record for White. (Courtesy of Halifax Historical Society.)

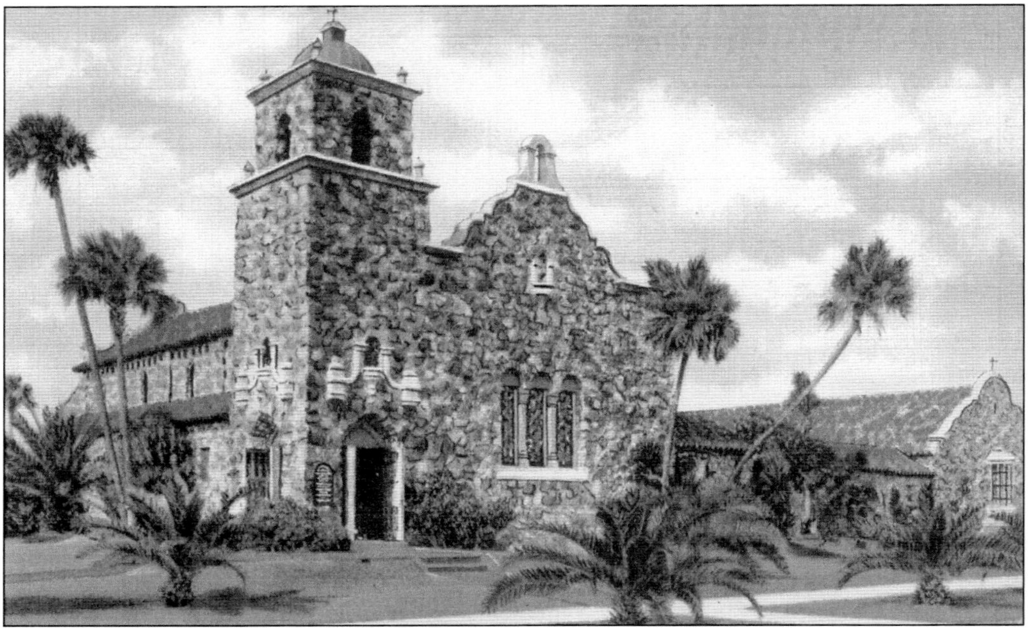

Seabreeze United Church of Christ at 501 North Wild Olive Avenue in 1929. This outstanding Mission-style building designed by architect Harry Griffin is listed on the National Register of Historic Places. The exterior walls are made of "bog rock," a solidified marlstone collected from open fields west of Daytona. The roof is a red barrel tile with a domed bell-tower and arched entrances. During the winter season so many tourists came for the services that it was called "The Tourist Church." (Courtesy of Cardwell Family Collection.)

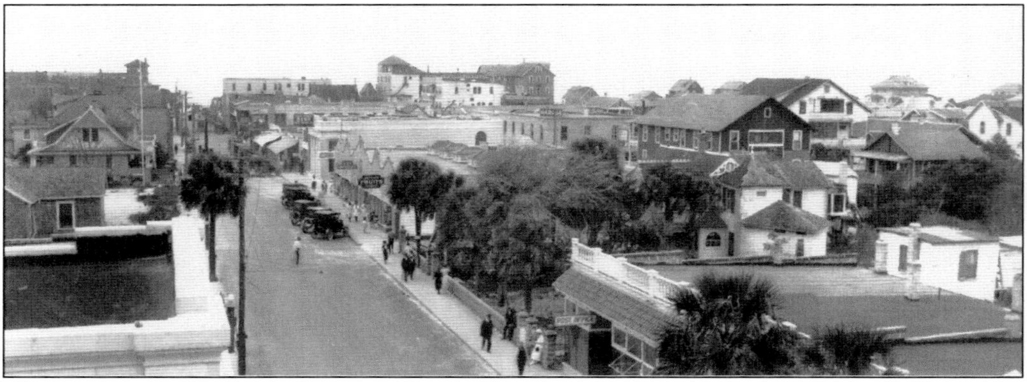

Main Street c. 1930. Some of the identified businesses, looking east on the south (right) side, are the post office, Cortell Fruits, G and S Cafeteria, and the East Coast Bank and Trust Company. In the distance on the left is Seaside Inn and on the immediate right is the Pier Hotel. At the beach is the Ocean Pier and Casino and further to the right is the Breakers Hotel. (Courtesy of Cardwell Family Collection.)

Six

The Depression Years 1931–1941

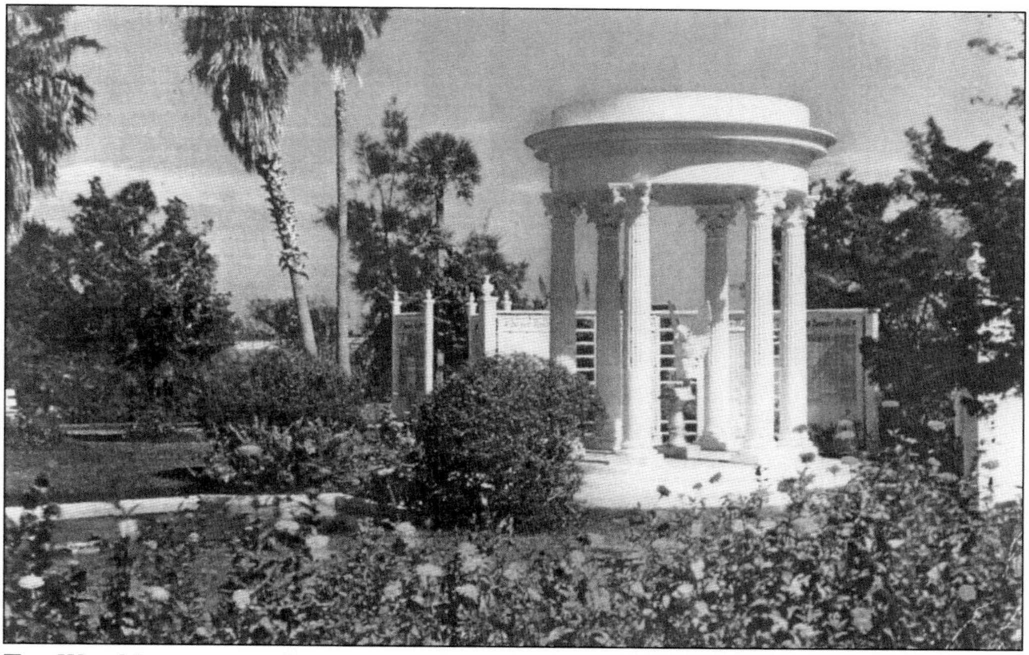

The War Memorial at Riverfront Park, Built in 1932. This memorial honors veterans of World War I and was later expanded to include World War II veterans. In the background a register of World War II veterans is visible. In years gone by parades with color guards stopped to honor all veterans. For many years the Daytona Beach Drum and Bugle Corps was a part of these patriotic ceremonies. Today this memorial stands in Tuscawilla Park. (Courtesy of Cardwell Family Collection.)

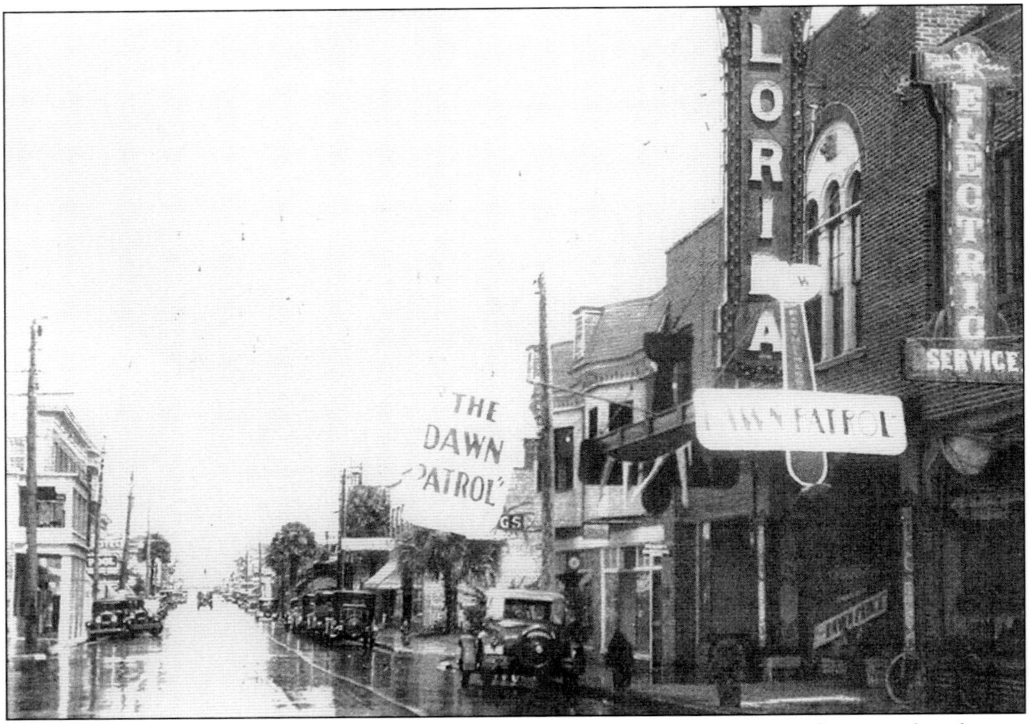

The Florida Theatre at 510 Main Street in the Early 1930s. This popular theater featured the latest films, vaudeville acts, minstrels, and magic shows. Often they had live demonstrations on the sidewalk to attract attention for the movie that was being featured. In later years it was renamed the Beach Theatre. (Courtesy of Cardwell Family Collection.)

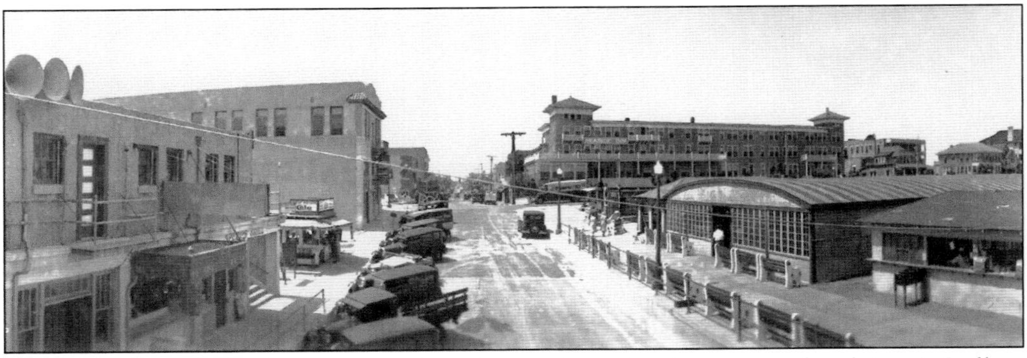

Main Street in 1932. Looking west from the beach, notice the Pier Hotel and Spiro's Grill on the south side and the Seaside Inn on the north side, with other unidentified buildings visible in the far distance. Many makes of automobiles and trucks can be seen parked along the busy Main Street. Two hot dog stands can be seen in the near distance to accommodate beachgoers. (Courtesy of John Gontner.)

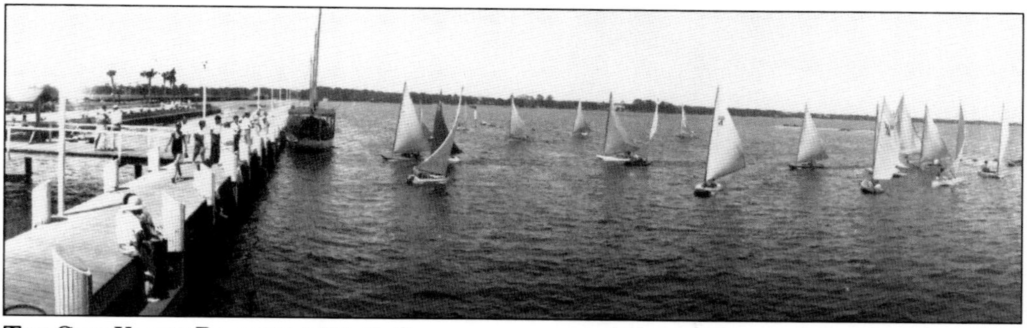

THE CITY YACHT BASIN IN 1932. Sailing regattas were held here each year. A number of sailboats can be seen near the dock in preparation for a racing event. (Courtesy of John Gontner.)

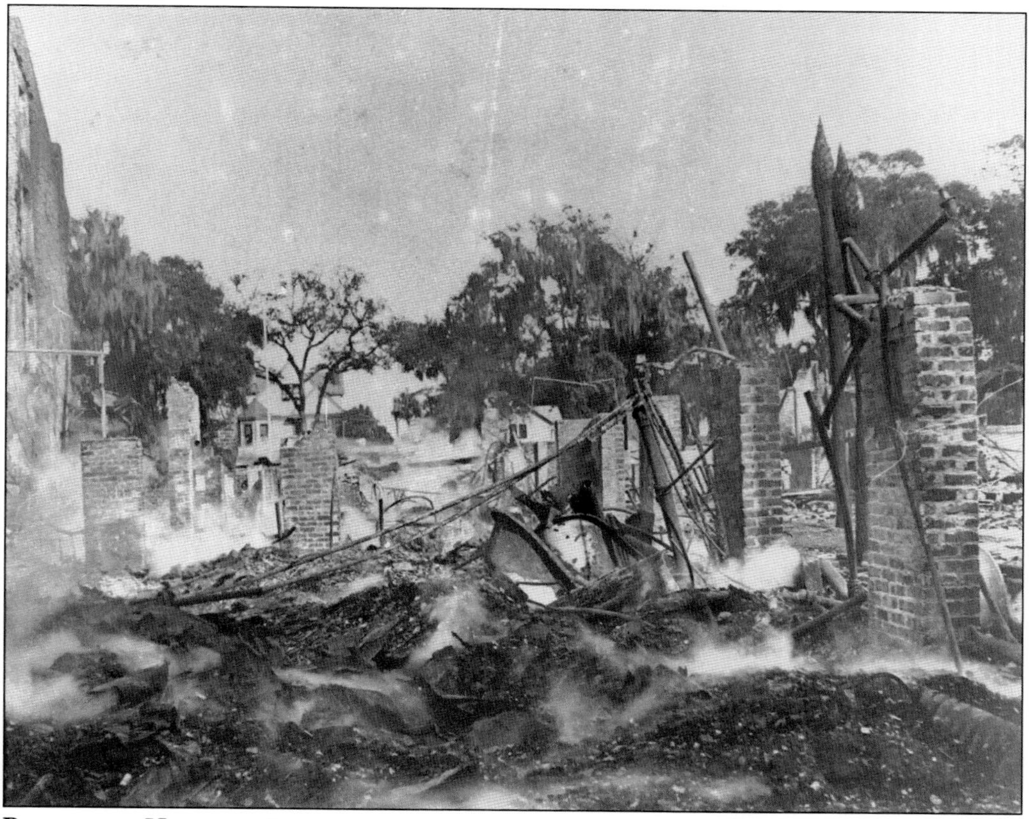

RIDGEWOOD HOTEL ON DECEMBER 6, 1932. The hotel is pictured in ruins on the morning after a fire. This was a prominent hotel for winter guests who came back each year and often reserved the same room. This hotel featured a gourmet restaurant and a chef of renown. (Courtesy of John Gontner.)

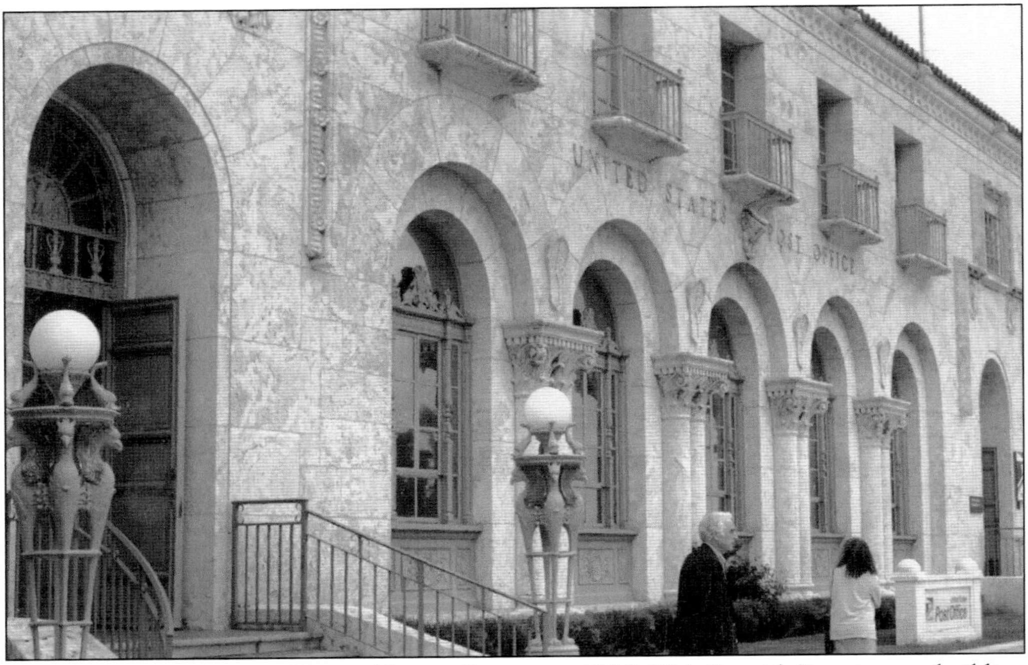

The Post Office at 220 North Beach Street in 1996. This Spanish-Renaissance building was designed by architect Harry Griffin and is listed on the National Register of Historic Places. Stained-glass windows are set in both the north and south sides. This structure, built in 1932, is constructed from coral rock from the Florida Keys, called keystone, and you can see fossils imbedded in some of the stones. This is one of the most outstanding buildings in Daytona Beach. (Courtesy of Cardwell Family Collection.)

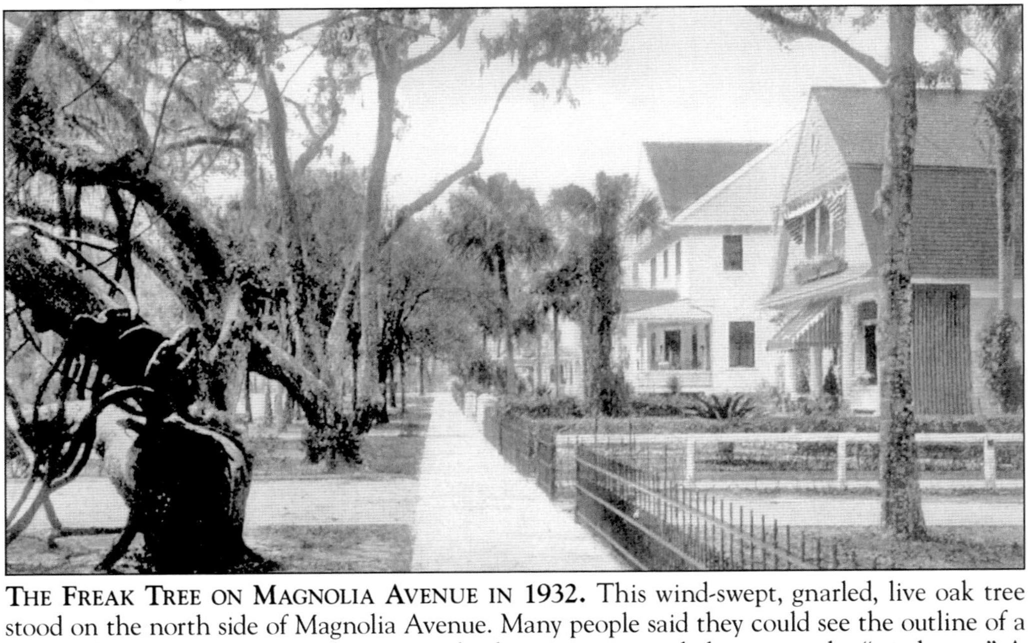

The Freak Tree on Magnolia Avenue in 1932. This wind-swept, gnarled, live oak tree stood on the north side of Magnolia Avenue. Many people said they could see the outline of a witch riding a broomstick in the tree, and it became commonly known as the "witch tree." A woman who lived in a house nearby was said to hate her son-in-law so much that the tree took on her characteristics after her death. (Courtesy of Cardwell Family Collection.)

SIMON J. PEABODY, 1851–1933. A philanthropist and well-known lumber baron, Peabody contributed a large sum of money to build the city auditorium named after him. He also gave money for a playground next to the auditorium and a Young Women's Christian Association (YWCA) home on South Beach Street in what was previously the White-Edmonds Home. His permanent home was at 21 North Halifax Drive. (Courtesy of Cardwell Family Collection.)

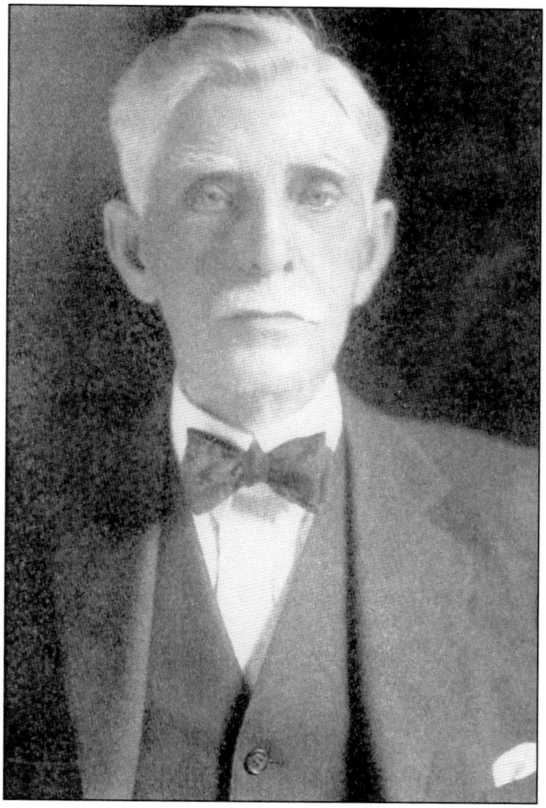

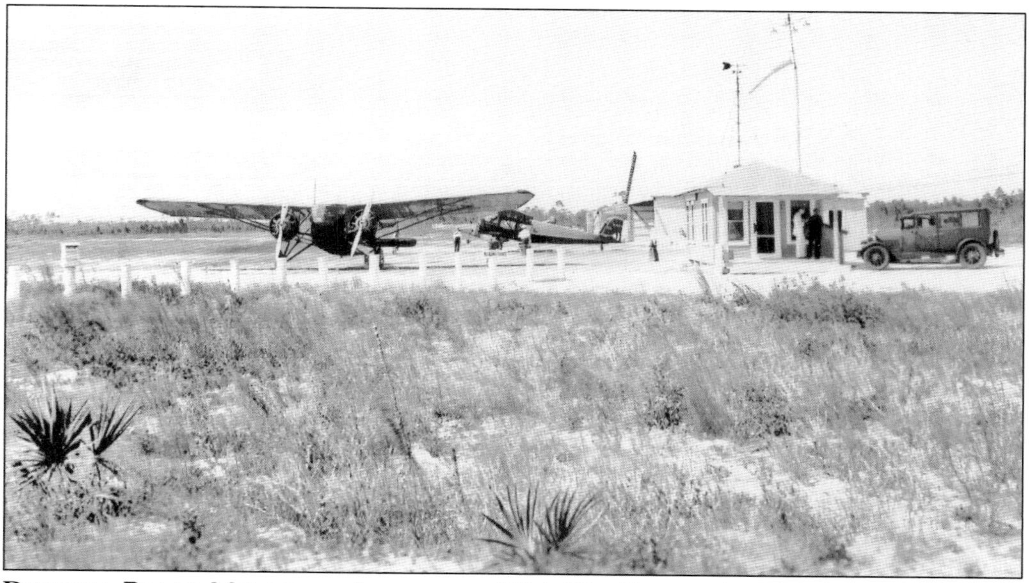

DAYTONA BEACH MUNICIPAL AIRPORT C. 1934. The Eastern Air Transport terminal and hangar was located on the old DeLand Road, today's Bellevue Avenue. This new field could accommodate larger commercial planes. In the early days, planes used the beach for landings and take-offs; in the late 1920s they used Bethune Point Airstrip. (Courtesy of John Gontner.)

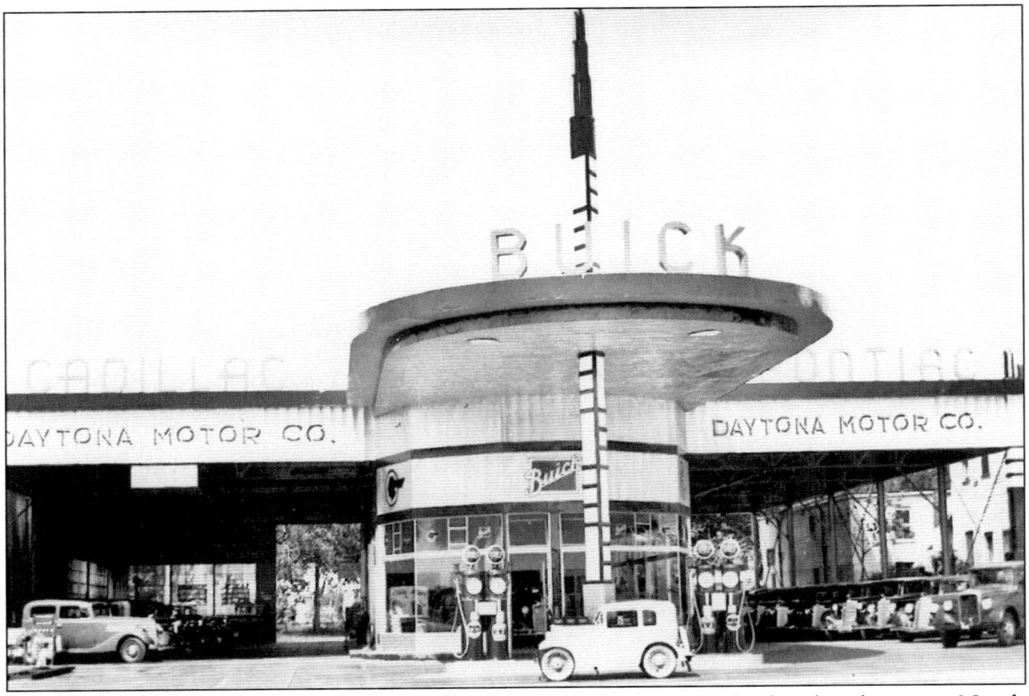

LLOYD BUICK, PONTIAC, CADILLAC IN 1934. The Lloyd car dealership has been on North Beach Street for many years. It was established by J. Saxton Lloyd as Daytona Motor Company and was operated by his two sons after his death. Today it is no longer family-owned, but it is still known as Lloyd Buick-Cadillac Sales and Services. (Courtesy of John Gontner.)

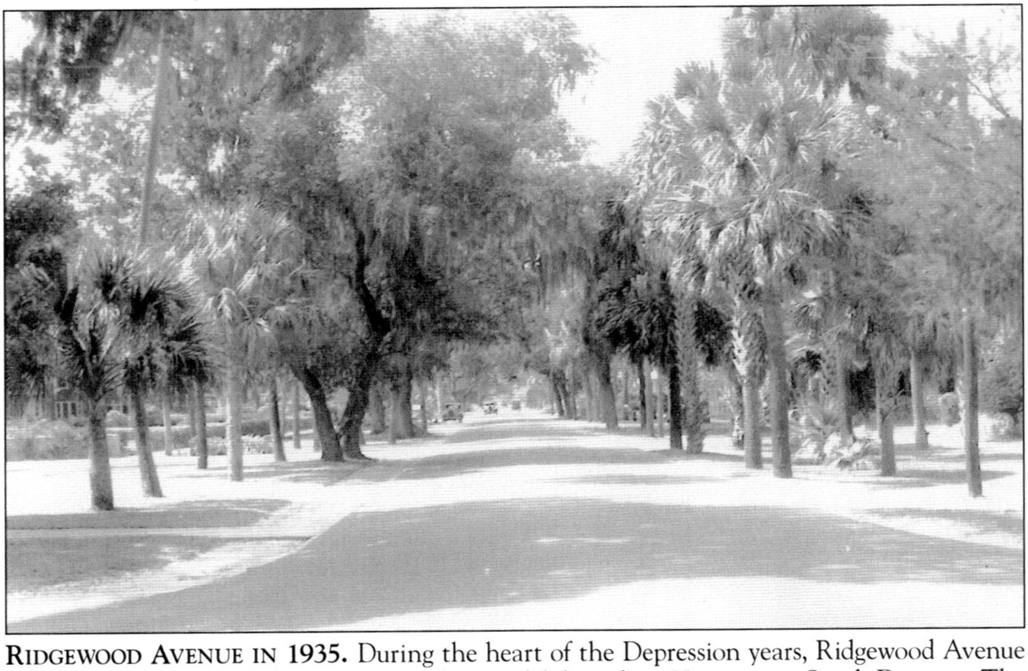

RIDGEWOOD AVENUE IN 1935. During the heart of the Depression years, Ridgewood Avenue was tree-lined and shaded. It was a restful, peaceful drive from Kingston to South Daytona. The sidewalks were some distance from the two-lane street and allowed for drainage of the roadway into the wide grassy area. (Courtesy of John Gontner.)

SIR MALCOLM CAMPBELL (MARCH 11, 1885–DECEMBER 31, 1948). An English country gentleman born to achieve, Campbell inherited his wealth from his diamond-merchant father, and Malcolm was a financier and underwriter for Lloyds of London. He piloted aircraft during World War I. From 1928 to 1935 Campbell set five world records in his famed Bluebirds on Daytona Beach. In 1931 Campbell was knighted by King George V for his 245.73 mile-per-hour world record at Daytona Beach in his Bluebird II. (Courtesy of Halifax Historical Society.)

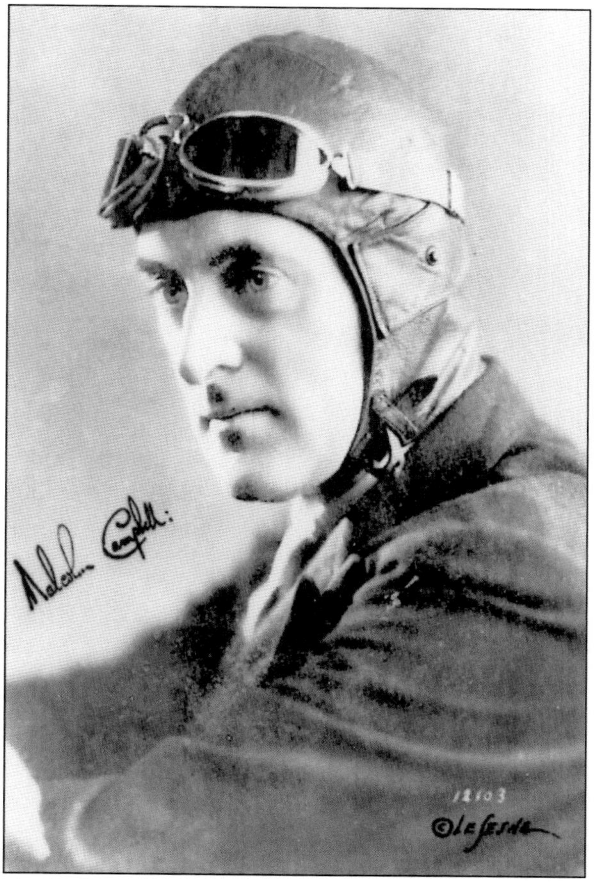

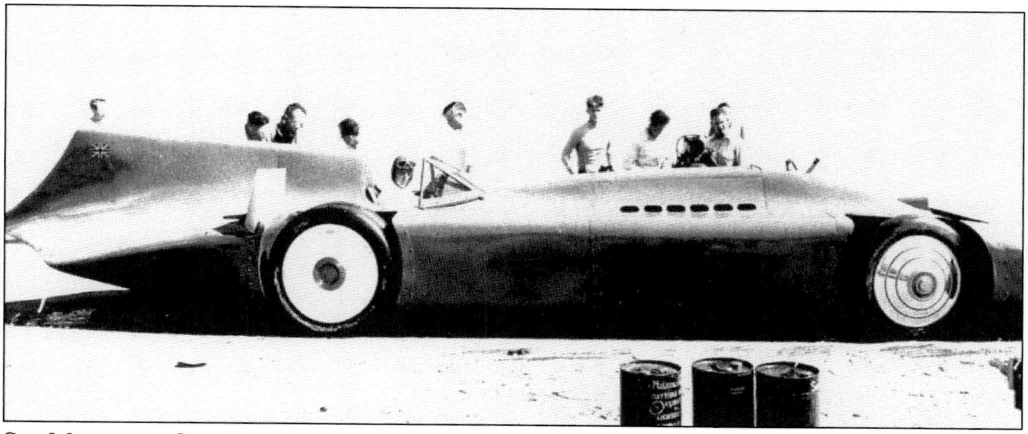

SIR MALCOLM CAMPBELL AND HIS BLUEBIRD V ON MARCH 7, 1935. Campbell's record still stands at 276.82 miles per hour. This car had dual rear wheels to help eliminate the wheel-spin that plagued the 1933 car. The Rolls Royce engine, with special spark plugs and supercharger, was engineered to break 300 miles per hour. The engine was monitored by the British Defense Ministry's special team responsible for improved airplane development. Today the car remains on display at the Daytona U.S.A. Museum. (Courtesy of Halifax Historical Society.)

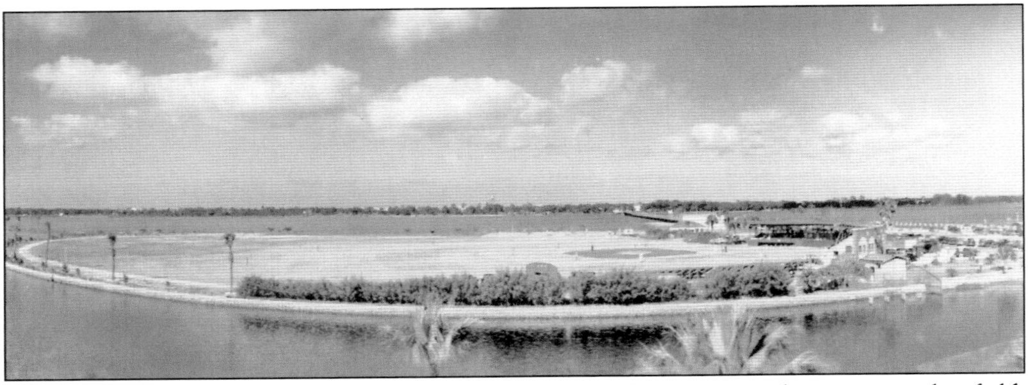

CITY ISLAND BALLPARK C. 1936. Many famous baseball players got their start at this field. Over the years it has provided special sporting events that have entertained the citizens of the area. Today this ballpark honors Jackie Robinson, who played here and broke baseball's racial barrier in 1946. (Courtesy of John Gontner.)

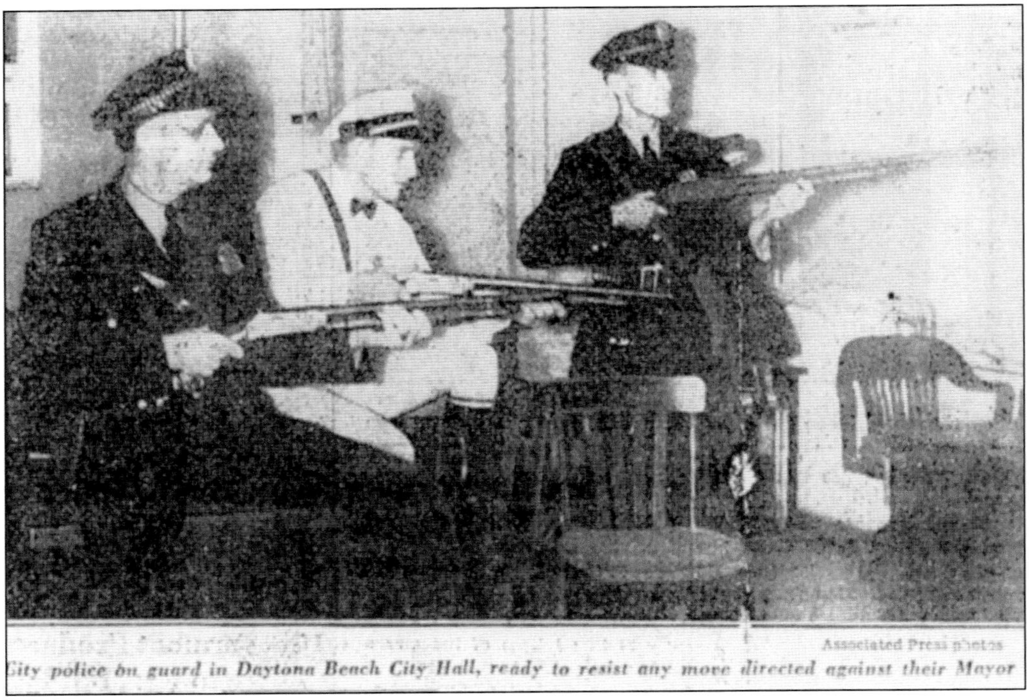

THE BATTLE OF DAYTONA, DECEMBER 30, 1936. Edward H. Armstrong was sometimes called a strong leader with power, while opponents called him a corrupt, heavy-handed tyrant. Due to irregularities in the city government, Gov. Dave Sholtz announced he would remove Armstrong from office. Armstrong resigned immediately and swore in his wife Irene as mayor. The governor ordered 200 national guardsmen to Daytona Beach to remove Mrs. Armstrong. When word arrived, police and armed citizens barricaded themselves inside City Hall. A court order averted a confrontation and on January 4, 1937, the Florida Supreme Court ordered Mayor E.H. Armstrong to resume his office. He died the morning of January 2, 1938, just days before his inauguration for a fifth term. (Courtesy of Daytona Beach News-Journal Corporation.)

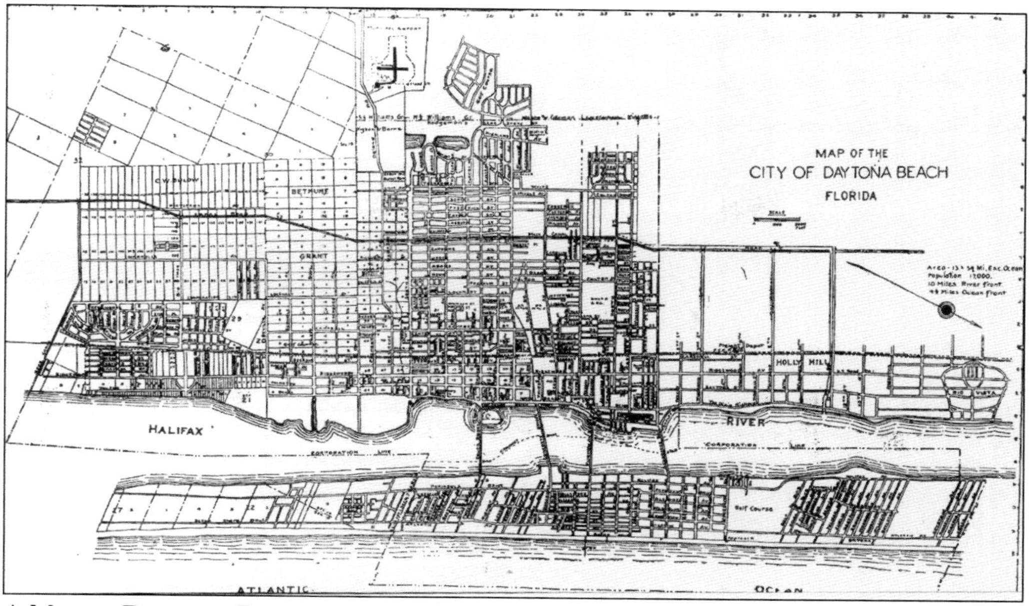

A Map of Daytona Beach c. 1937. This map was made to promote tourism in 1937. The city was just beginning to grow out of the Depression. President Franklin D. Roosevelt had initiated the WPA, which created jobs for workers building civic and tourist accommodations and other needed facilities. (Courtesy of Cardwell Family Collection.)

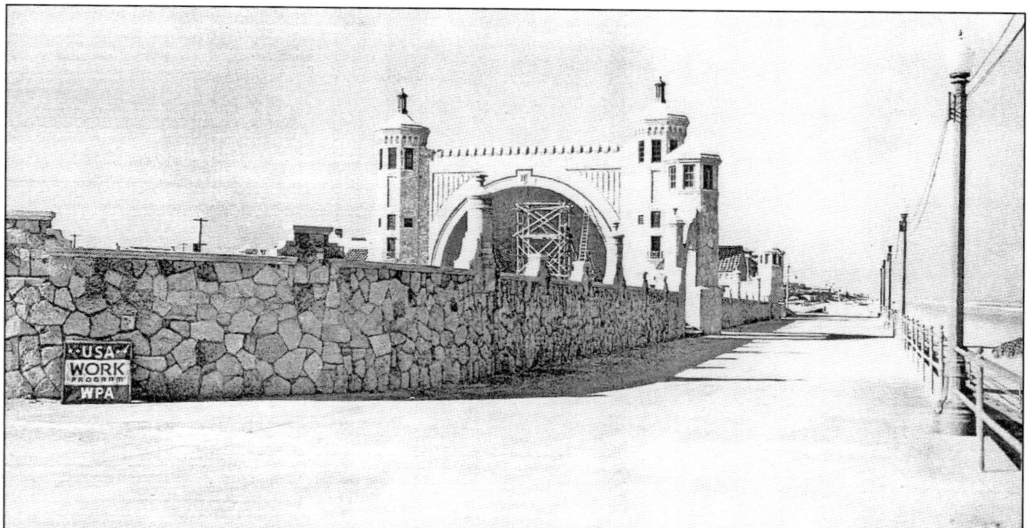

The Daytona Beach Band Shell under Construction in 1937. The Daytona Beach Boardwalk and Band Shell was constructed with funds from the Works Progress Administration (WPA). The band shell, constructed out of local coquina rock, provided work for hundreds of men who were unemployed during the Depression years in the 1930s. It was unique as an outdoor theater for concerts and other types of social programs. (Courtesy of Halifax Historical Society.)

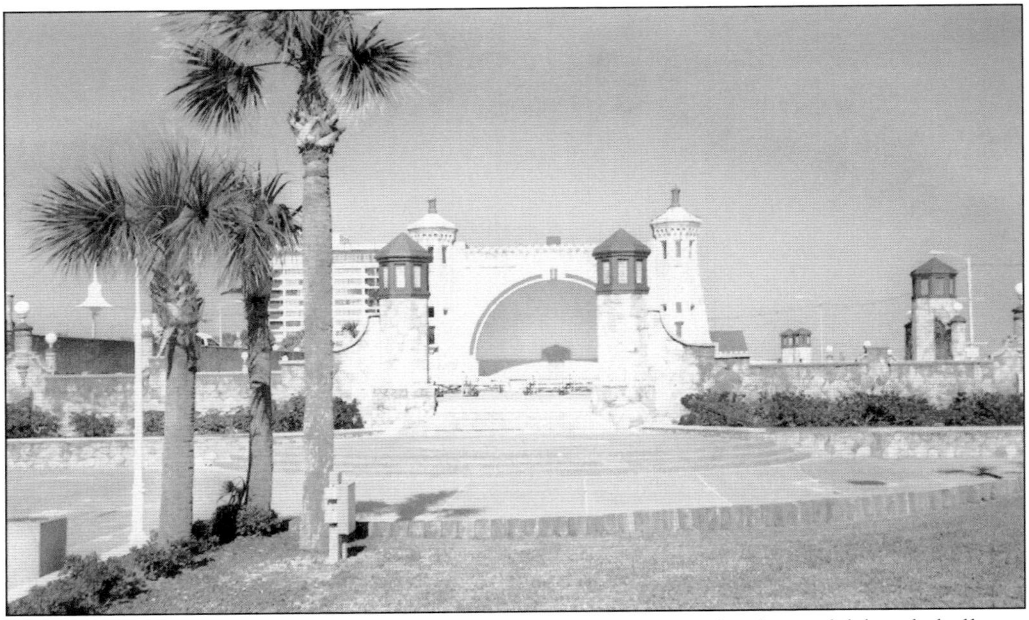

Daytona Beach Band Shell at the Boardwalk, 1999. This beautiful band shell was built by the WPA in 1937. Throughout the years it has provided outdoor entertainment, band concerts, beauty contests, Easter sunrise services, and other specialized programs. This outdoor amphitheater can only serve the public in dry weather, and when it rains programs have to be postponed. (Courtesy of Cardwell Family Collection.)

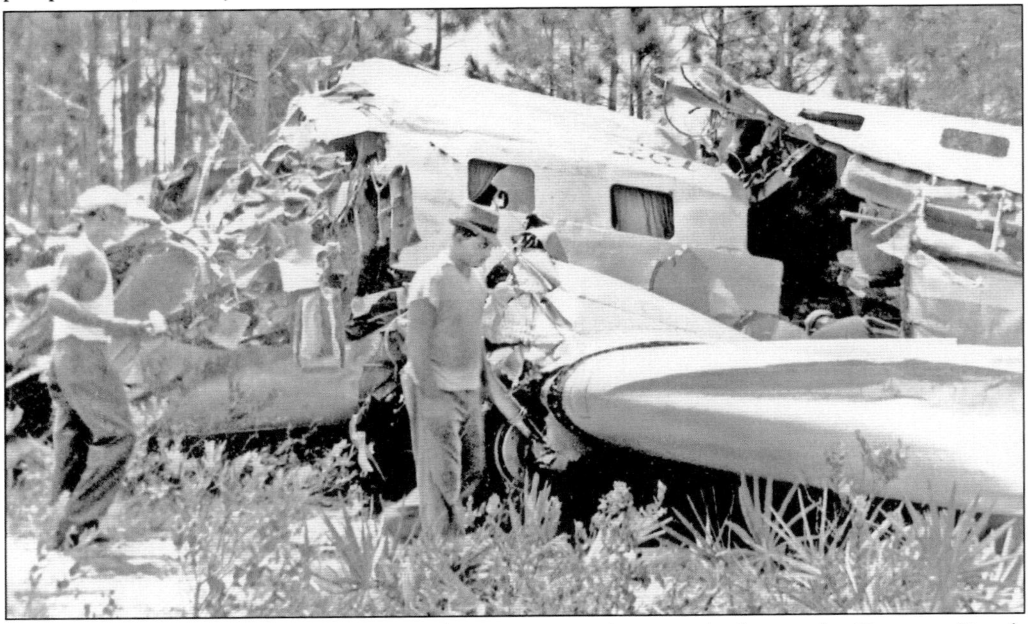

Eastern Airlines Crash in 1937. This passenger plane crashed near the Daytona Beach Airport and killed four. Among the survivors was a young boy wandering dazed near the crash site when rescue workers arrived. A temporary utility pole had been placed near the end of the runway, and somehow the plane failed to gain altitude and struck the pole with a wingtip. The crash created considerable attention, and the president of Eastern Airlines, Eddie Rickenbacker, came to Daytona to oversee the investigation of the crash. (Courtesy of John Gontner.)

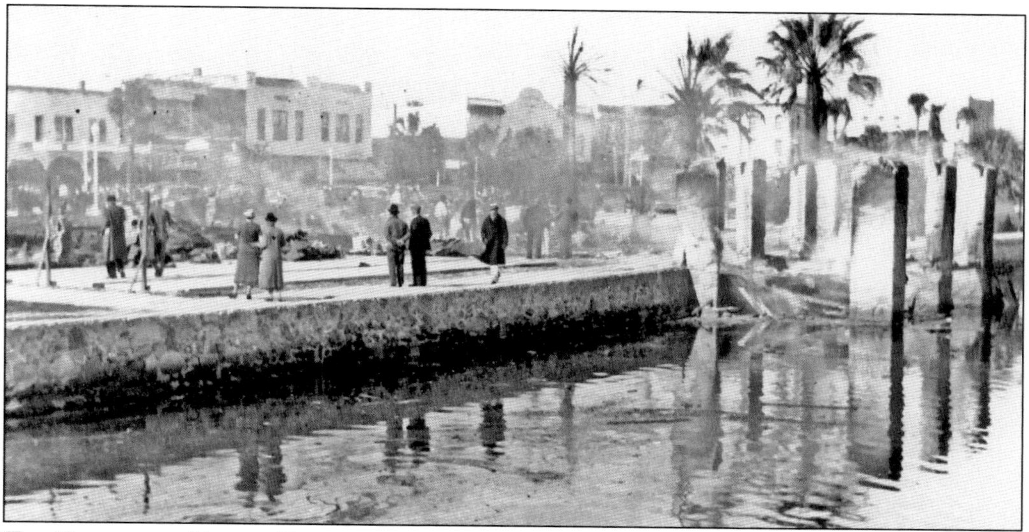

THE BURGOYNE CASINO DESTROYED BY FIRE ON DECEMBER 8, 1937. A fire of undetermined origin destroyed the casino in an early morning blaze. The heat from the intense fire cracked windows in the Florida Bank and Trust Company Building across the street and scorched other buildings nearby. This casino was a landmark of Daytona Beach and was built and sponsored by Charles Burgoyne as a gift to promote civic activities. (Courtesy of John Gontner.)

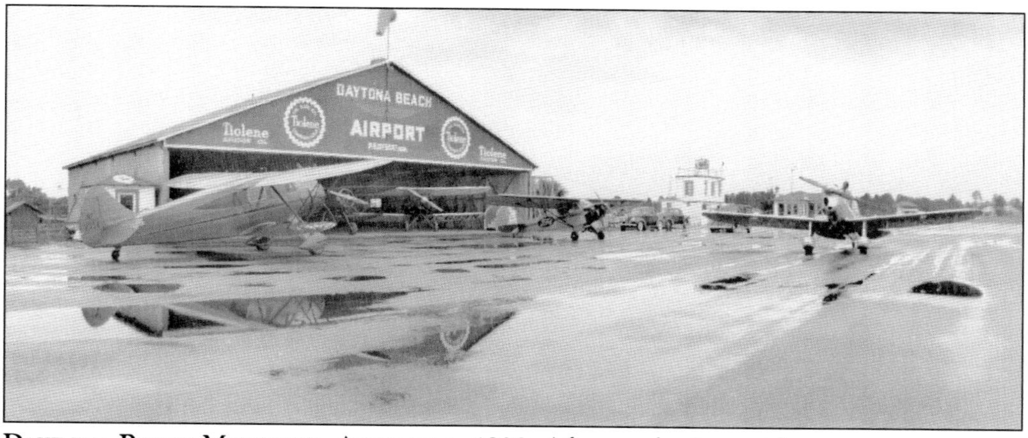

DAYTONA BEACH MUNICIPAL AIRPORT C. 1938. After purchasing a ticket, passengers waiting for their flight could visit a small animal zoo adjacent to the main hangar, perhaps feeding peanuts to the monkeys. This city airport opened May 15, 1930, and by 1931 it had a lighted runway. The terminal was located on the old DeLand Road, Bellevue Avenue today. (Courtesy of John Gontner.)

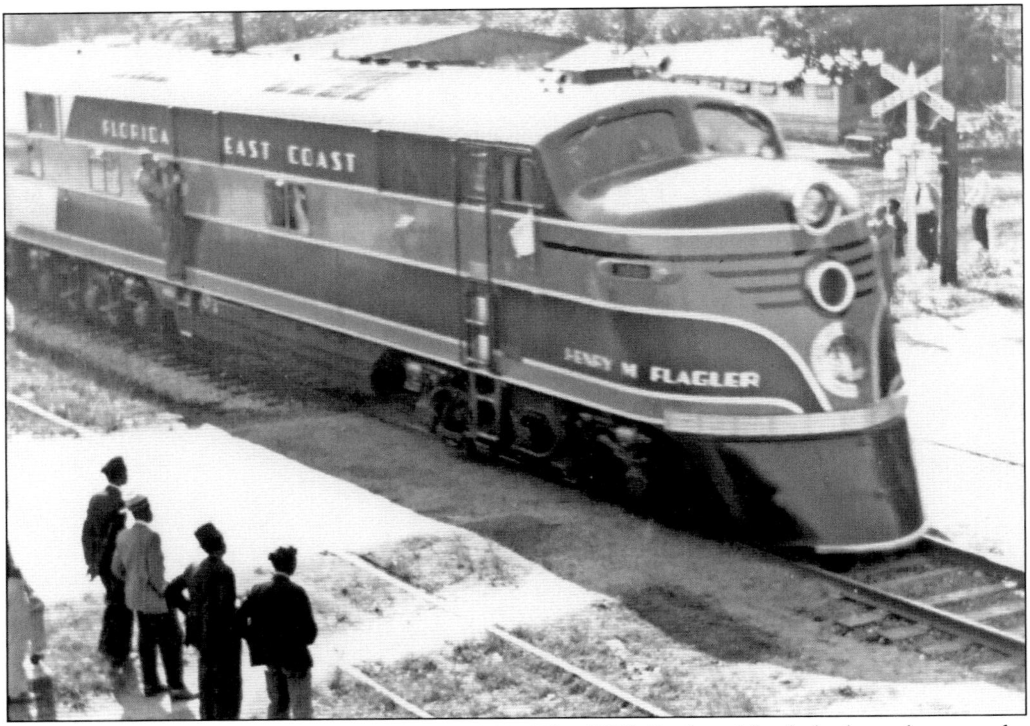

HENRY M. *FLAGLER* STREAMLINER IN 1939. The FEC Railroad had dual tracks, one for northbound trains and one for southbound trains. The peak of railroad travel was 1939. Northern tourists came to Florida in the winter season, and all passengers wished to travel on the *Henry M. Flagler* special. (Courtesy of John Gontner.)

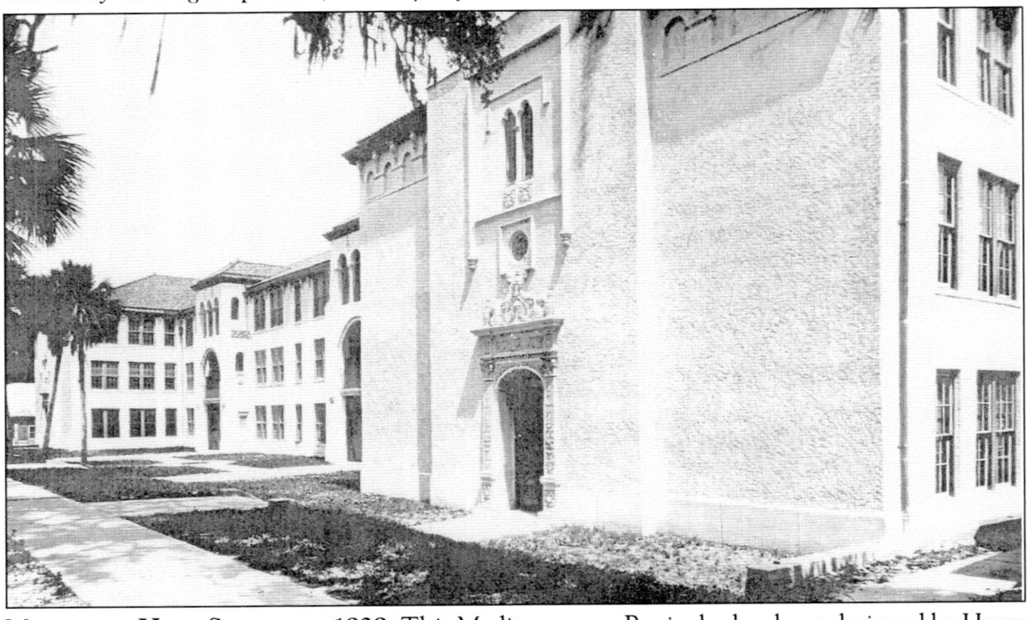

MAINLAND HIGH SCHOOL C. 1939. This Mediterranean-Revival school was designed by Harry Griffin and built in 1926. It operated on Third Avenue for many years until it was demolished in the 1980s. Today a state building stands on this site, housing the Children and Family Services Agency. The authors graduated from this school. (Courtesy of Halifax Historical Society.)

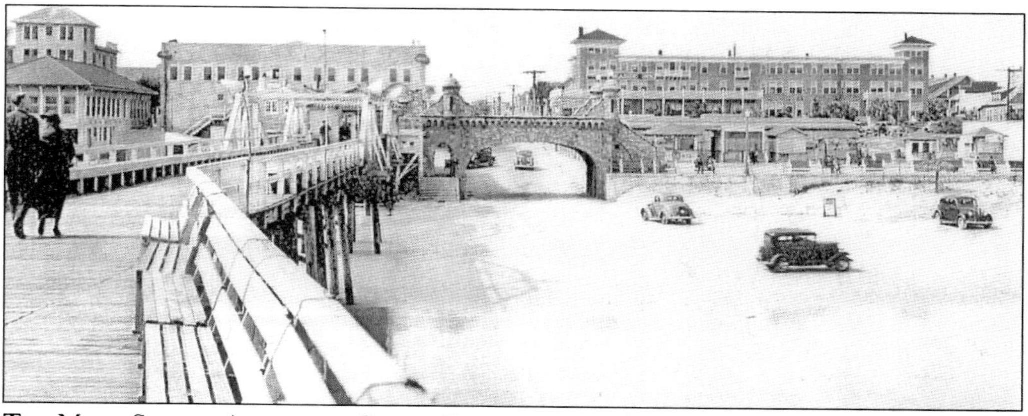

The Main Street Arch and Ocean Pier c. 1939. This famous walkway leads to the Pier Casino and all the way north to the band shell on the boardwalk. The Seaside Inn can be seen in the background on the corner of Main Street and Ocean Avenue. (Courtesy of Halifax Historical Society.)

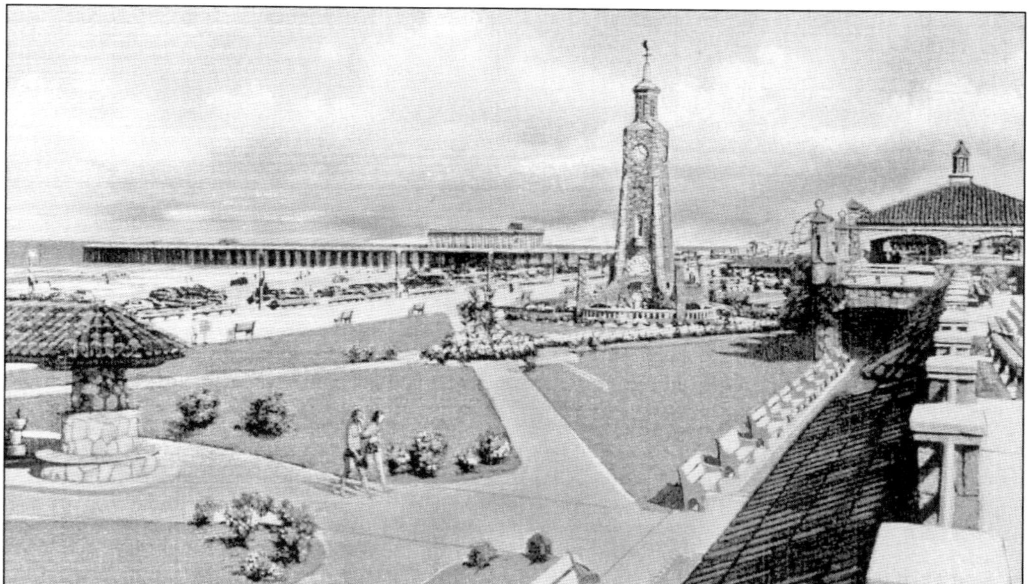

Overlooking Oceanfront Park and the Boardwalk in 1939. This was a place that families liked to visit on vacation where they could get a "far-away" feeling. Many of these visitors were only a day's drive from their home. The oceanfront provided a peaceful and relaxing environment, ideal for vacationers. (Courtesy of Cardwell Family Collection.)

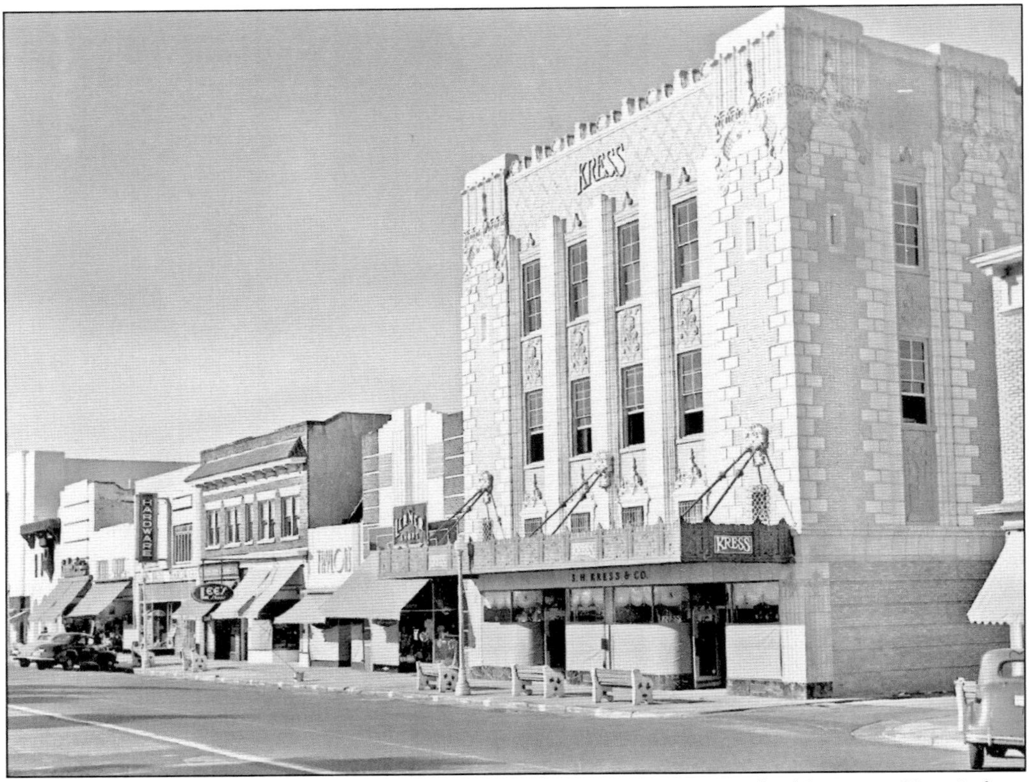

BEACH STREET AT MYRTLE LANE IN 1941. The beautiful Art Deco building was Kress's five-and-dime store. Looking south is Lerner Shop, Taylor's, Lee's Shoes, Curtis Dry Goods, Dunn Brothers Hardware, and, at the end of the block, Yowell-Drew. All of these businesses are gone, and the Dunn Brothers Hardware has moved to the southwest corner of Magnolia and Segrave at the railroad tracks. (Courtesy of John Gontner.)

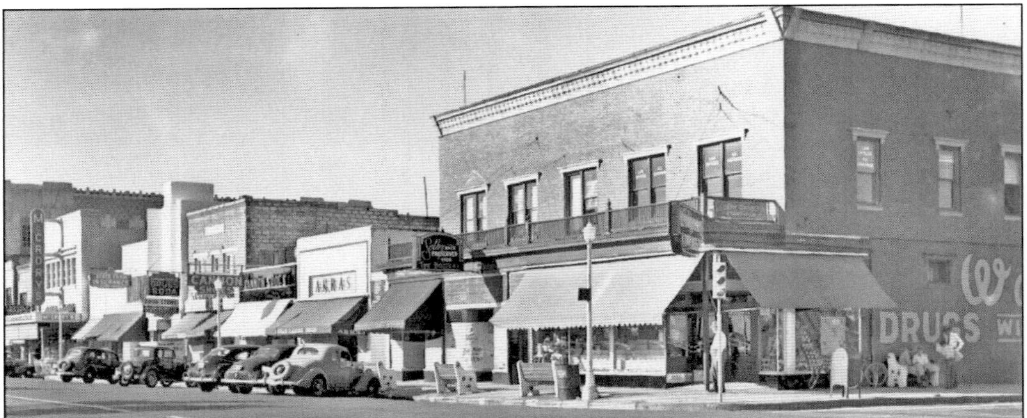

LOOKING SOUTH AT THE INTERSECTION OF BEACH STREET AND VOLUSIA AVENUE IN 1941. Today this intersection is Beach Street and International Speedway Boulevard. Looking south are Walgreen's Drug Store on the corner, the Bootery, Pat Parkers and Akras Women's Stores, Cannon Shoes, and a luncheonette. In the distance is McCrory's and Kress's five-and-dime stores. All of these businesses are gone; however, today Jessup's Jewelers is in the old Walgreen's Store. (Courtesy of John Gontner.)

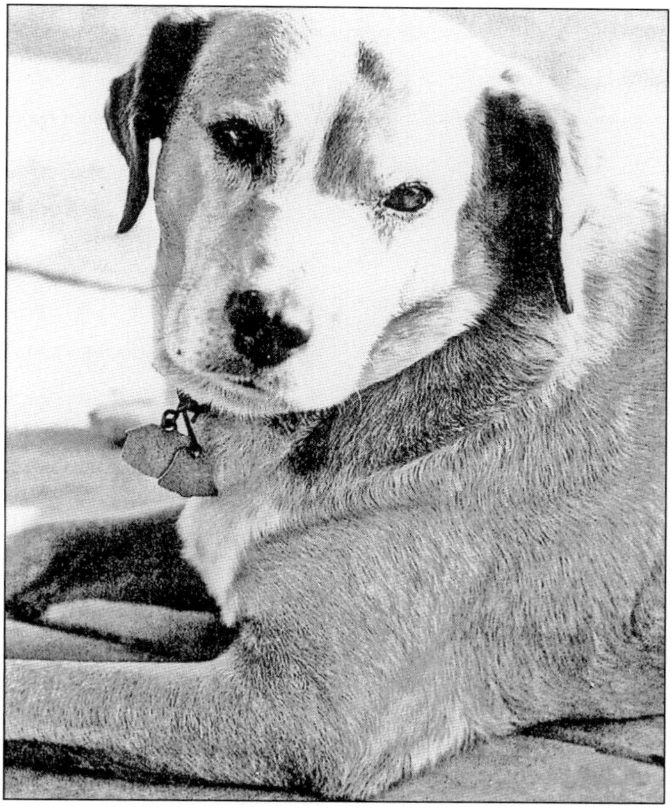

Brownie, Daytona's Most Celebrated Dog, in 1941. Brownie showed up at the Daytona Cab Company stand at the corner of Beach Street and Orange Avenue in 1940. Cab drivers and locals took a liking to the friendly dog. Brownie quickly gained fame and was rewarded almost daily with a bone from a nearby steakhouse. A doghouse was constructed near the taxi telephone booth, and he lived there until his death in 1954. The burial service was eulogized by the mayor as a large crowd said goodbye to Brownie. He is buried in Riverfront Park. (Courtesy of Halifax Historical Society.)

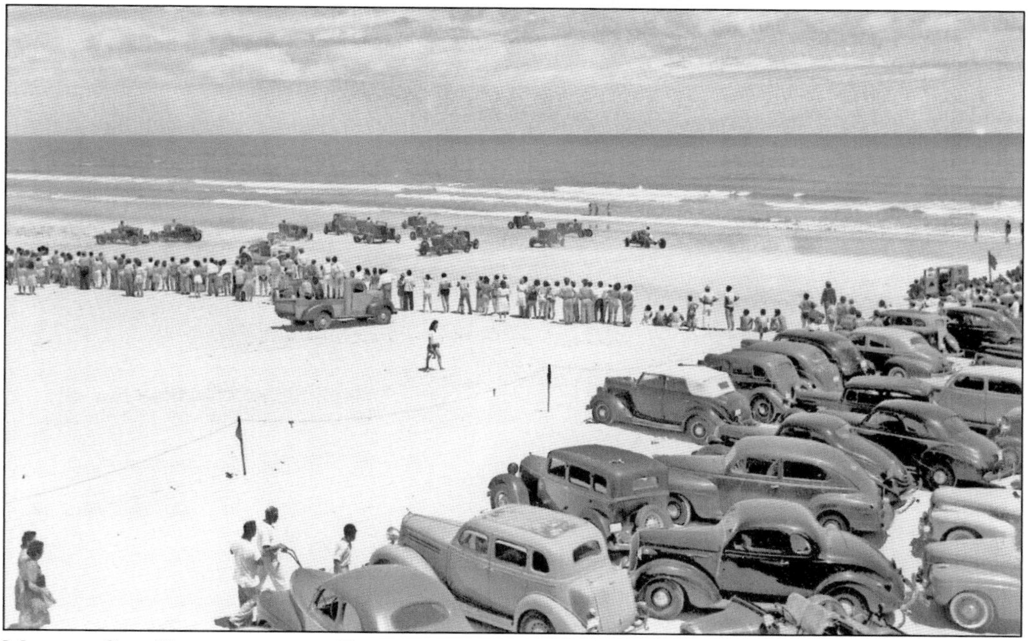

Midget-Car Races on the Beach in 1941. Barrel or pillar races were often held on the beach near the boardwalk. Pictured here are midget cars rounding the south turn, marked by a pillar, and heading north. Occasionally junk-car races were held in this area. Stock car and motorcycle races were held farther south on the beach. (Courtesy of John Gontner.)

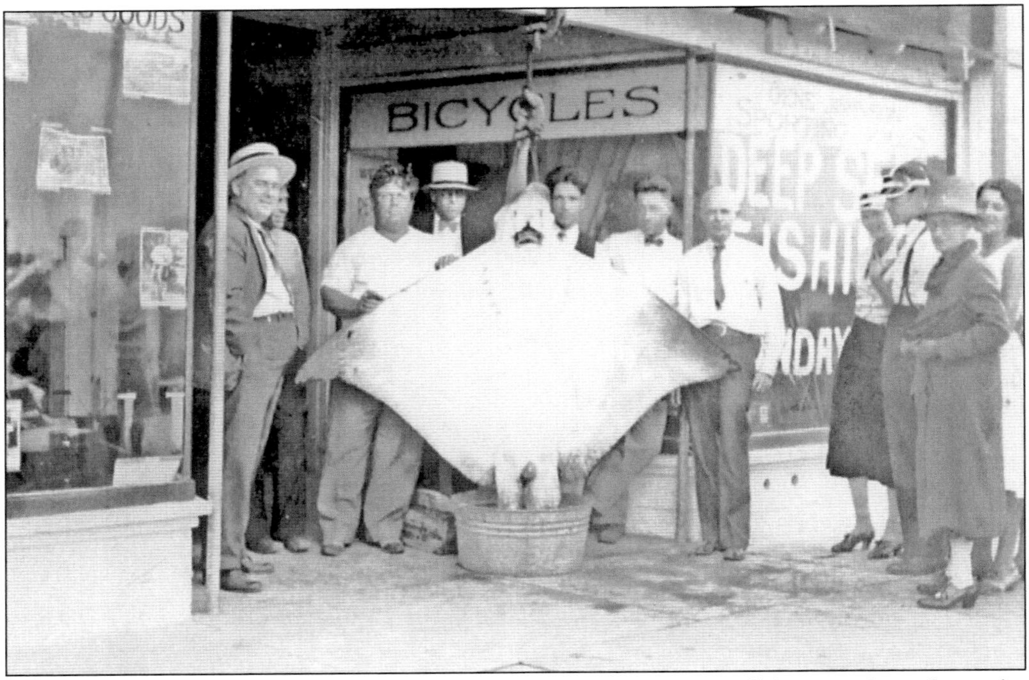

Gene Johnson's Sporting Goods Shop in 1941. Gene was well known throughout the Daytona Beach area for his fishing tackle supplies and bicycle sales and repair. His shop was located at 103 Fairview Avenue. Local enthusiasts went to him for reliable fishing information. This unidentified angler is proud of his "catch of the day." The unidentified onlookers are amazed at the size of the stingray. (Courtesy of Cardwell Family Collection.)

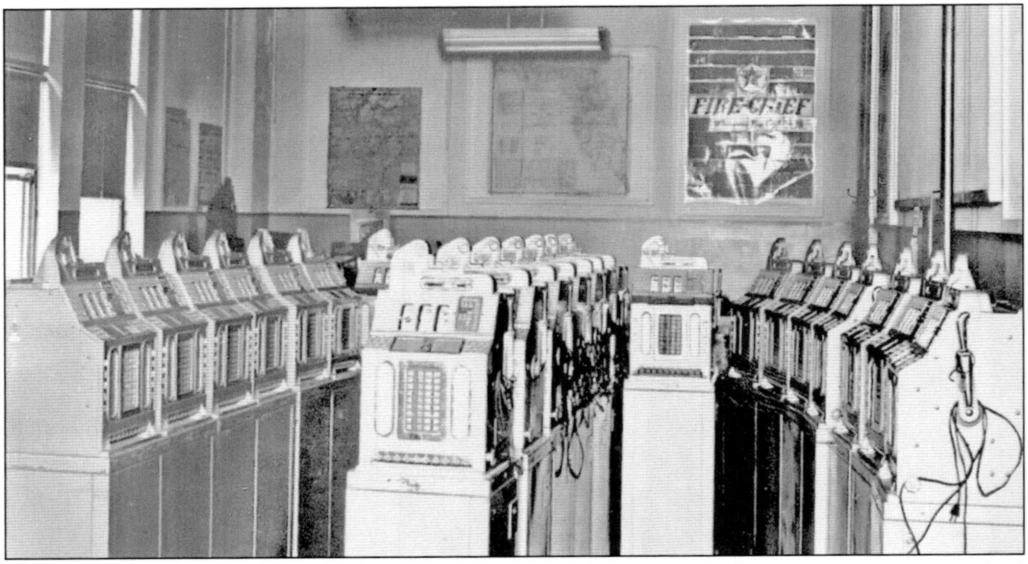

Illegal Gambling in Secret Hideaways in 1941. Daytona, being a tourist town, had speakeasies and taverns. Some had their secret hide-a-ways where gaming and horse-racing results were tallied. Each week small-time gamblers would head for their favorite spot to play "bolita" and place a bet on a horse–that would never win! These places usually had "one-arm bandits," roulette, and of course, poker. This picture shows a cache of confiscated gambling equipment rounded up by local law enforcement. (Courtesy of Florida State Archives.)

Seven

World War II to the New Boom Era 1942–1970

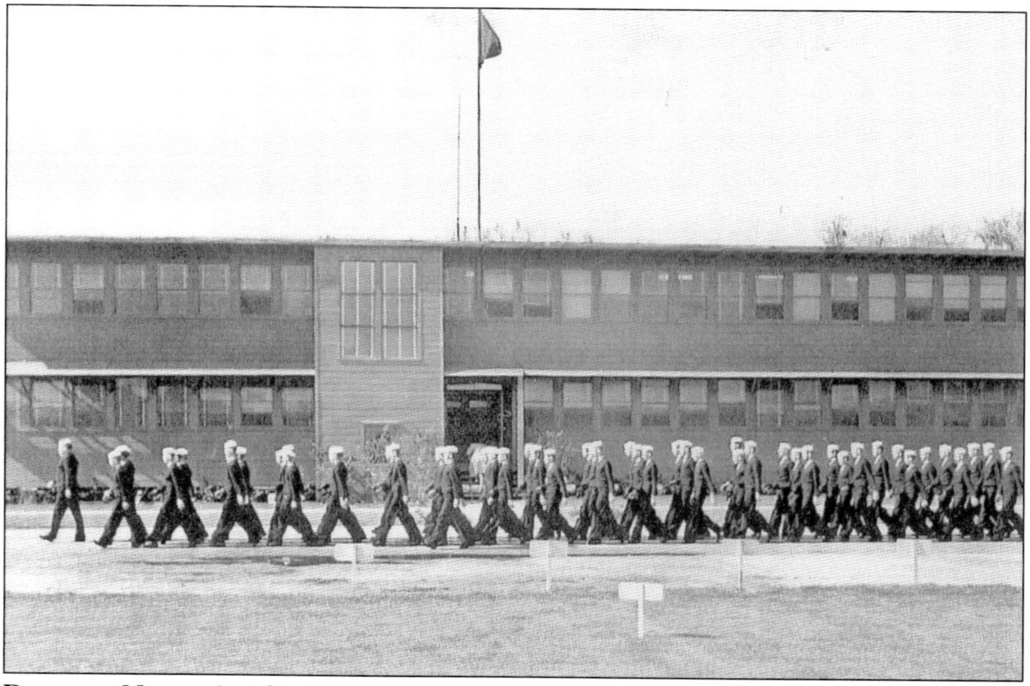

Daytona Naval Air Station in 1943, with a Unit in Training. This base operated from 1942 to 1946. At its peak there were 350 navy airmen training for aircraft-carrier landings on auxiliary fields. Upon graduation they went directly to the Pacific theatre and were assigned to aircraft carriers. (Courtesy of Halifax Historical Society.)

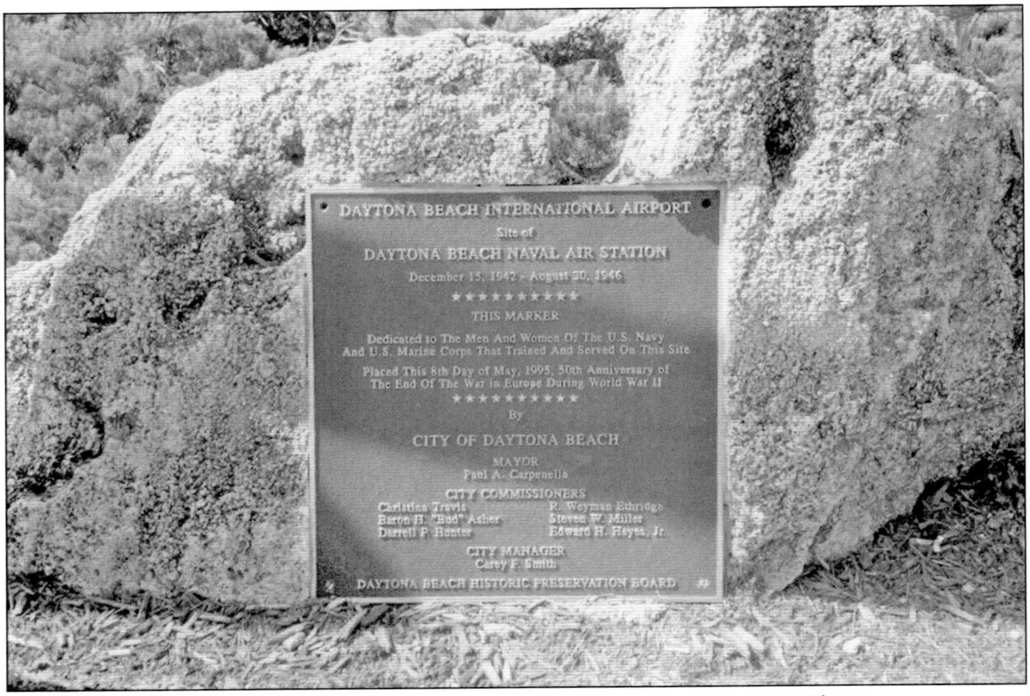

UNITED STATES NAVAL AIR STATION DAYTONA BEACH, 1942–1946. The city airport was constructed from 1930 to 1932 and served the community until World War II. The U.S. Navy took over the airfield in 1942 and added four new runways, a control tower, several barracks buildings, a hangar, and other service buildings. The navy also eliminated the city golf course and dug drainage canals and other necessary base improvements. The base closed in 1946. (Courtesy of Cardwell Family Collection.)

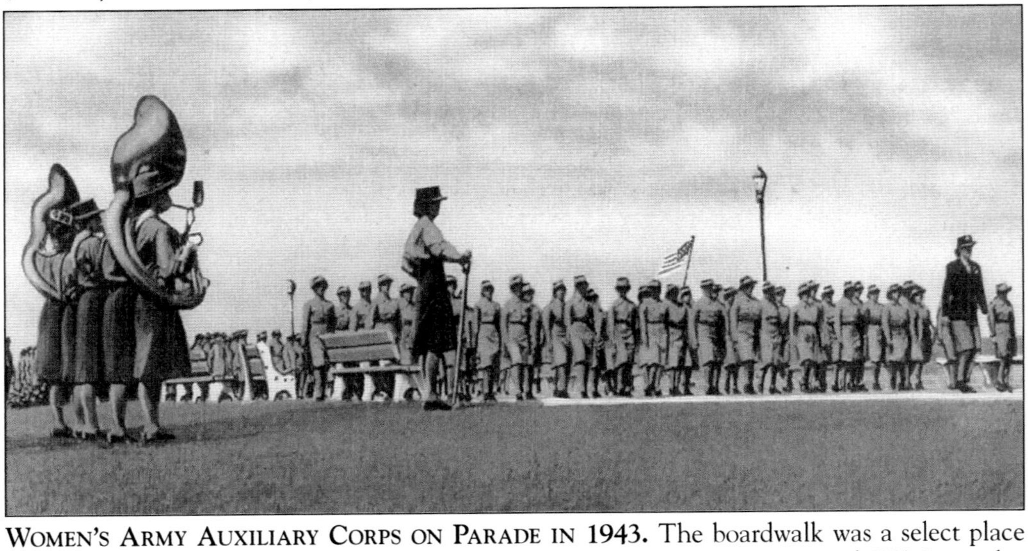

WOMEN'S ARMY AUXILIARY CORPS ON PARADE IN 1943. The boardwalk was a select place for dress parades. In the beginning hotels were used to house WAACs and WACs, and a hutment village was hastily constructed on South Beach Street. Finally a WAC cantonment was completed on Volusia Avenue. At the peak of training there were 14,000 women soldiers in training at Daytona Beach. In August of 1943 the name WAAC was changed to WAC (Women's Army Corps). (Courtesy of Cardwell Family Collection.)

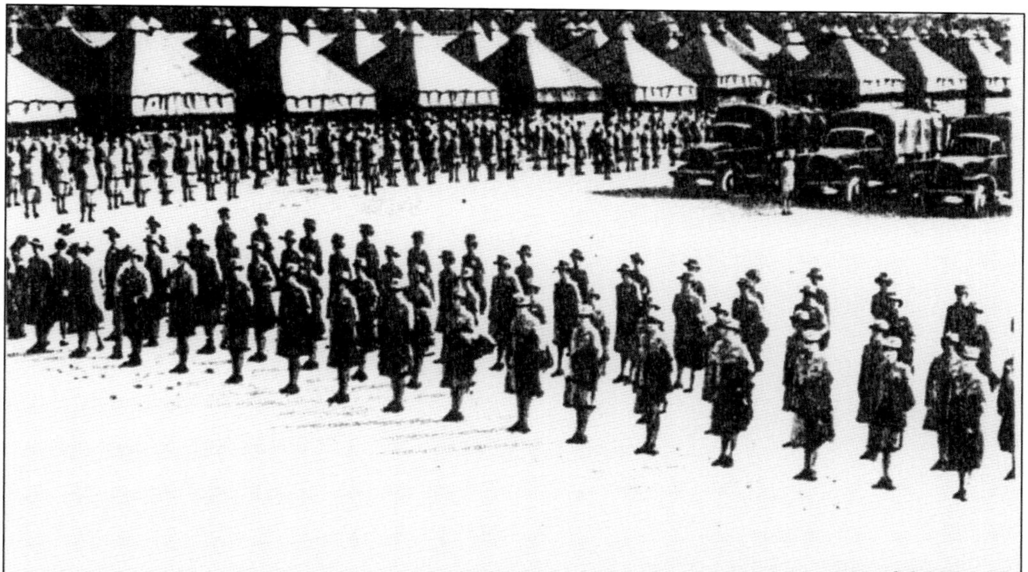

Daytona Beach was an important WAC Training Center during World War II. This is the last inspection for a group of women who have completed basic training and are leaving for their assigned units, 1944.

The Second WAC, 1942–1944. These women soldiers are undergoing final inspection at "Tent City" on South Beach Street in Daytona Beach. (Courtesy of Halifax Historical Society.)

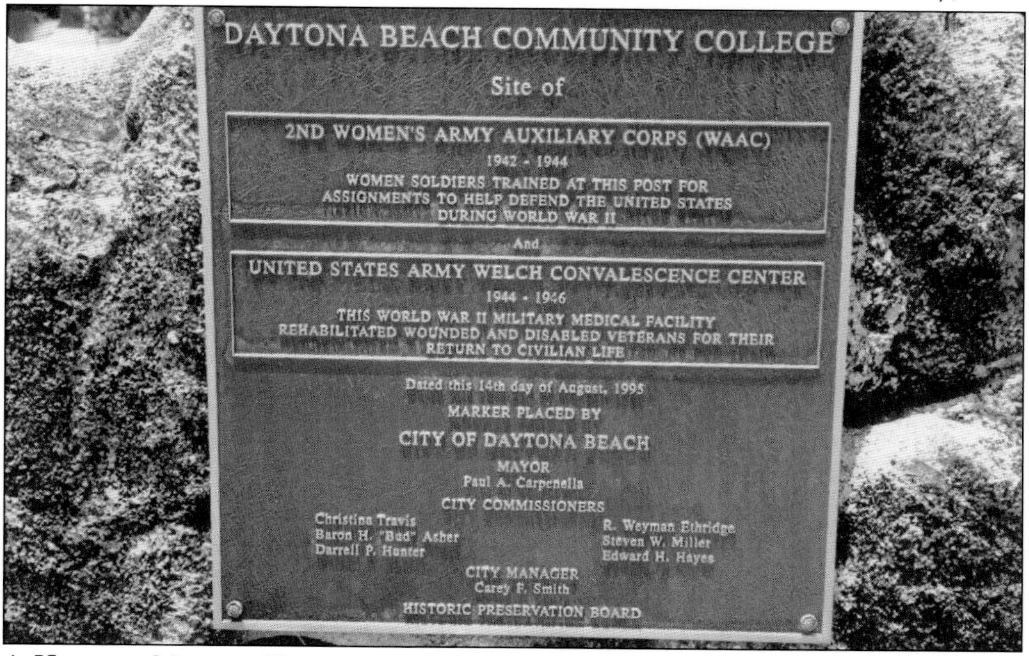

A Historic Marker Honoring the Second WAAC and the United States Army Welch Convalescence Center. This plaque is located on the campus of the Daytona Beach Community College, almost on the exact spot where the former entrance gate to both the WAAC cantonment and the Welch Convalescence Center was once located. The Daytona Beach City Commission and the Daytona Beach Historic Preservation Board placed this historic marker on August 14, 1995. (Courtesy of Cardwell Family Collection.)

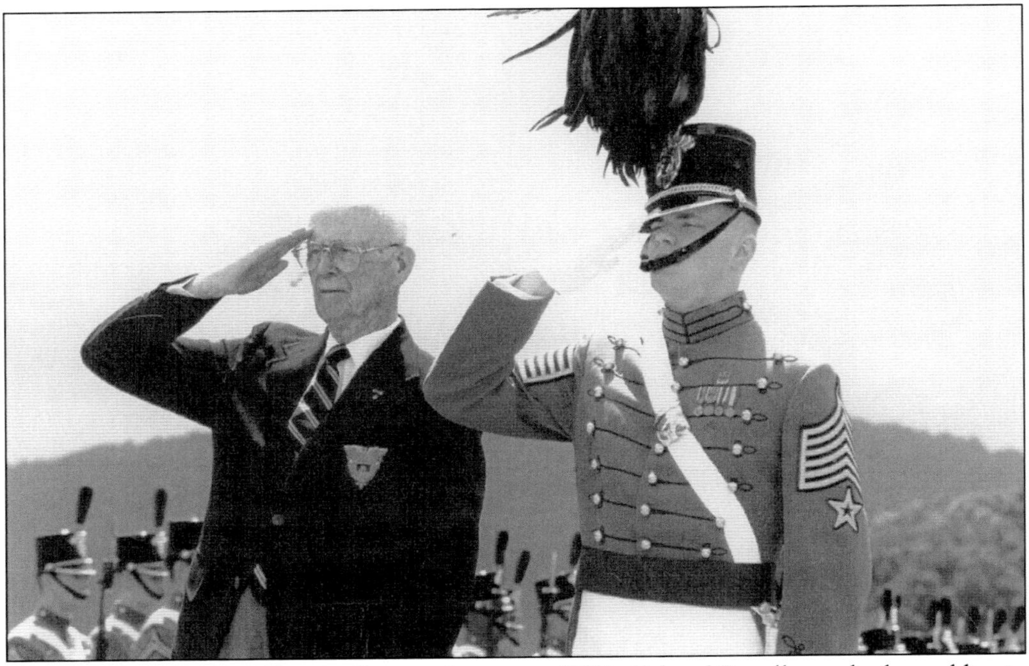

COL. HENRY ROYALL, UNITED STATES ARMY, IN 1999. Colonel Royall was the last soldier to leave the United States Army Welch Convalescent Center when it closed in August 1946. He was wounded in the European campaign in 1945 and was sent to the hospital for rehabilitation. Following his rehabilitation and retirement, he often returned to Daytona Beach to visit his close friend and fellow officer Gen. Paul Thompson. Each year Colonel Royall visited West Point for the alumni review and graduation exercises. (Courtesy of Cardwell Family Collection.)

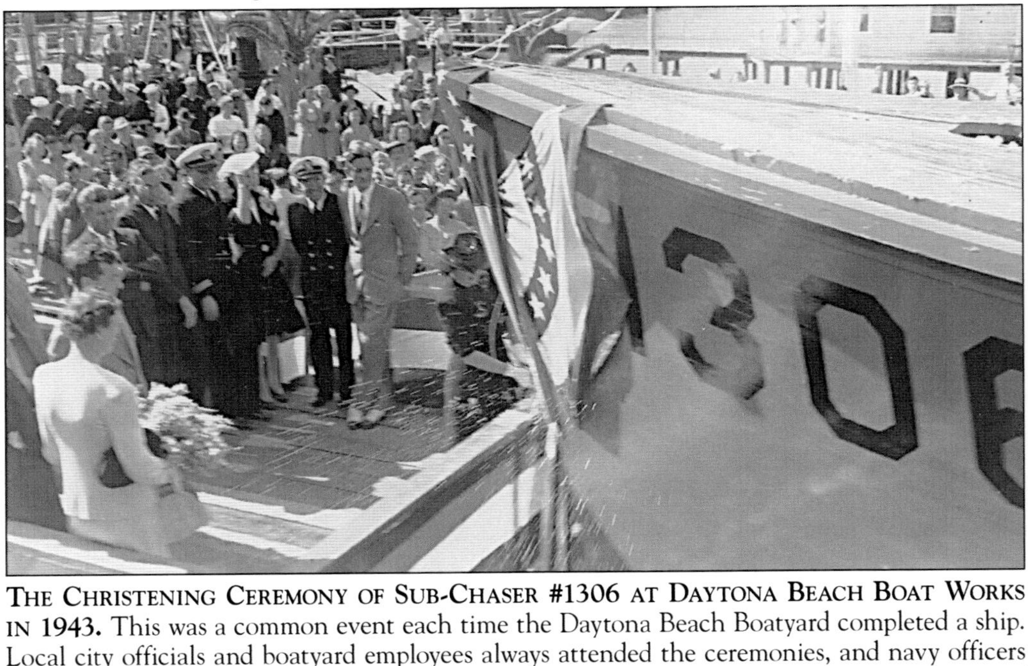

THE CHRISTENING CEREMONY OF SUB-CHASER #1306 AT DAYTONA BEACH BOAT WORKS IN 1943. This was a common event each time the Daytona Beach Boatyard completed a ship. Local city officials and boatyard employees always attended the ceremonies, and navy officers were there to take title. After christening, the ship went into active service. (Courtesy of Cardwell Family Collection.)

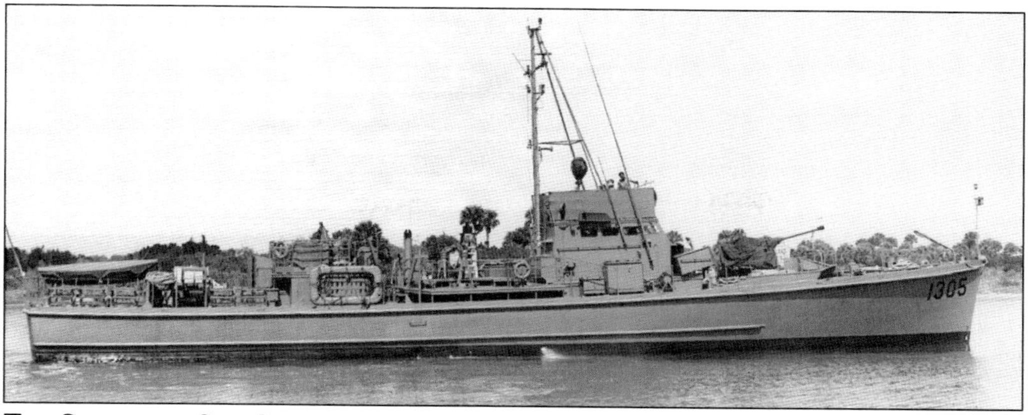

The Completed Sub-Chaser #1305, Built by the Daytona Boat Works in 1943. This sub-chaser was built by employees of the boat works at Daytona Beach. The boat works built sub-chasers, air/sea rescue vessels, and Liberty boats. This was Daytona's contribution to World War II. (Courtesy of Cardwell Family Collection.)

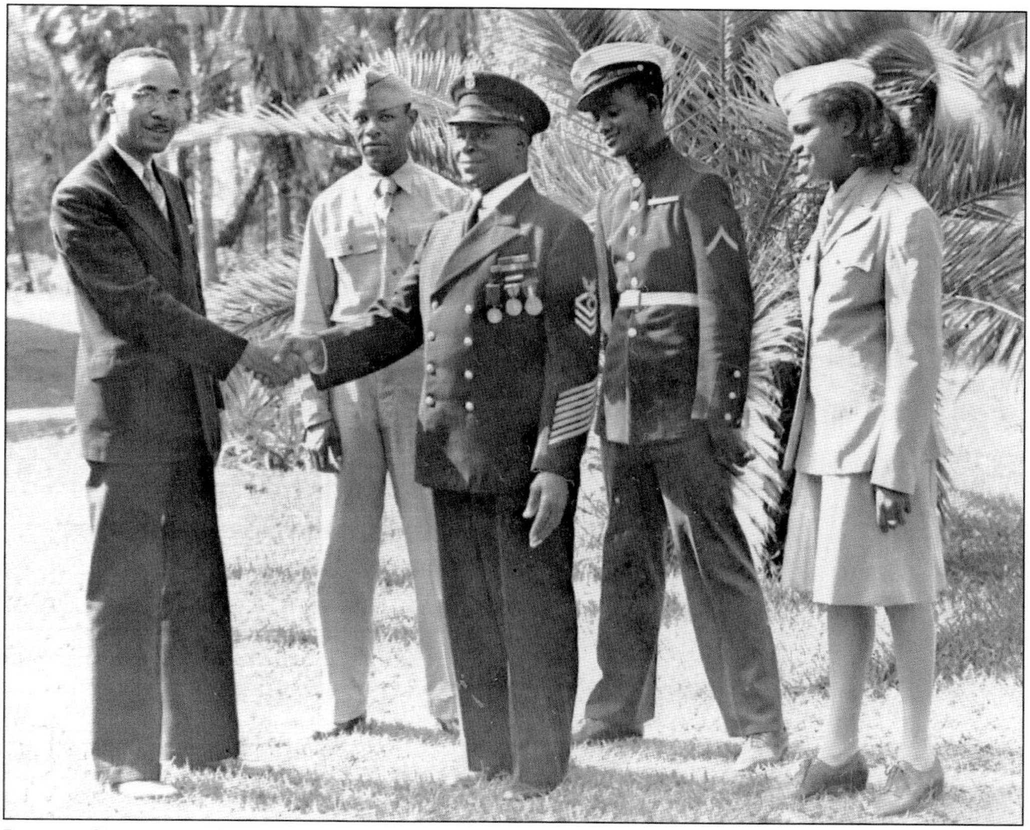

James Colston, Administrator of Bethune-Cookman College, 1943–1946. Mr. Colston, at left, greets World War II veterans on the campus of Bethune-Cookman College. When veterans returned after World War II, there was an increase in enrollment and the college grew. In 1943 the first baccalaureate degree was awarded under Mr. Colston's administration. The school was founded by Mary McLeod Bethune, and when her first classroom building was completed in 1907, she named it Faith Hall. (Courtesy of Florida State Archives.)

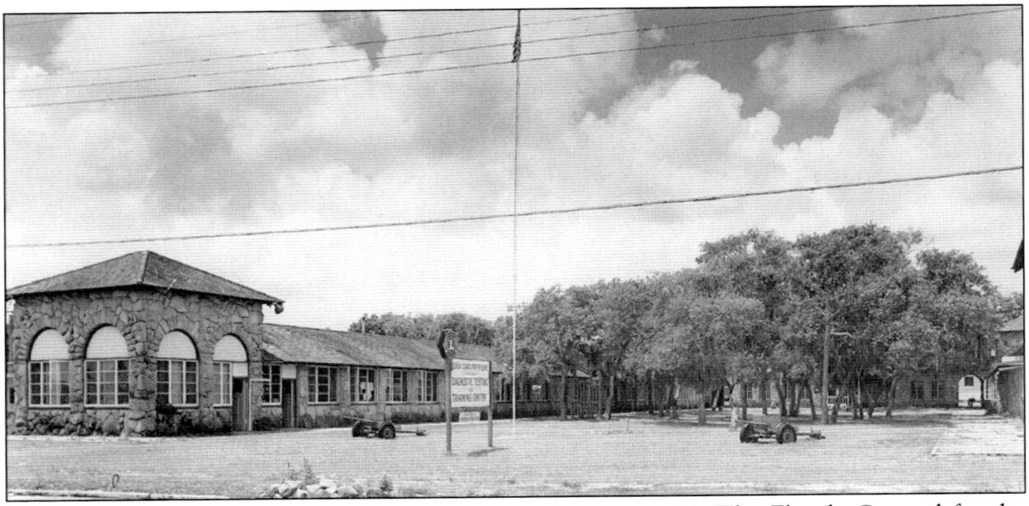

FLORIDA STATE FARMERS' MARKET AT HOLLY HILL IN 1946. The Florida Council for the Blind (FCB) leased this farmers' market in 1946 from the State of Florida for the first diagnostic testing and training center for the blind. The facility was used until 1949, when larger quarters were made available at the abandoned Welch Convalescence Center. Today a modern training center occupies the grounds of the old convalescence center. The farmers' market is now the Volusia County Law Center. (Courtesy of Cardwell Family Collection.)

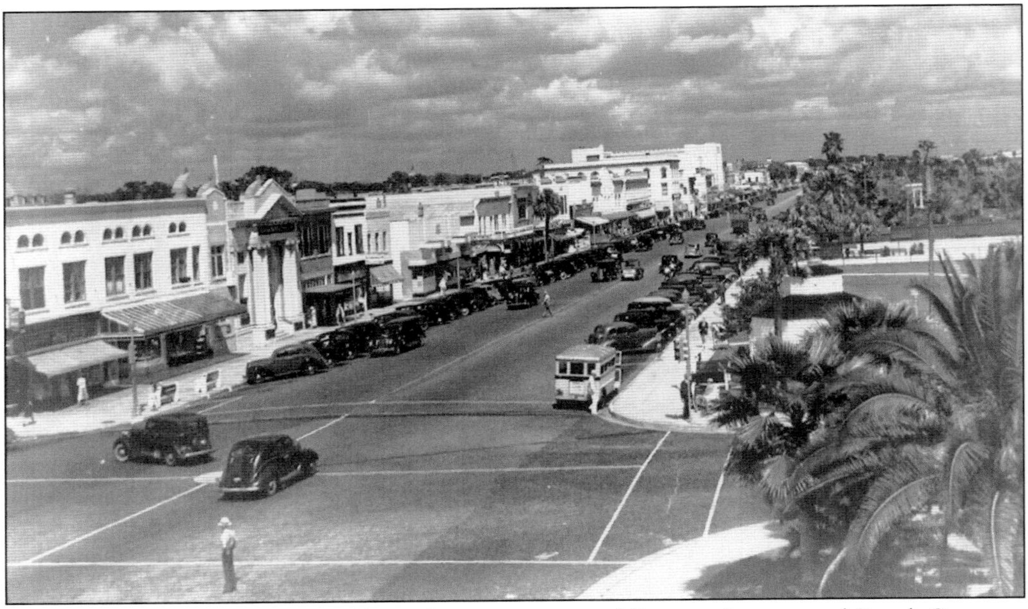

BEACH STREET IN THE 1940S. From the intersection of Orange Avenue and Beach Street to the east (at right) is the city bus station; to the west (at left) heading north are Liggett's Drug Store, Hegenwald Jewelers, Florida Bank and Trust Company, and Davidson Brothers Fruits. On the south corner of Magnolia Avenue and Beach Street is Woolworth's and on the north is Yowell-Drew Company Department Store. On the east side going north from the bus station is the City Riverfront Park. (Courtesy of Cardwell Family Collection.)

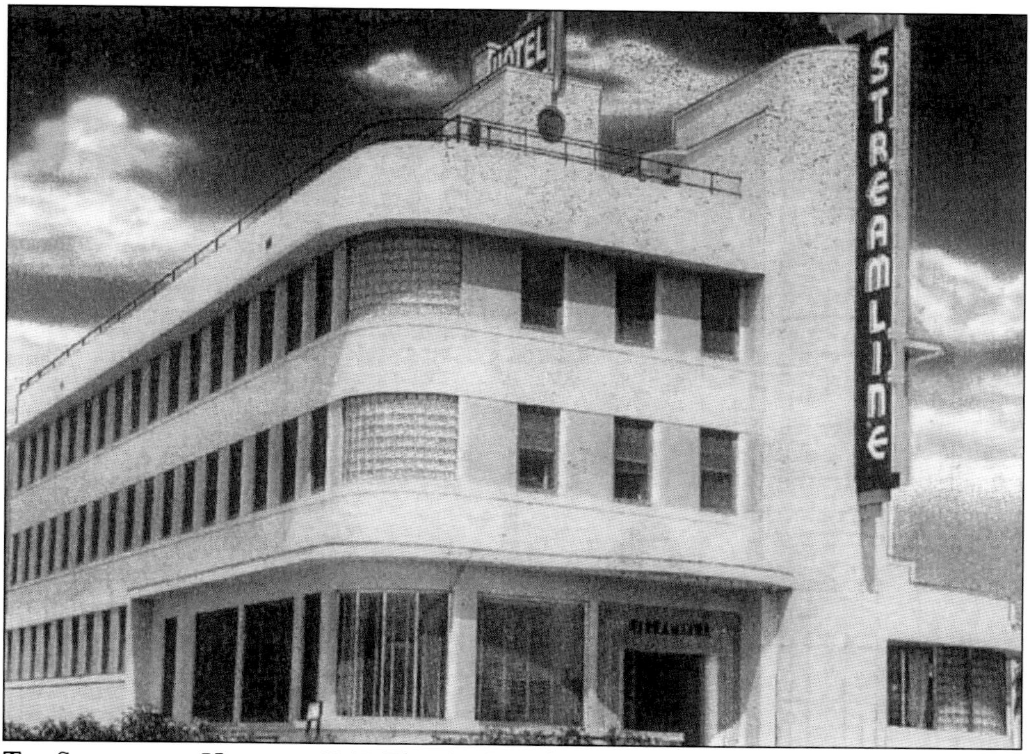

THE STREAMLINE HOTEL IN 1947. This Art Deco hotel on Atlantic Avenue was the birthplace of the National Association for Stock Car Auto Racing (NASCAR); on December 14, 1947, at 1:00 p.m., this new organization was formed in the rooftop penthouse lounge. Bill France was elected president, Bill Tuthill was elected national secretary, and Erwin G. "Cannonball" Baker was elected national commissioner. From this humble beginning NASCAR has emerged into a large corporation headquartered in Daytona Beach. (Courtesy of Midkiff Family Collection.)

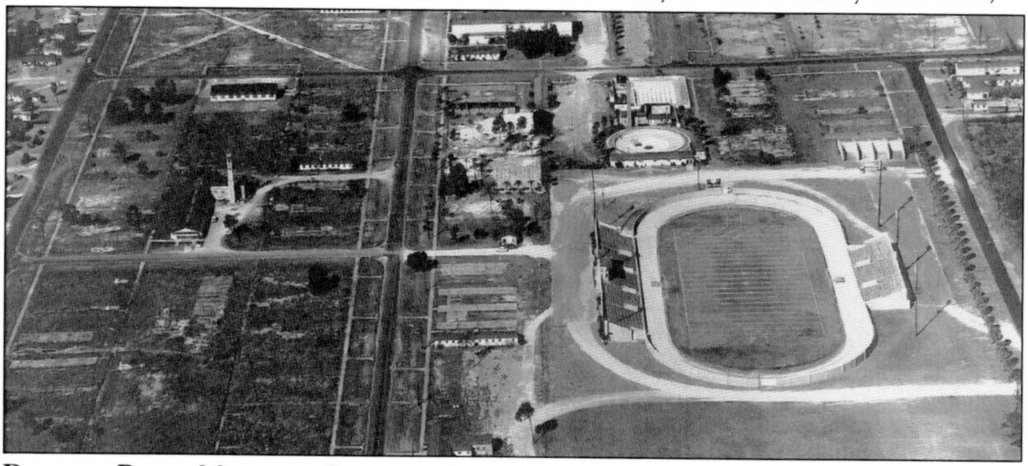

DAYTONA BEACH MEMORIAL STADIUM, CONSTRUCTED IN THE LATE 1940S. This area was the location of the WAC cantonment and the Welch Convalescence Center during World War II. The surrounding buildings are mostly World War II military structures and include circular and square swimming pools, a bowling alley, laundry, and barracks. The stadium was demolished c. 1990. Today there is no physical evidence of this structure or military buildings on the Daytona Beach Community College Campus. (Courtesy Halifax Historical Society.)

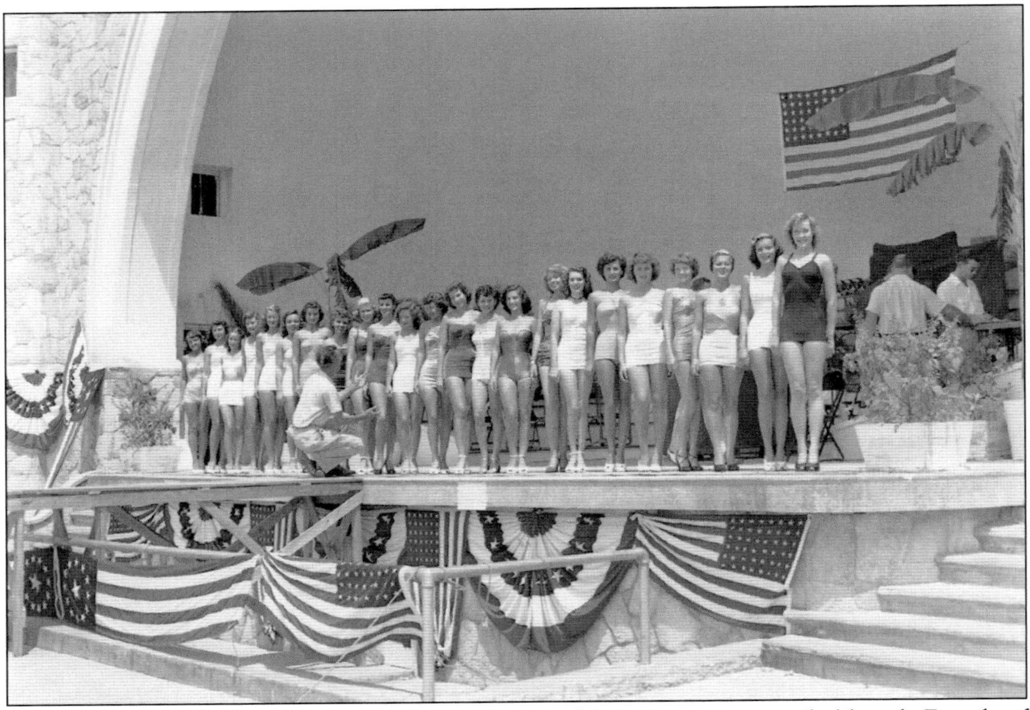

A BEAUTY PAGEANT ON JULY 4, 1949. An annual beauty contest was held each Fourth of July and sponsored by businesses in Daytona Beach. "Dixie Frolics" was one title used to help promote summer holiday tourism. (Courtesy of Florida State Archives.)

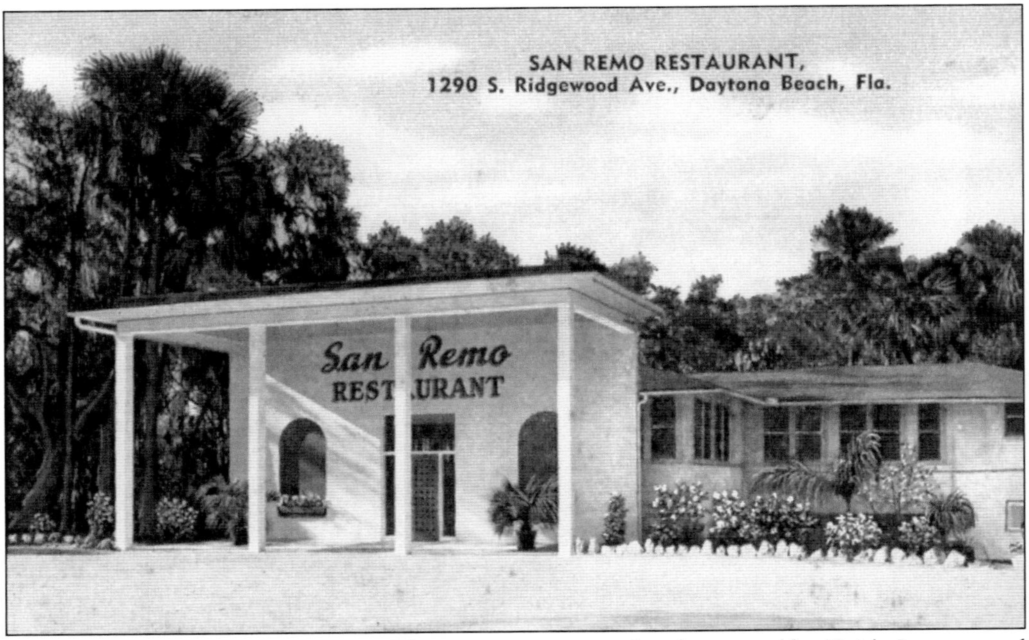

SAN REMO RESTAURANT C. 1949. This restaurant, owned and operated by Guido Levetto and his parents for many years, was located at 1290 South Ridgewood Avenue. It had three names: the Plantation, the Brook, and lastly the San Remo. (Courtesy of Cardwell Family Collection.)

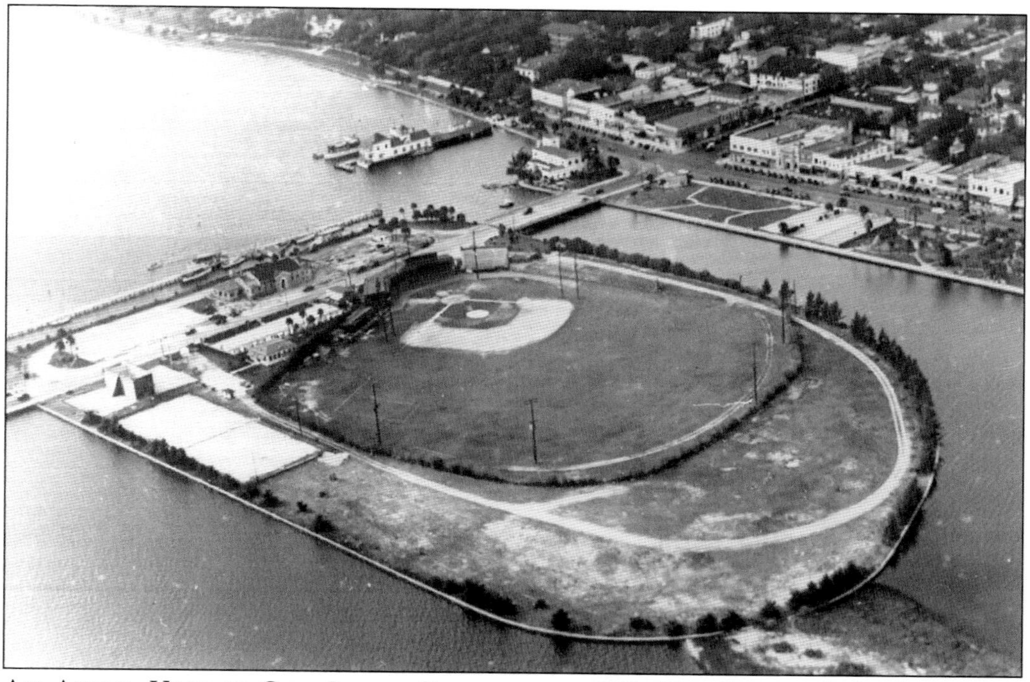

AN AERIAL VIEW OF CITY ISLAND BALLPARK IN 1950. This Daytona ballpark has been renamed Jackie Robinson Ballpark. He broke the baseball color barrier at this field in 1946. A bronze statue of Jackie Robinson in uniform stands at the front entrance to the main grandstand. The field was constructed in 1914, and improvements have been made throughout the years. (Courtesy of John Gontner.)

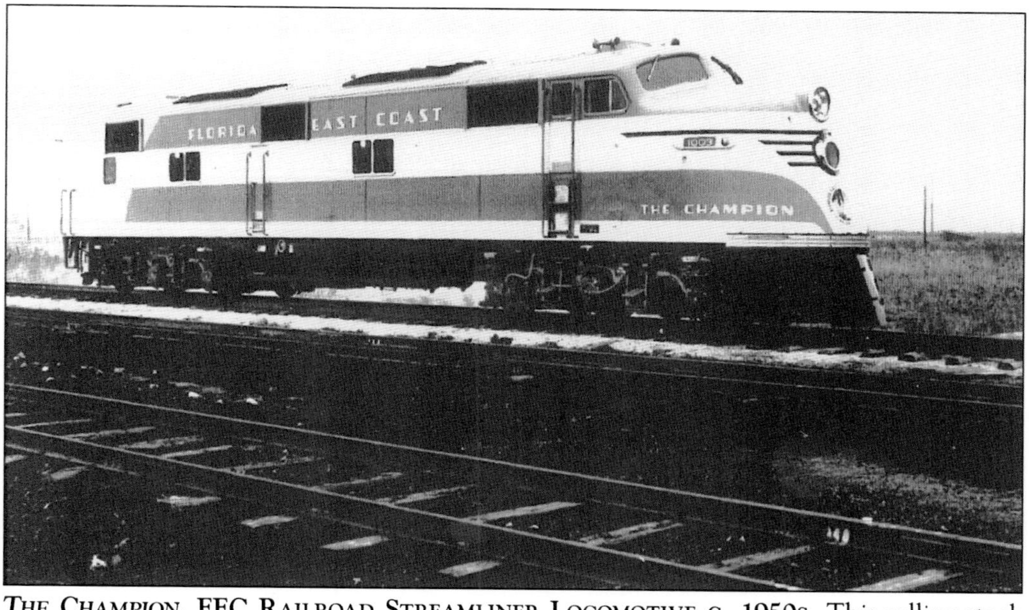

***THE CHAMPION*, FEC RAILROAD STREAMLINER LOCOMOTIVE C. 1950S.** This rolling stock of streamliners passed through Daytona Beach year after year when passenger service was in its heyday. In the early 1960s, a crippling railroad-employee strike caused the FEC Railroad service to disband passenger service. To this day it has not been re-inaugurated. (Courtesy of Port Orange Historical Trust.)

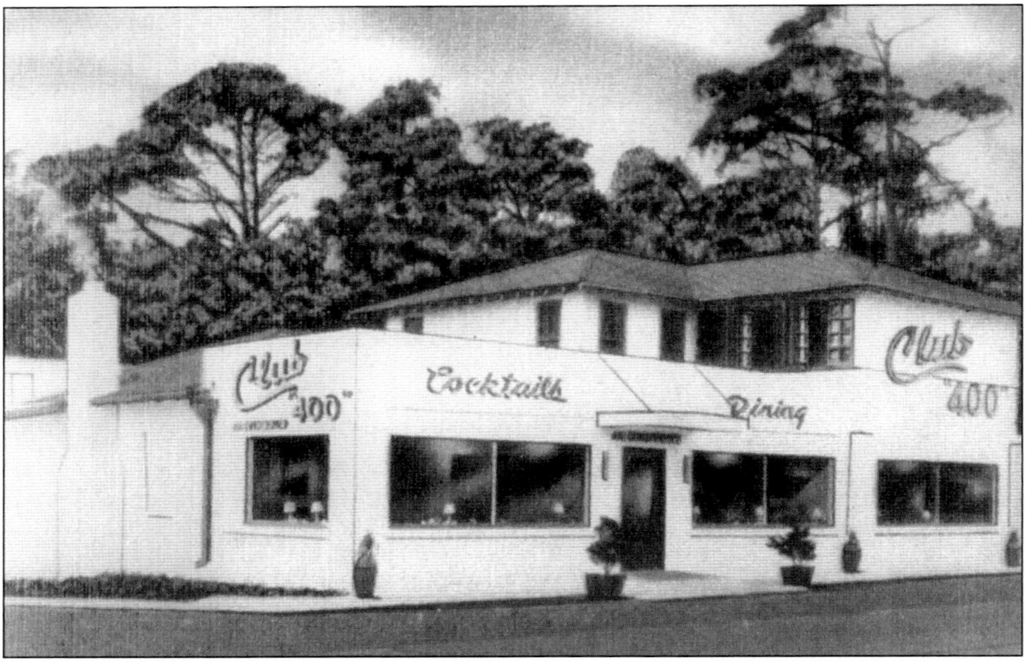

THE "FOUR O'CLOCK CLUB" IN THE LATE 1950S. This popular nightclub kept late hours, closing at 4:00 a.m. each morning. Revelers could go just outside the Daytona city limits to South Daytona to continue their night of drinking, dancing, and shows that featured striptease dancers, as most of the Daytona clubs closed at 2:00 a.m. (Courtesy of Port Orange Historical Trust.)

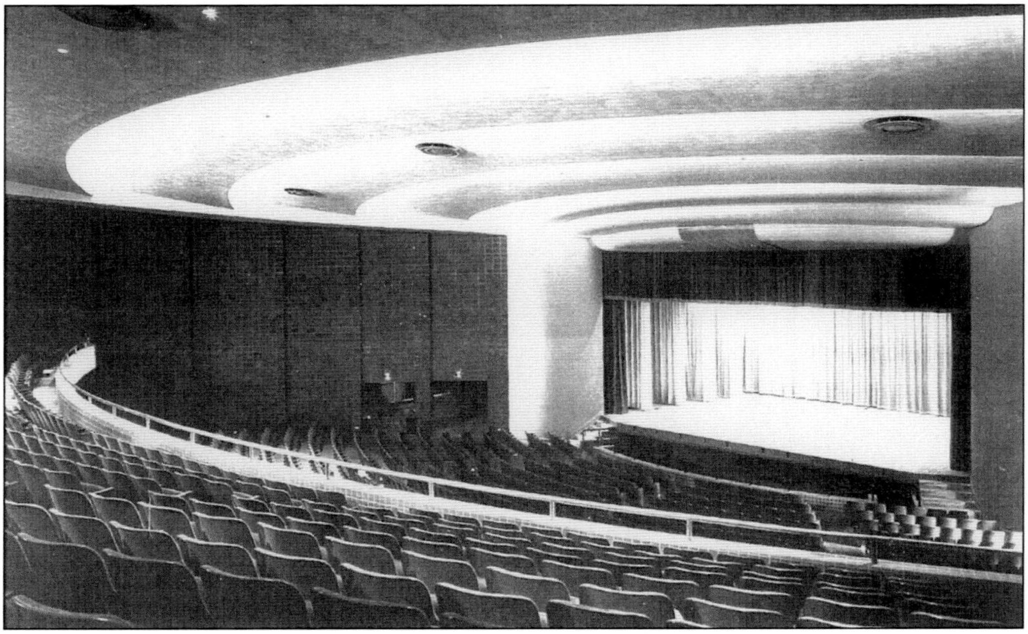

THE PEABODY AUDITORIUM IN 1950. This new facility at 600 Auditorium Boulevard replaced the old wooden one that burned several years before. Henry DeVerne, manager and director of the new auditorium, was in charge of the outstanding programs that started in 1950. (Courtesy of Leonard Lempel, Ph.D.)

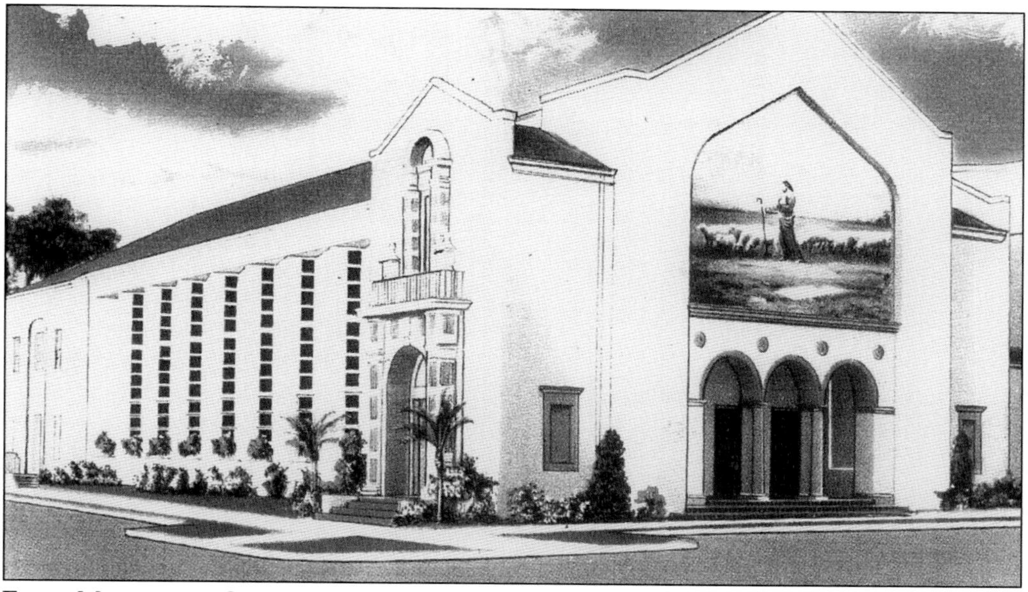

First Methodist Church of Daytona Beach in 1952. This church was organized in 1877. The present sanctuary and other renovation work, including the beautiful mural at the entrance, were completed for the first service and dedication in March 1952. The Methodist church closed in January 2002. (Courtesy of Cardwell Family Collection.)

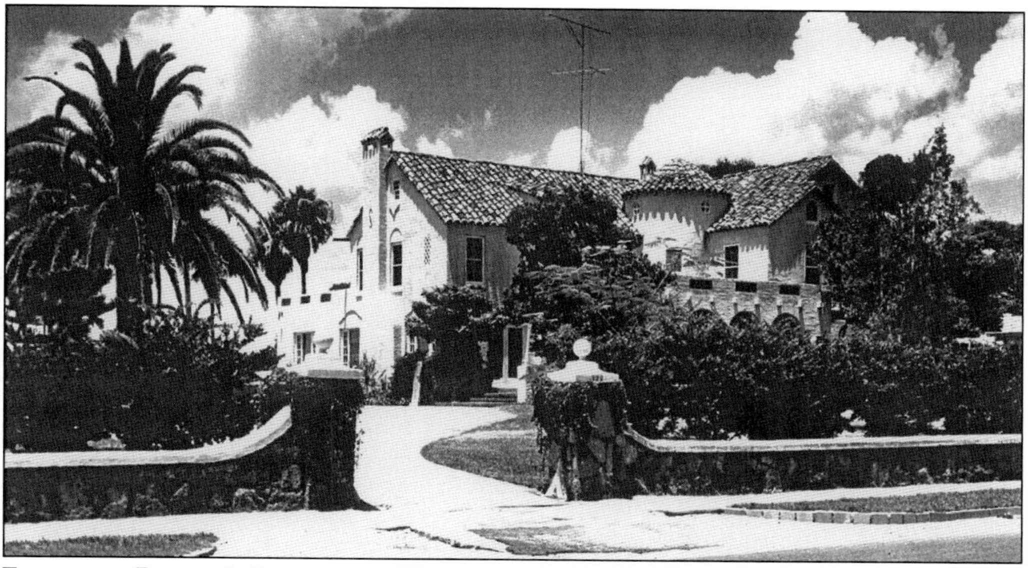

Fulgencio Batista's Riverfront Home in 1953. This beautiful home at 137 North Halifax Drive was originally built as a winter home for Ransom E. Olds. Olds, an automobile manufacturer, made a name by racing his car "The Pirate" on the beach in 1903. He also established Olds Hall at 340 South Ridgewood Avenue, a home for retired ministers and missionaries. President Batista established his home here in Daytona Beach before being exiled from Cuba. (Courtesy of Halifax Historical Society.)

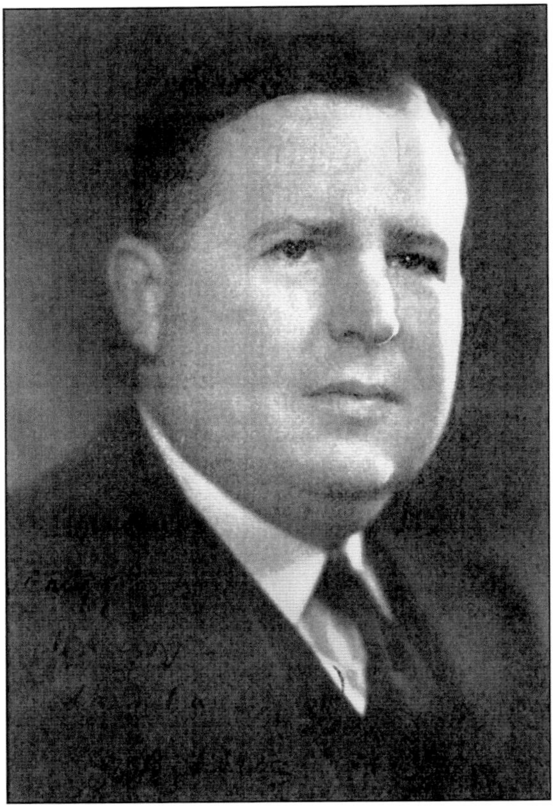

David Sholtz, 1891–1953. A practicing attorney and civic leader, Sholtz established the law firm of Sholtz, Green, Daniels, and West at 226 South Beach Street. He was a World War I veteran, and in 1917 he was elected to the Florida State Legislature. In 1919 he was appointed municipal judge and was eventually elected governor in 1933. After serving as governor he ran for U.S. senator and was defeated. He lived at 240 Anita Street on the Halifax River. (Courtesy of Halifax Historical Society.)

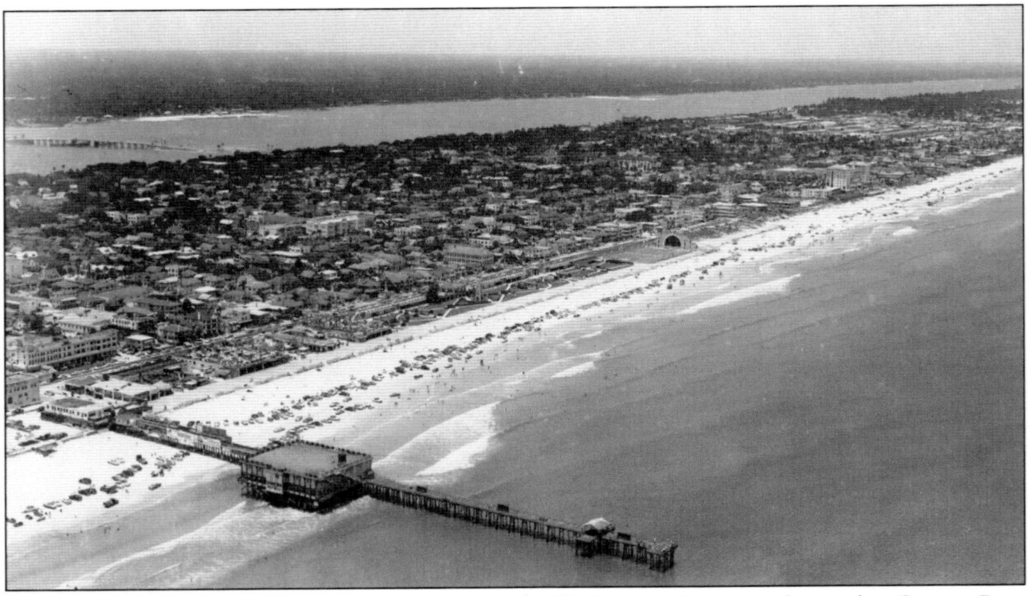

An Aerial View of Daytona Beach in 1957. In the foreground are the Ocean Pier, boardwalk, band shell, and Seabreeze Boulevard Bridge, with Halifax River to the west. (Courtesy of John Gontner.)

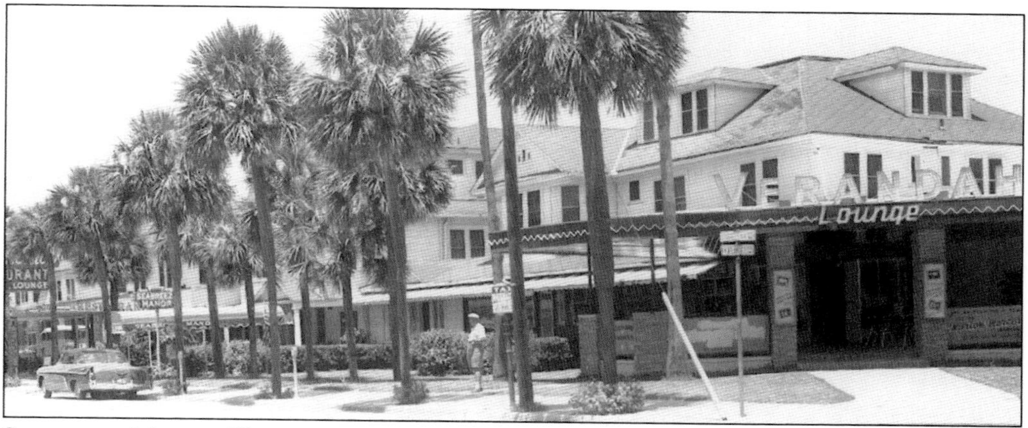

SEABREEZE MANOR HOTEL AND LOUNGE IN 1957. This was a favorite nightspot for tourists and locals alike. The Veranda Lounge had a famous bar and an adjoining restaurant. The establishment was owned by the Howard Dayton Hotel chain. Mr. Dayton lived in Daytona Beach in the former R.E. Olds home on Halifax Drive. (Courtesy of John Gontner).

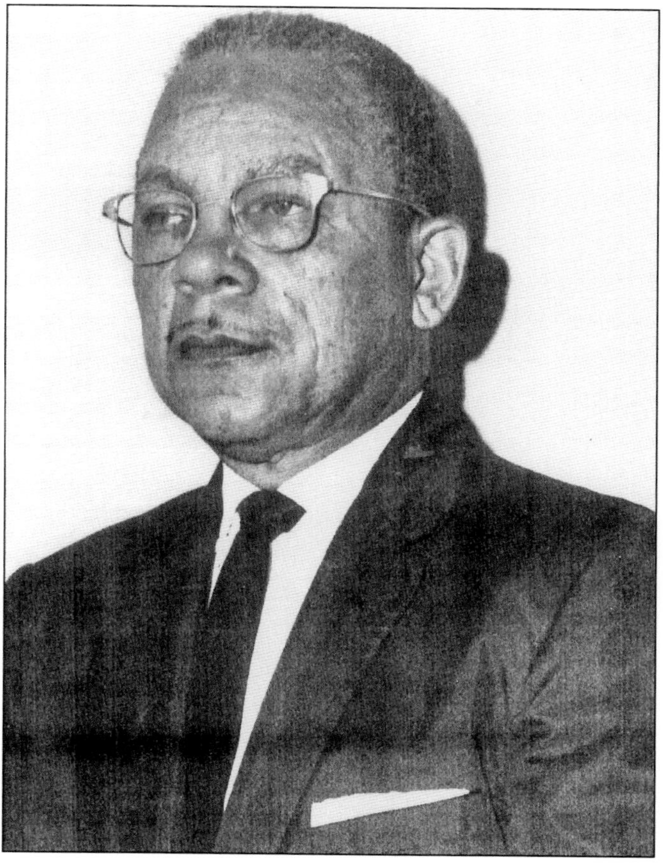

JAMES GRIFFEN GREENE IN 1958. Dr. Greene was a respected educator and president of the segregated, two-year Volusia County Junior College on Loomis Street. After integration and relocation to the International Speedway campus in 1965, the Volusia County School Board took over the building, and today it is used as the east Volusia offices. The college merged in 1971, and the name changed from Daytona Beach Junior College to Daytona Beach Community College. (Courtesy of Leonard Lempel, Ph.D.)

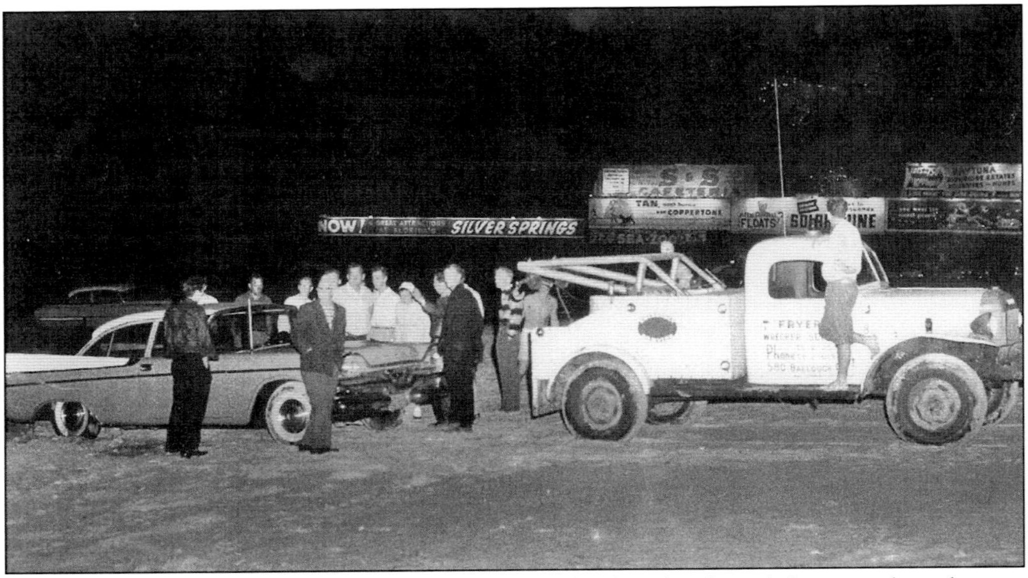

Fryer's Towing Service c. 1959. Visitors to the beach often did not realize that an incoming tide could overrun their car and cause them to be stuck in the sand of the ocean surf. Towing services stayed busy during the beach season. Often this was costly and ruined a beach outing. Notice the Ocean Pier walkway in the background. (Courtesy of Port Orange Historical Trust.)

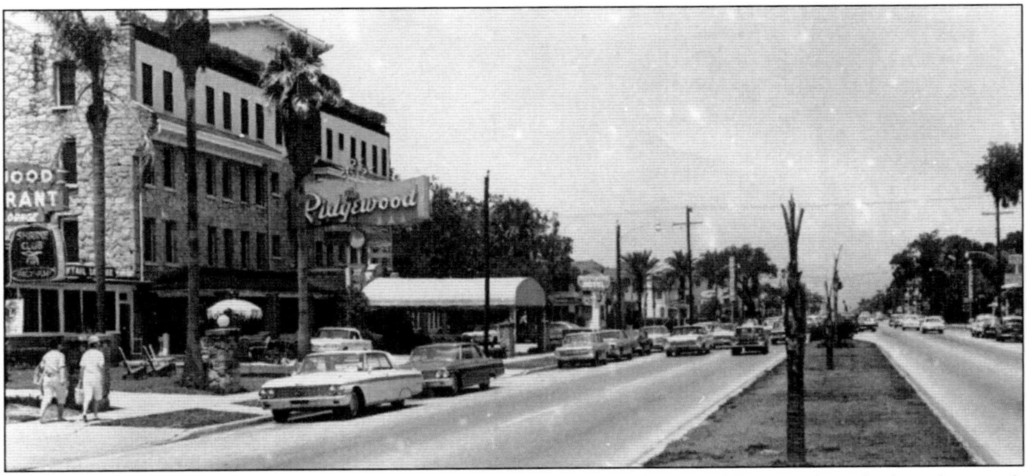

The Ridgewood Hotel in 1960. This hotel replaced the old 1932 hotel that burned. The exterior façade was stone veneer made from locally cut coquina rock, giving the front elevation a unique architecture that identified it throughout the years. The cocktail lounge featured a piano player who was the owner's brother. The dining was cafeteria style, which was popular with local folks, and it was always crowded on Sunday after church service. (Courtesy of John Gontner.)

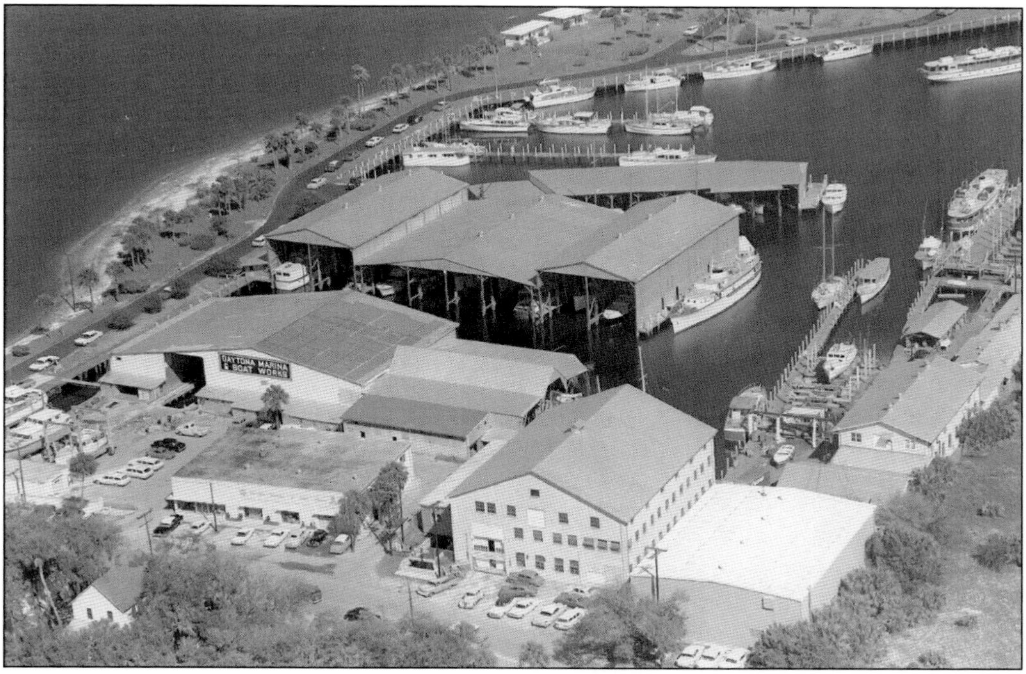

DAYTONA MARINA AND BOAT WORKS, 645 SOUTH BEACH STREET, IN 1960. This active boatyard, which had a dry dock and repaired all types of watercraft, built ships for the navy during World War II. They built sub-chasers, air/sea rescue vessels, and Liberty boats. (Courtesy of Cardwell Family Collection.)

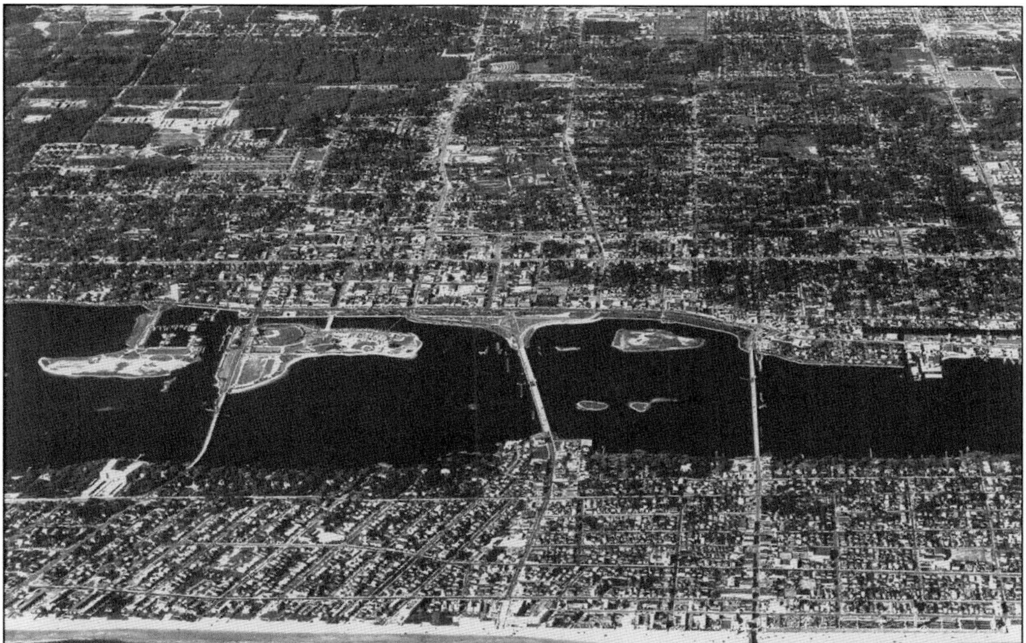

DAYTONA BEACH AERIAL VIEW LOOKING WEST FROM THE OCEAN IN 1964. Notice the shade trees, Ocean Pier, boardwalk, Beach Street along the west side of Halifax River, and other landmarks. (Courtesy of Cardwell Family Collection.)

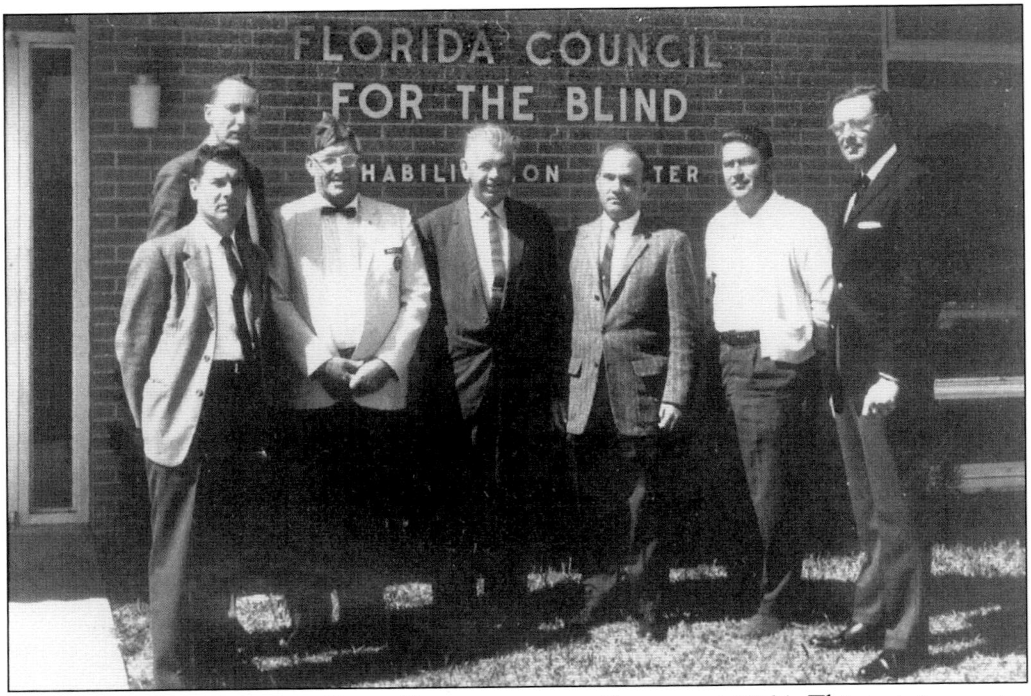

FLORIDA COUNCIL FOR THE BLIND REHABILITATION CENTER IN 1964. This training center for the blind is located at 1111 Willis Avenue. The Lions Club provided funds for landscaping the campus. Carl McCoy was the administrator and Matthew Hyland was the supervisor of training. Members of the South Halifax Lions Club are, from left to right, Wayne Campbell (front), Walter Snell (rear), Floyd Filman, Matthew Hyland, Carl McCoy, James Toole, and Harold Cardwell Sr. (Courtesy of Cardwell Family Collection.)

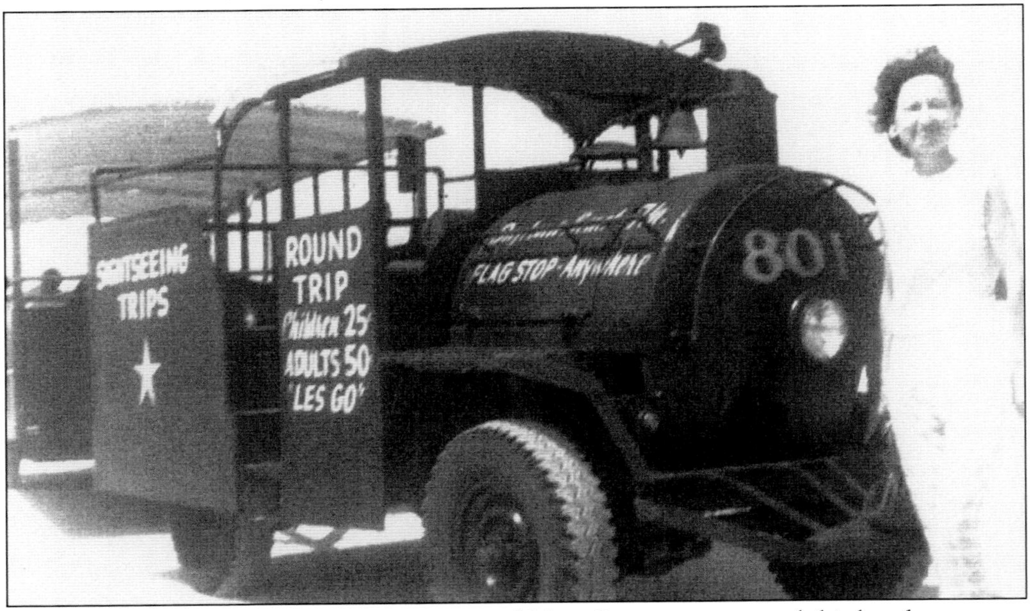

BEACH SIGHTSEEING TRAM C. 1965. James and Mary Stevenson operated this beach transport on Daytona Beach for many years. Note the prices posted on the side of the vehicle. (Courtesy of Port Orange Historical Trust.)

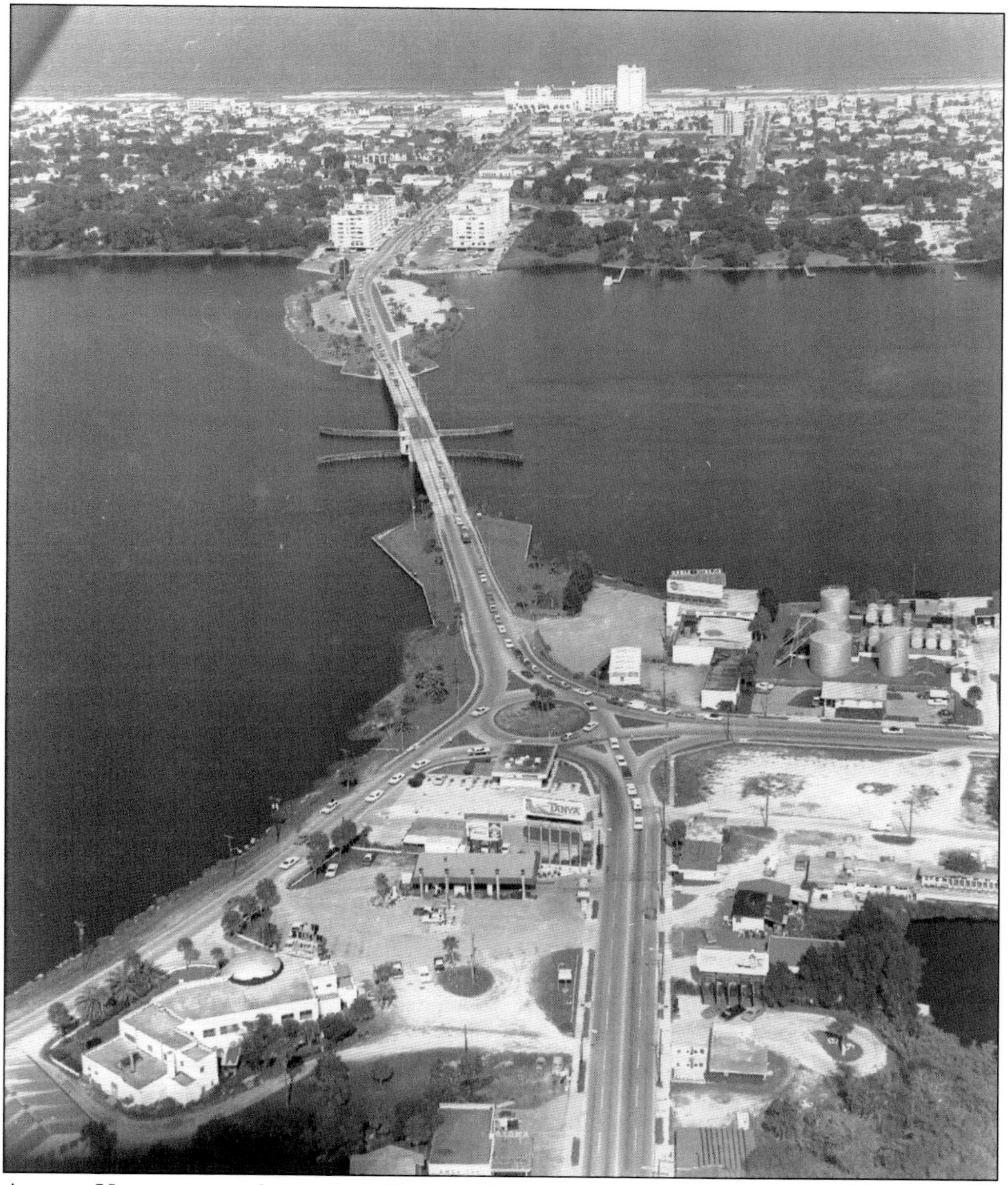

AERIAL VIEW OF THE SEABREEZE TRAFFIC CIRCLE IN 1969. The circle was located at the intersection of Sickler Drive, Ballough Road, Seabreeze Bridge, and Mason Avenue. The Loyal Order of Moose clubhouse, a two-story building with a rotunda, can be seen in the left foreground. The Diplomat Center can be seen on the east side of the bridge. The bridge was replaced at the millennium by a new high-rise, twin-span bridge, making the old drawbridge span obsolete. (Courtesy of John Gontner.)

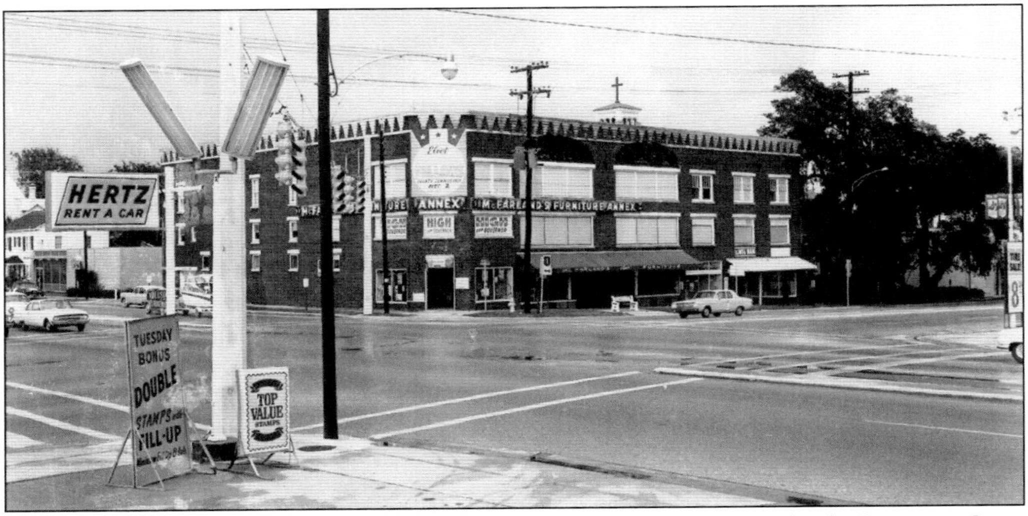

McFarland's Furniture Store Annex in 1966. The main McFarland's Furniture Store was located on Magnolia Avenue. The annex was on the corner of Ridgewood Avenue and Volusia Avenue, today's International Speedway Boulevard. This furniture store was formerly the Mather-Barnes Furniture Company, and the land was owned by Sumner Hale Gove, who designed the building c. 1914. (Courtesy of John Gontner.)

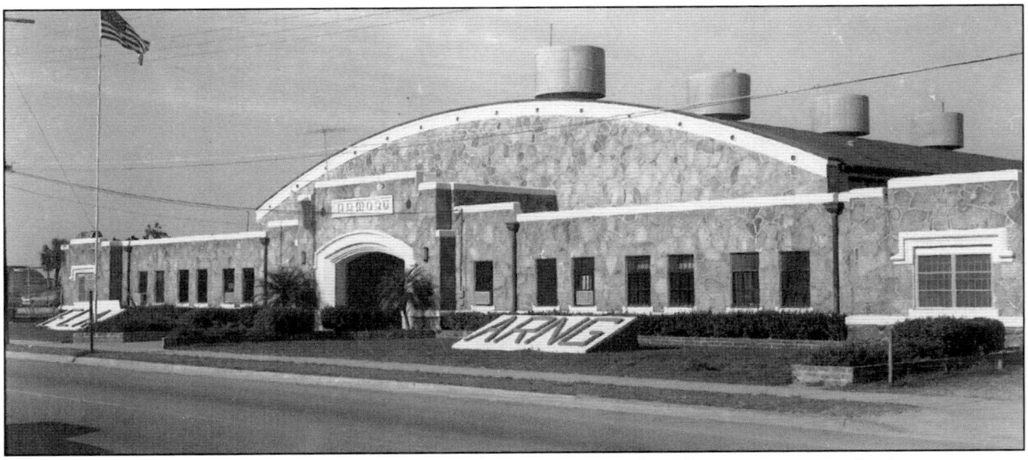

Daytona Beach Armory in 1970. This large, masonry building constructed of cut coquina stone was built by the WPA in 1940. During World War II men trained here for the Florida State Militia and later the Florida National Guard. The author Harold Cardwell, who was a private in the Florida State Guard, trained in this building. Today this building is owned by Bill and Jim France, officers in the International Speedway Corporation (ISC). The first armory was built by Sumner Hale Gove in 1896. The second armory was headquartered in an arcade on North Beach Street. (Courtesy of John Gontner.)

Eight

The New Boom Era to the Millennium 1971–2004

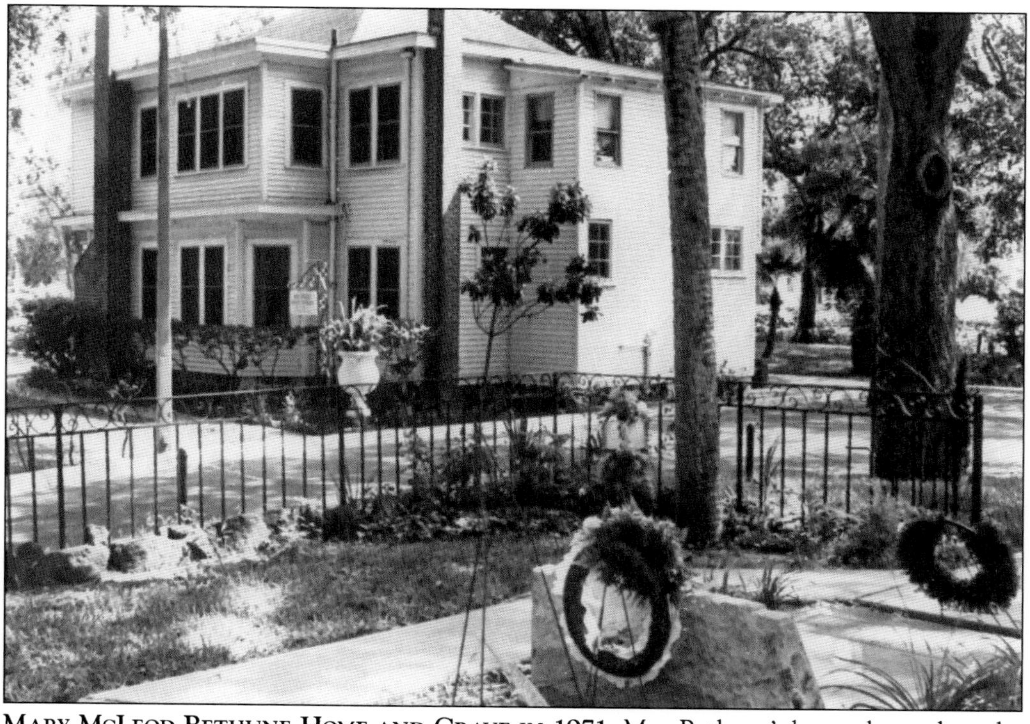

Mary McLeod Bethune Home and Grave in 1971. Mrs. Bethune's home, located on the Bethune-Cookman College campus facing Dr. Martin Luther King Jr. Boulevard, was built in 1915. The home is on the National Register of Historic Places and is in the National Historic District. (Courtesy of John Gontner.)

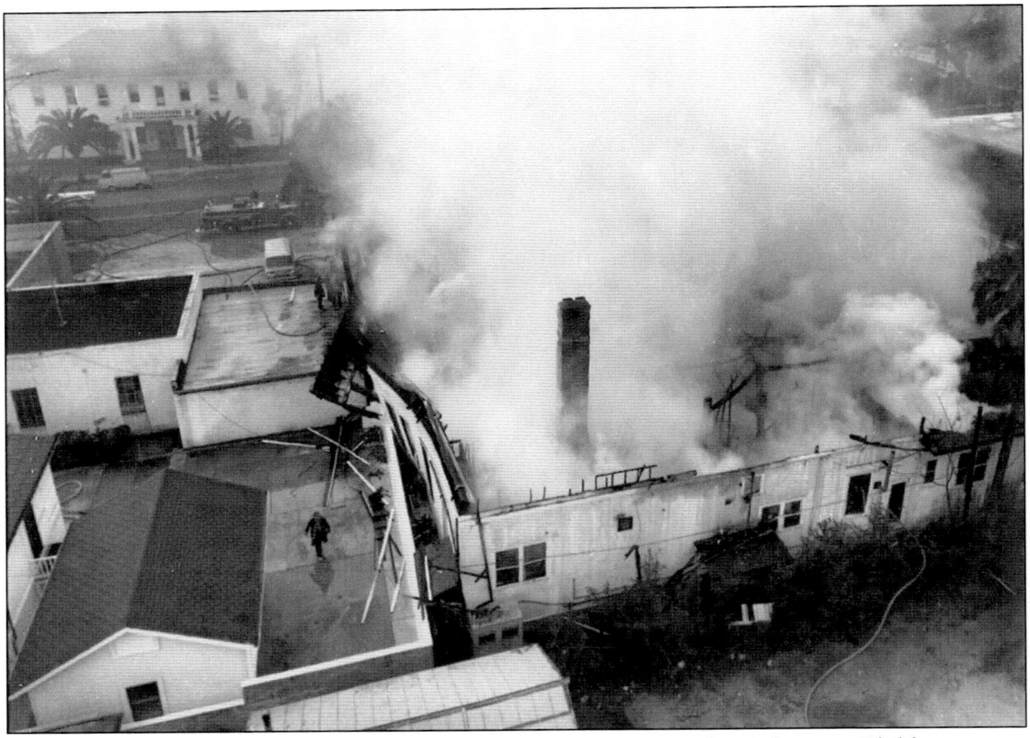

PALMETTO CLUBHOUSE ON FIRE ON FEBRUARY 2, 1971. The Palmetto Clubhouse was operated by club members and was a place for special programs featuring live entertainment, often including well-known artists and singing and dancing acts that drew large crowds. The first clubhouse, built by L.Z. Burdick in the late 1890s, was destroyed by fire. (Courtesy of John Gontner.)

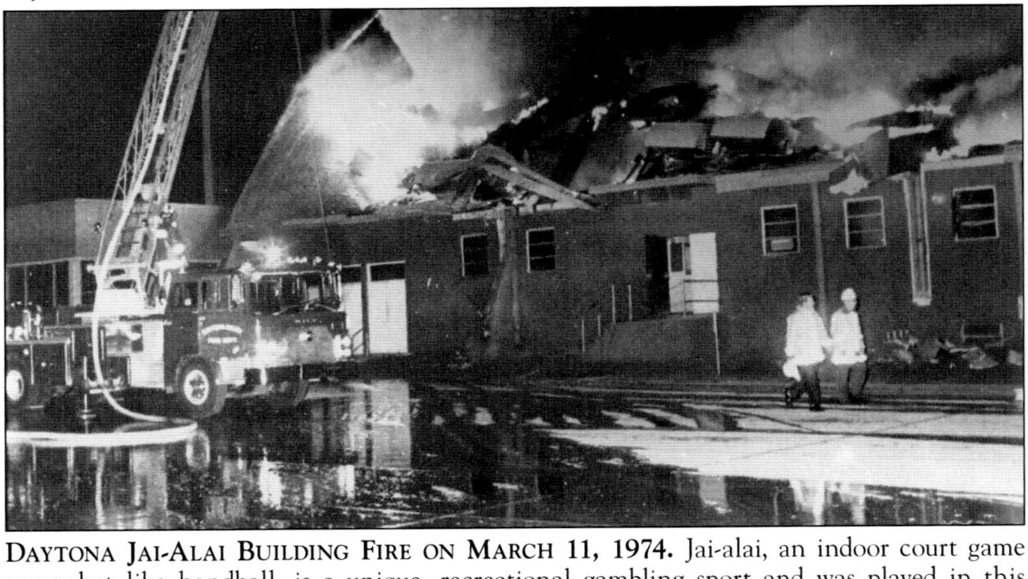

DAYTONA JAI-ALAI BUILDING FIRE ON MARCH 11, 1974. Jai-alai, an indoor court game somewhat like handball, is a unique, recreational gambling sport and was played in this building, known as a fronton. Played by two or four players with a ball and a long curved wicker basket strapped to one's wrist, Jai-alai is a fast-action game that requires speed and skill. (Courtesy of John Gontner.)

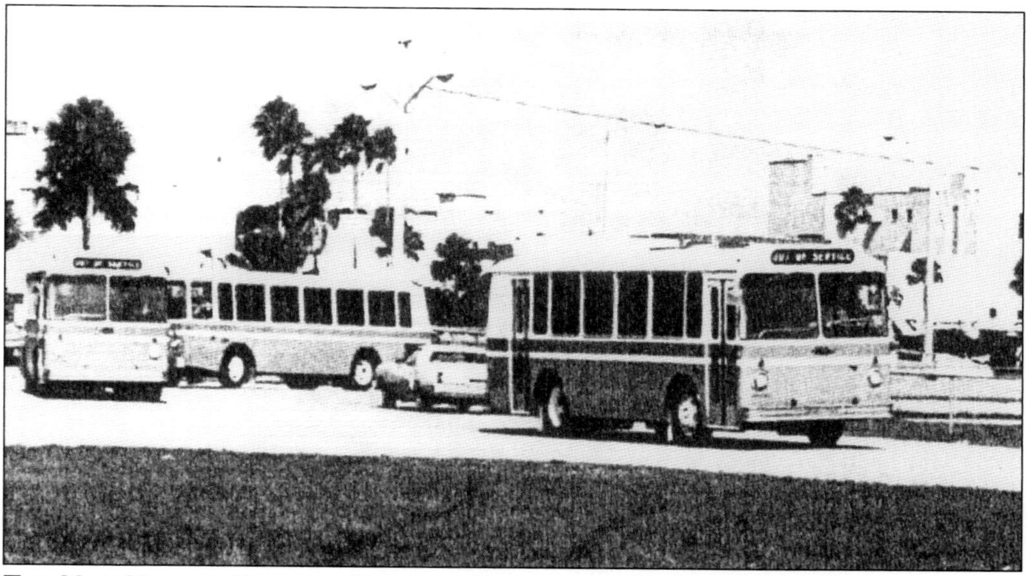

The New Votran Buses in Daytona Beach in 1975. Daytona Beach was very proud of the new Volusia County bus system; the diesel-powered buses ushered in a modern era. These special buses were adapted to be handicap accessible. (Courtesy of Daytona Beach News Journal Corporation.)

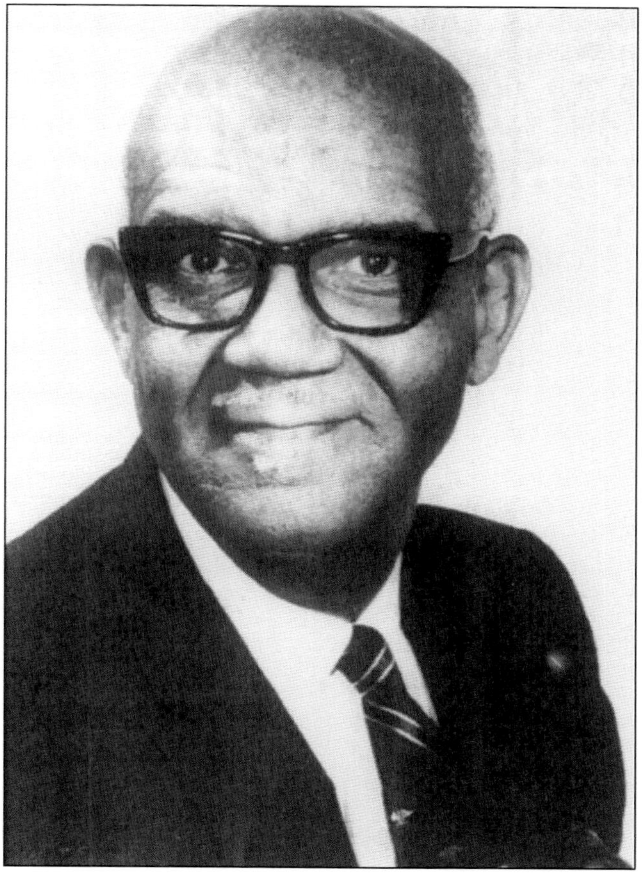

Dr. Richard V. Moore in 1979. Moore was an outstanding educator, former president of Bethune-Cookman College, civic leader, and organizer of many community projects. A strong black leader, he was instrumental in the transition from segregation to integration in public schools. (Courtesy of Halifax Historical Society.)

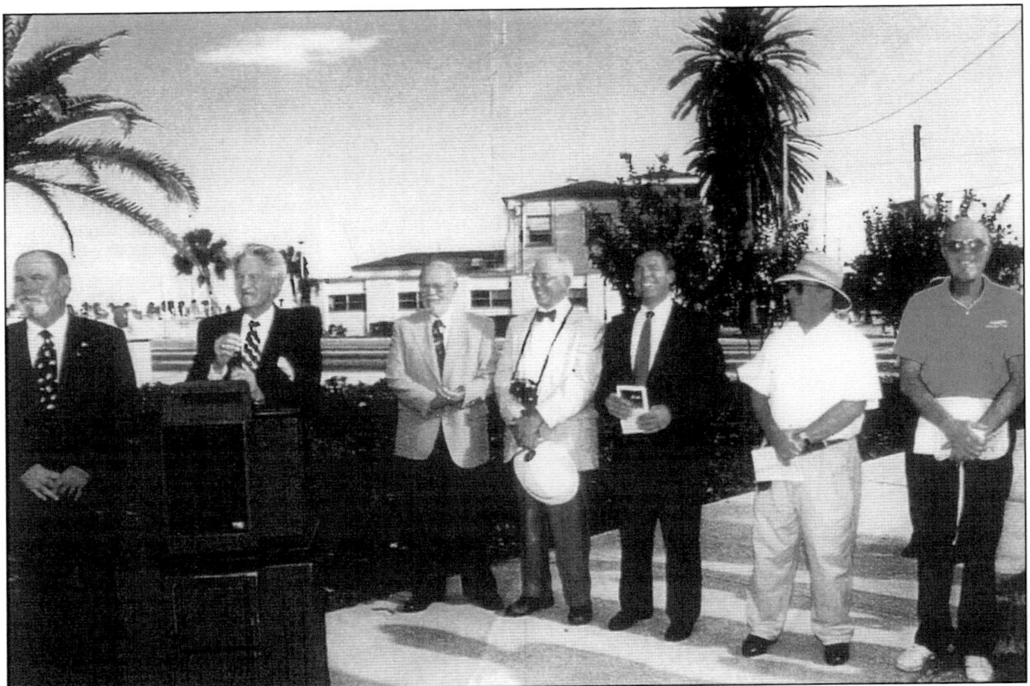

THE FIVE CITY MAYORS IN 1997. This photo shows, from left to right, city commissioner Daryl Hunter; Mayor Baron H. "Bud" Asher; former mayors Jack Tamm, Hart Long, Paul Carpenella, and Larry Kelly; and program-chairman Bill Seitz. The photo was taken at a rare gathering of Daytona Beach mayors at the city's 121st anniversary on July 26, 1997. (Courtesy of Cardwell Family Collection.)

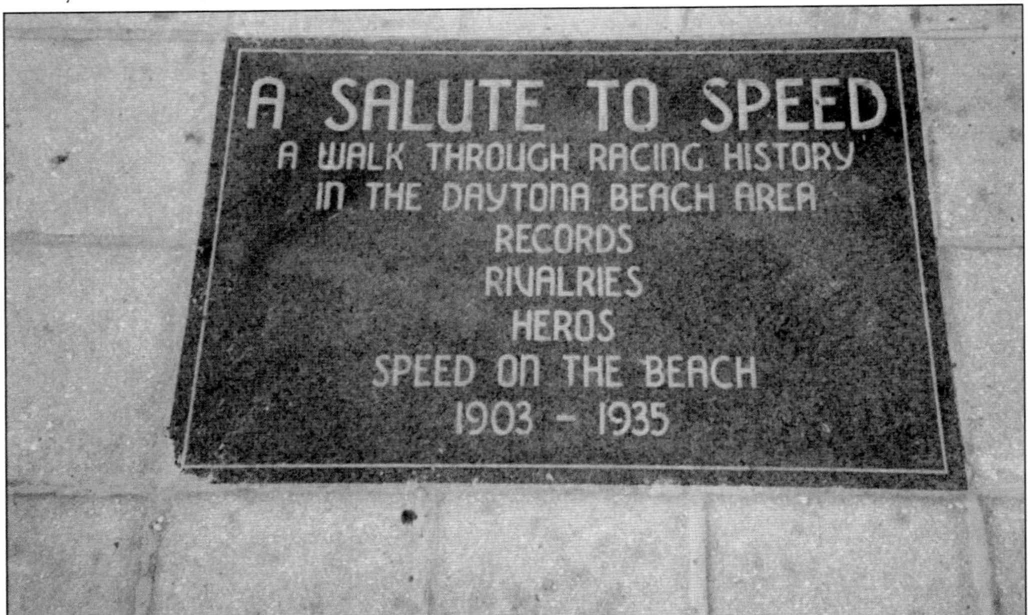

A WALK THROUGH RACING HISTORY IN 1997. The Daytona Beach City Commission and the Daytona Beach Historic Preservation Board Special Committee had this milestone placed in a section of the beachside boardwalk. (Courtesy of Cardwell Family Collection.)

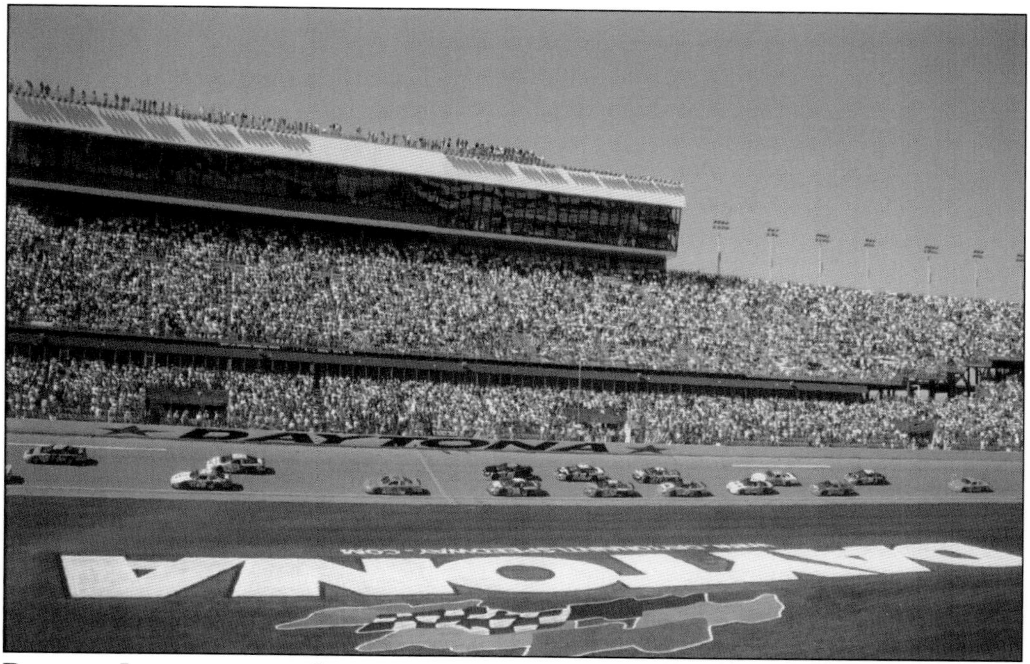

Daytona International Speedway in 2000. The start/finish line is visible, as are spotters on the Winston Tower, and the press suites can be seen in the upper level. Among the many drivers in this race are Jeff Gordon, the late Dale Earnhardt Sr., Dale Jarrett, Rusty Wallace, and Mark Martin. Dale Earnhardt Sr. was killed in a crash on February 18, 2001, during the Daytona 500. (Courtesy of ISC Archives.)

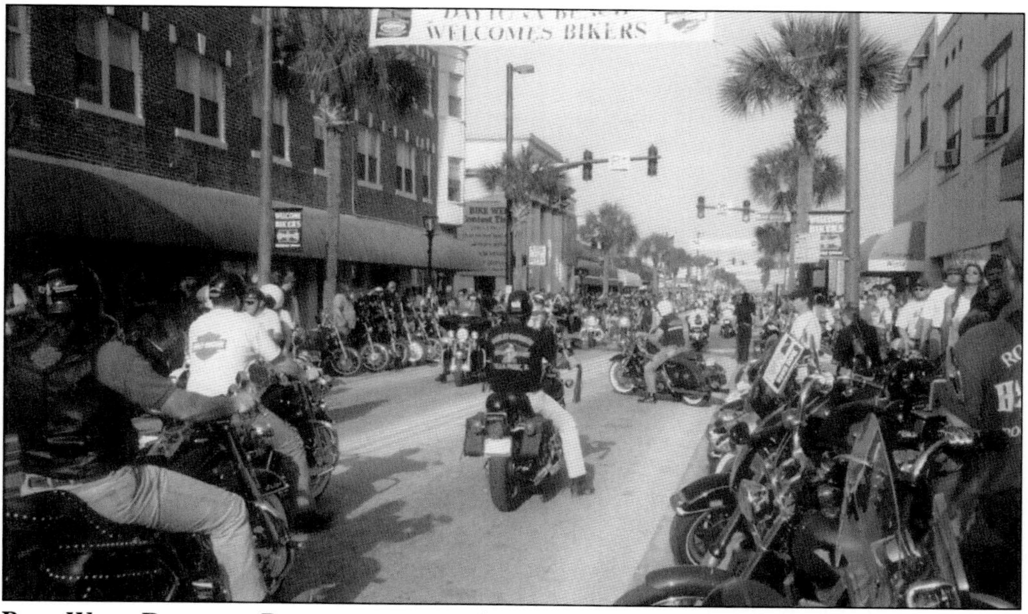

Bike Week Daytona Beach in 2000. Thousands come here each year to see the events, including the Daytona 200 Motorcycle Race at the speedway. The most highly sought-after parking places are on Main Street, where spectators stroll the sidewalks to look over those magnificent machines. Many bike riders are creative and innovative in adding accessories to their motorcycles. (Courtesy of Russ Atwell.)

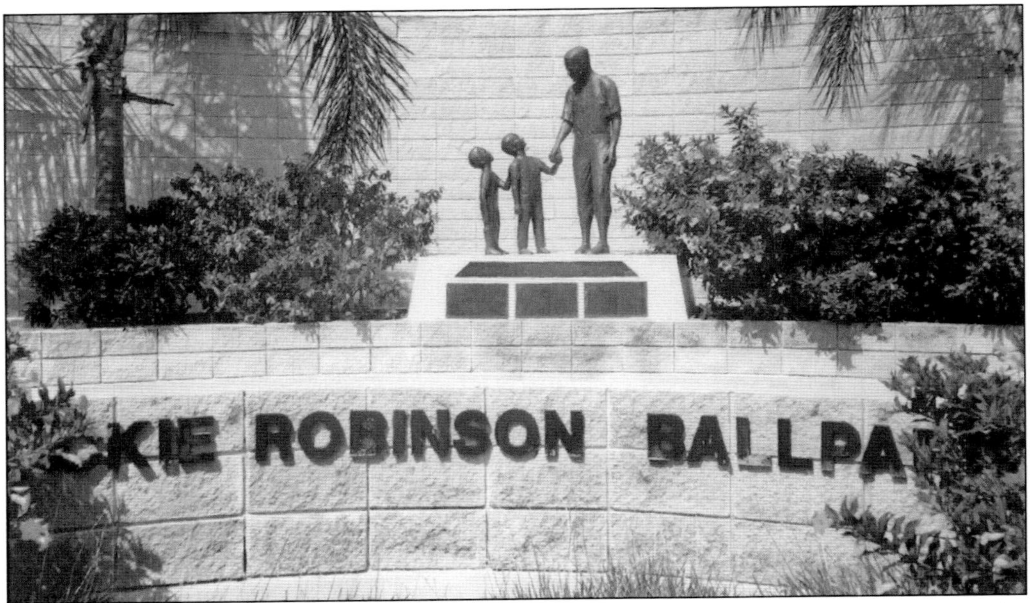

JACKIE ROBINSON BALLPARK MEMORIAL IN 2001. This statue of Jackie Robinson stands at the entrance to the ballpark. On March 17, 1946, he broke the baseball color barrier on this field playing for the Montreal Royals. One year later he broke the color barrier in the major leagues playing for the Brooklyn Dodgers. The City of Daytona Beach has a five-year plan for improving the field and constructing a museum to honor this great ball player. (Courtesy of Cardwell Family Collection.)

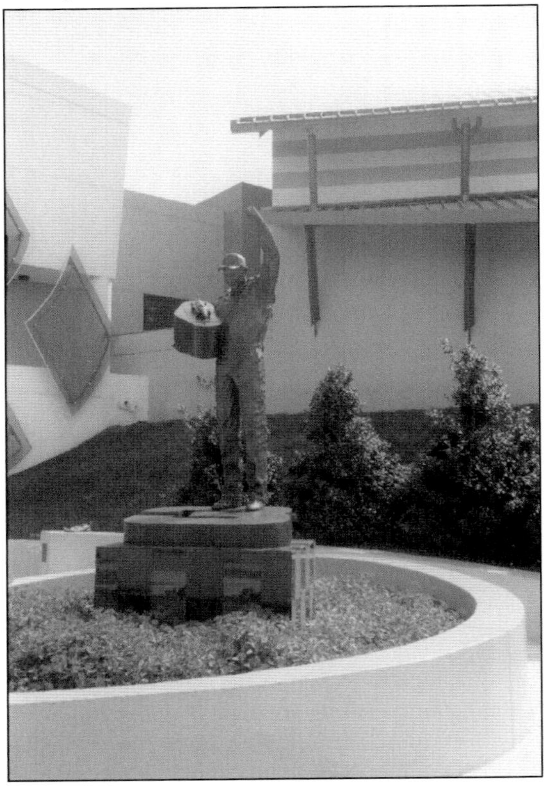

DALE EARNHARDT SR. MEMORIAL IN 2001. This likeness of Dale Earnhardt Sr. has attracted thousands of visitors since it was placed at the Daytona Beach International Speedway. He was killed in a crash on February 18, 2001, during the Daytona 500. He drove the number 3 car and was known as the "Great Intimidator." This statue is a fitting memorial for this great race driver. (Courtesy of Cardwell Family Collection.)

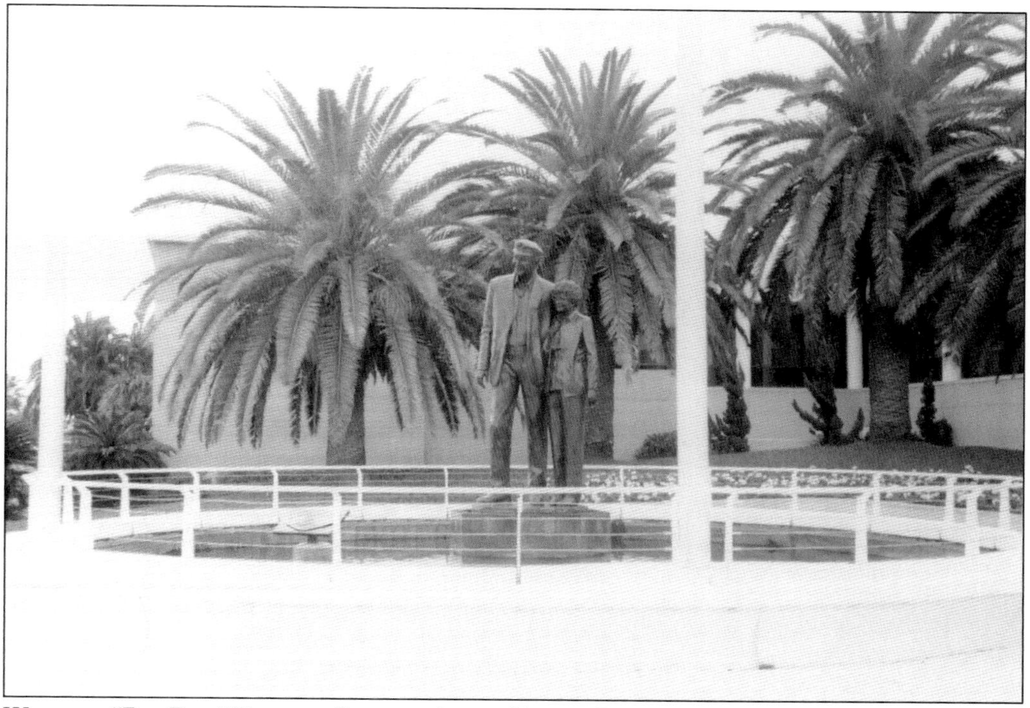

WILLIAM "BIG BILL" FRANCE SR. AND ANNE "ANNIE B." FRANCE MEMORIAL IN 2002. From a garage and filling station to the mammoth International Speedway at Daytona Beach, France's vision became a reality. His leadership and organization of NASCAR, with national speedway events each year, are a testament of the American Dream. The legacy lives on with his family members, who continue the tradition and growth of the International Speedway Corporation (ISC), Daytona U.S.A., and NASCAR. (Courtesy of Cardwell Family Collection.)

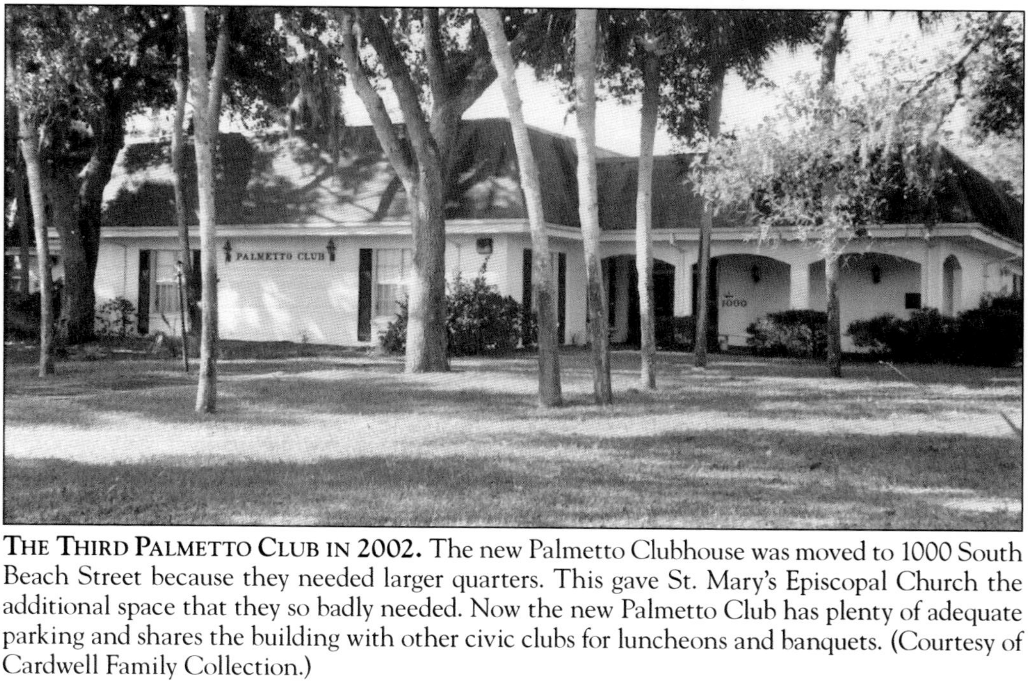

THE THIRD PALMETTO CLUB IN 2002. The new Palmetto Clubhouse was moved to 1000 South Beach Street because they needed larger quarters. This gave St. Mary's Episcopal Church the additional space that they so badly needed. Now the new Palmetto Club has plenty of adequate parking and shares the building with other civic clubs for luncheons and banquets. (Courtesy of Cardwell Family Collection.)

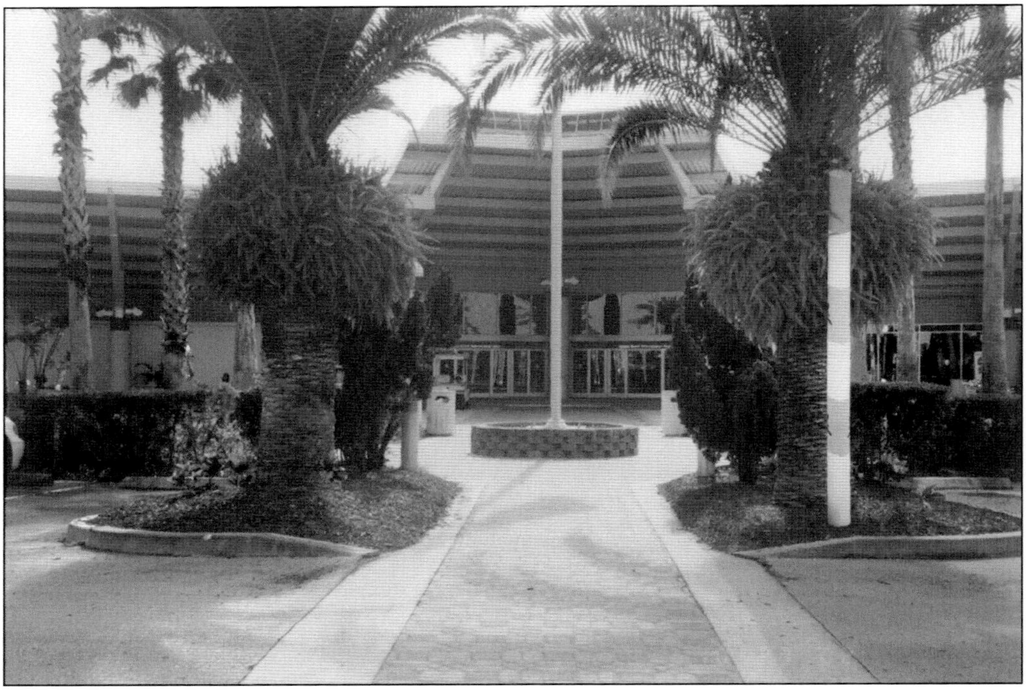

DAYTONA BEACH INTERNATIONAL AIRPORT IN 2002. This modern airport with its new terminal was completed in 1992 at a cost of $47 million. Hardly a trace is left of the U.S. Navy air base that once trained 350 navy fighter and dive-bomber pilots at a time during World War II. The navy base closed in 1946. (Courtesy of Cardwell Family Collection.)

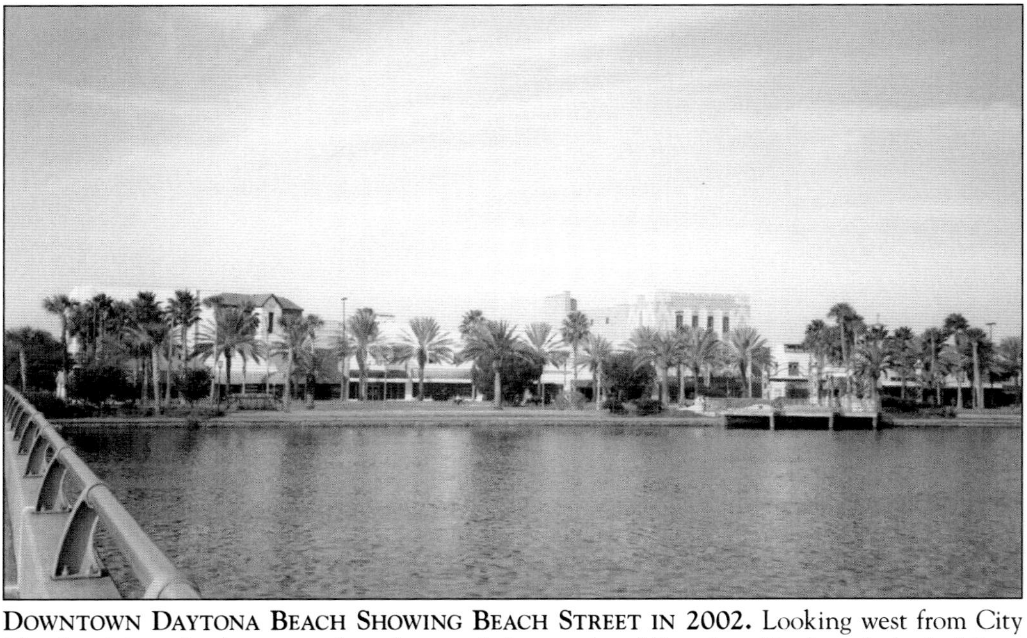

DOWNTOWN DAYTONA BEACH SHOWING BEACH STREET IN 2002. Looking west from City Island on Magnolia Avenue and north towards International Speedway Boulevard, the buildings in view are, from left to right, the Antique Emporium, Angell and Phelps, the former Kress Building, and the former McCrory Building; in the background to the west, the City Center Complex is visible. (Courtesy of Cardwell Family Collection.)

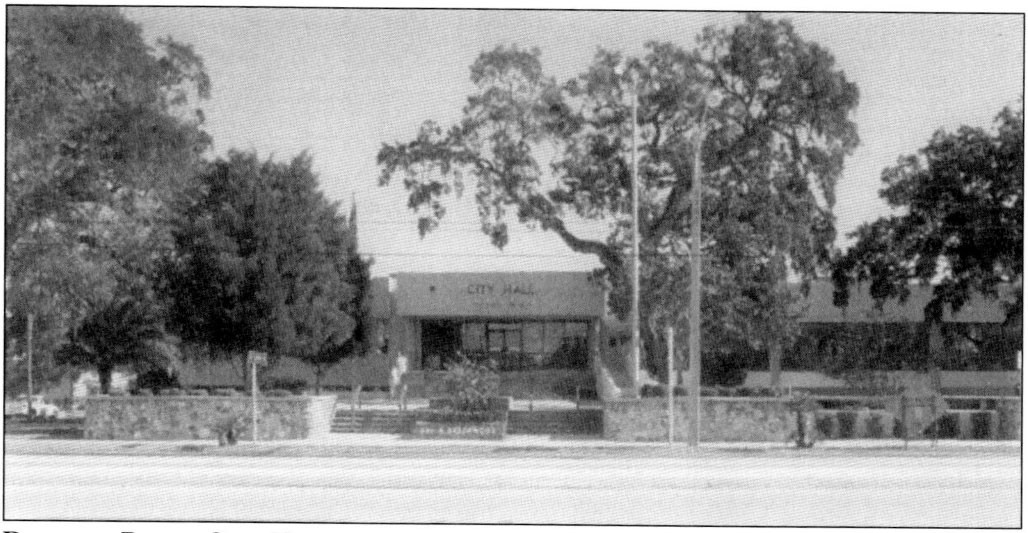

DAYTONA BEACH CITY HALL IN 2002. This new city hall at 301 South Ridgewood Avenue was built in 1976 in the International Modern style. For several years parking was available beneath the structure. However, in recent years it has been closed in to provide additional office space. There have been three city halls—the first was used from 1898 to 1920, the second from 1920 to 1976, and the third from 1976 to the present. Recently the City has acquired additional property nearby to accommodate parking for city employees and town hall meetings. (Courtesy of City of Daytona Beach.)

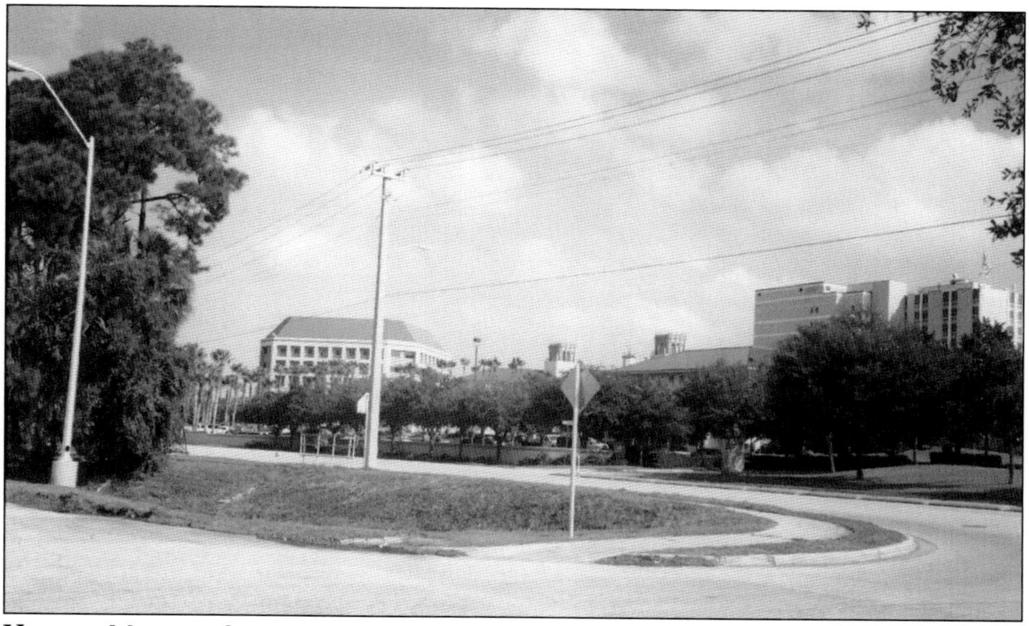

HALIFAX MEDICAL CENTER AT 303 NORTH CLYDE MORRIS BOULEVARD IN 2002. Today the Halifax Medical Center has grown to 10 floors and multiple side buildings, including a parking garage. This is a far cry from 1928, when the hospital was a three-story structure with 125 beds and support services. The hospital also has other facilities in Port Orange, Daytona Beach, and Ormond Beach. The main facility operates a trauma center with a receiving heliport for critical emergencies. The builders did incorporate a portion of the old hospital entrance lobby into the architectural plan of the new hospital. (Courtesy of Cardwell Family Collection.)

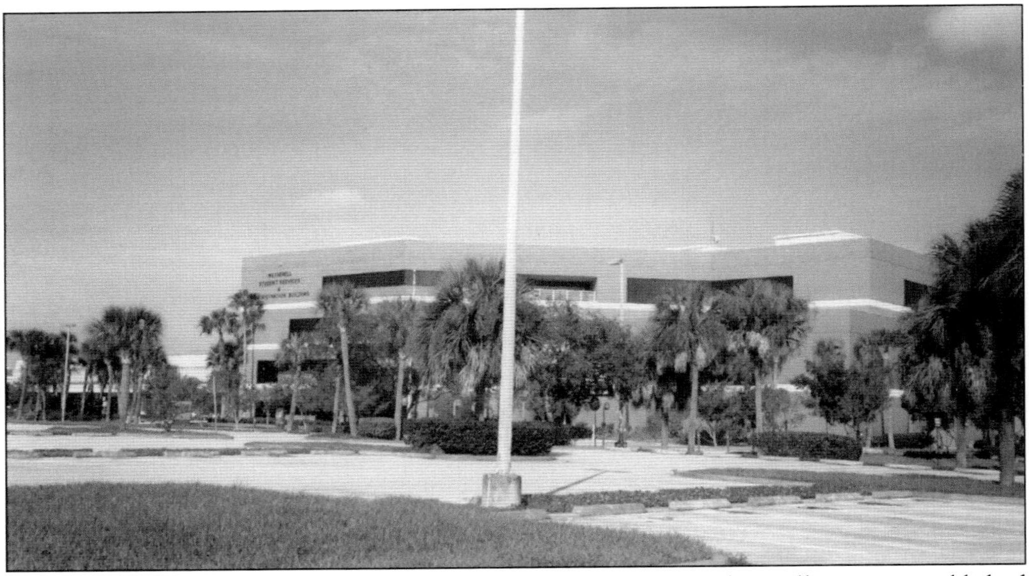

DAYTONA BEACH COMMUNITY COLLEGE CAMPUS IN 2002. This college was established in 1958 as a segregated community junior college. The present site was originally the WAC cantonment and the Welch Convalescent Center. After World War II this military post became the Mary Karl Vocational School. A portion of the classes were held at the Mary Karl School, and others were held temporarily at the Princess Issena Hotel. The first building constructed on the DBCC campus was the science center, followed by the library. By 1997 the Mary Karl School closed and extended campuses were added at DeLand, New Smyrna Beach, Deltona-DeBary, and Palm Coast. The college has become one of the largest community colleges in the state, offering apprenticeships and associate degrees in science and the arts. (Courtesy of Cardwell Family Collection.)

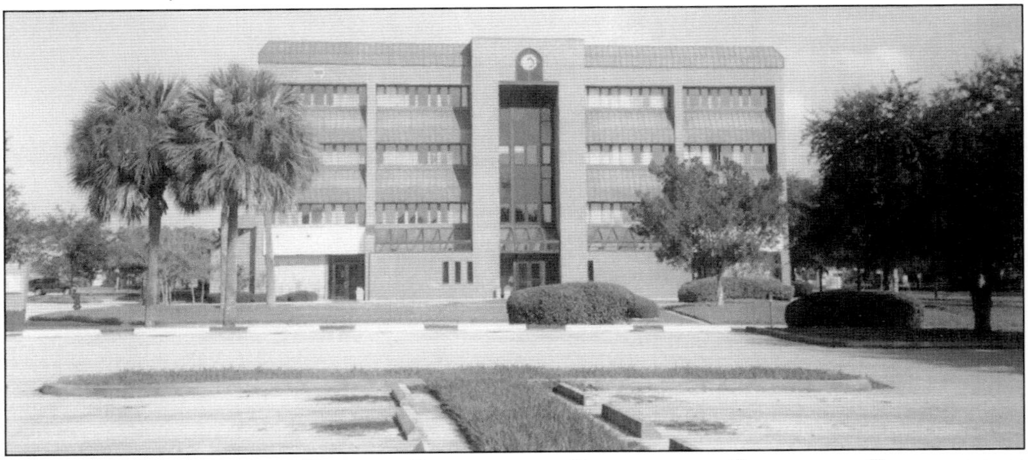

UNIVERSITY OF CENTRAL FLORIDA RESIDENTIAL CENTER AND CLASSROOM BUILDINGS IN 2002. The two-building center of the University of Central Florida (UCF) opened in September 1986. Dr. Sarah Pappas, director and associate vice president of the four-year undergraduate school, opened and guided this extended campus through outstanding growth. The president of UCF's main campus at Orlando, Dr. John Hitt, commended Dr. Pappas for being a forceful advocate and excellent contributor to education. When students receive their associate degrees from Daytona Beach Community College they can transfer to UCF to pursue education, business, and nursing degrees. (Courtesy of Cardwell Family Collection.)

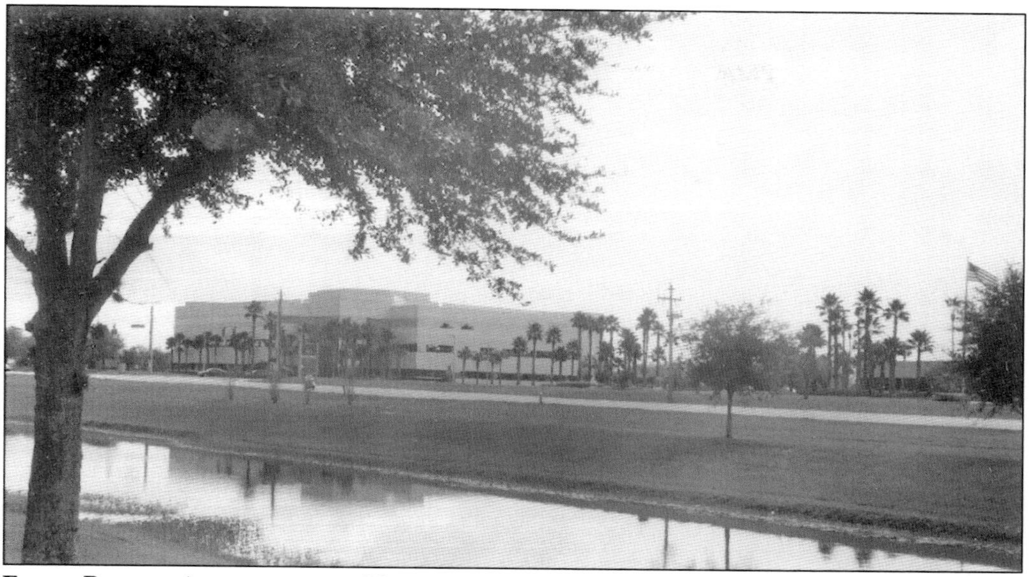

EMBRY-RIDDLE AERONAUTICAL UNIVERSITY AT 600 SOUTH CLYDE MORRIS BOULEVARD IN 2003. The Embry-Riddle Institute moved to Daytona Beach in 1965 from Dade County's Tamiami Airport. The school formed a partnership with Daytona Beach where they could come to an airport and grow into a large campus. Today they have a 95-acre campus featuring the Lehman Engineering and Technology Center; training aircraft; a field house, lecture auditorium, and classroom complex; dormitories, and the new, 1,000-bed, state-of-the art residential hall. Two new skywalks cross Richard Petty Boulevard and Clyde Morris Boulevard. In addition, they have numerous residential centers operating in other states and overseas, with many based at military installations. The vision of 1965 has become a reality, with outstanding recognition the world over. (Courtesy of Cardwell Family Collection.)

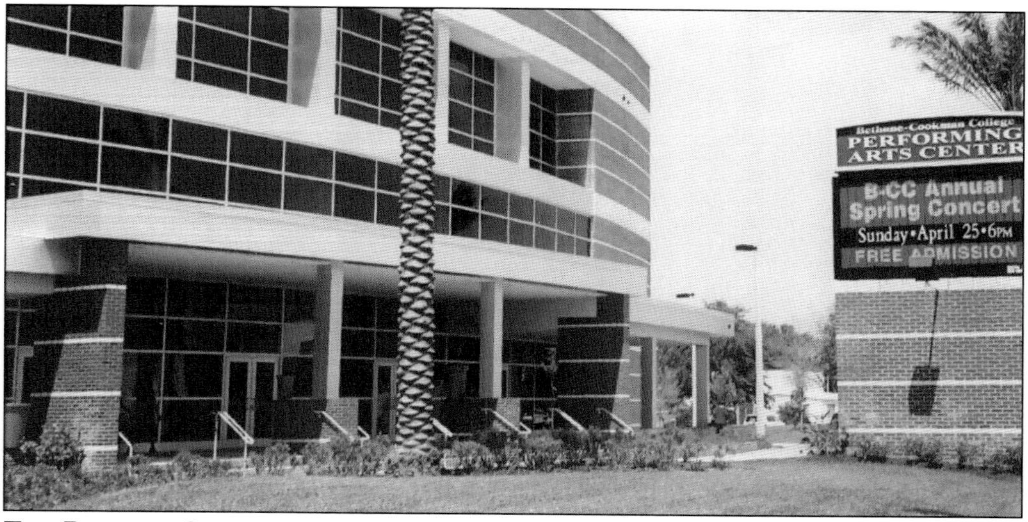

THE BETHUNE-COOKMAN COLLEGE PERFORMING ARTS CENTER. This beautiful modern architectural marvel, located at 698 West International Speedway Boulevard, is the newest addition to the Bethune-Cookman campus. The art center was opened in 2003 and is a prestigious landmark looking back at the time Mary McLeod Bethune established her school for girls in 1904 in a primitive wood schoolhouse not far from the railroad track. (Courtesy Cardwell Family Collection.)

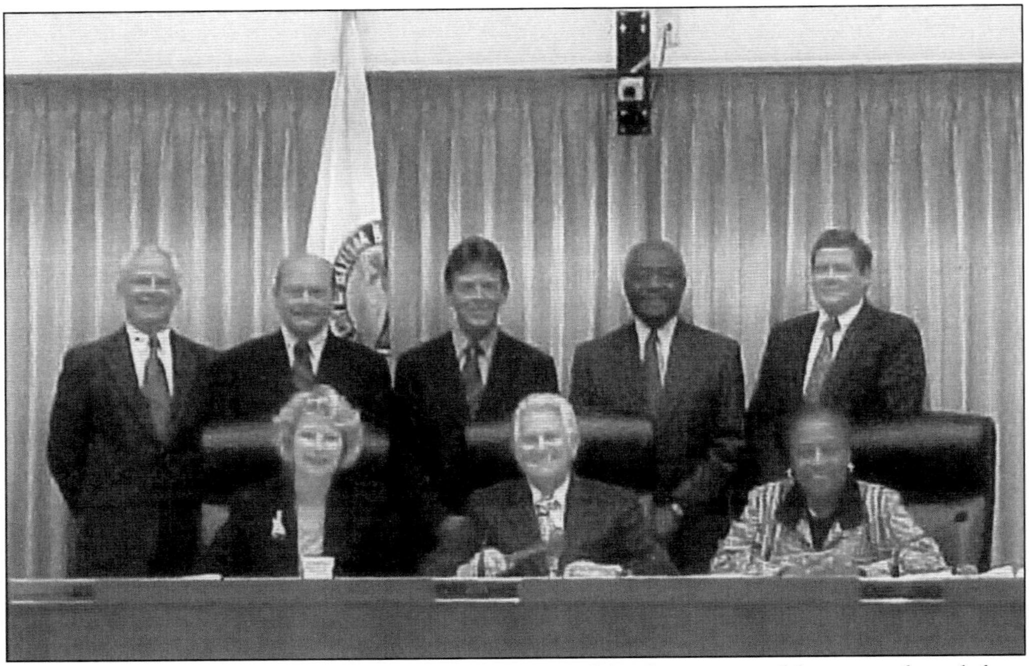

The Daytona Beach City Commission in 2002. Members pictured here are, from left to right, (front row) Darlene Yordon, Mayor Baron H. "Bud" Asher, and Yvonne Scarlett-Golden; (back row) city manager Carey Smith, Michael R. Shallow, Richard W. Shiver, Charles W. Cherry Sr., and Robert Brown. The commission meets twice a month. (Courtesy of City of Daytona Beach.)

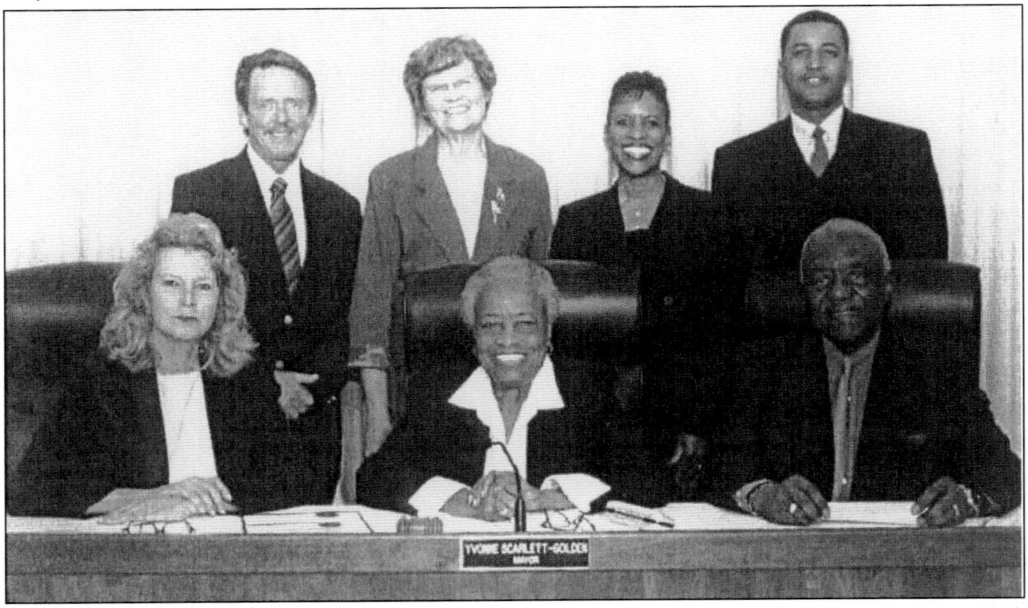

Daytona Beach Mayor and City Commissioners in 2004. Pictured here are, from left to right, (front row) city commissioner Darlene Yordon, Mayor Yvonne Scarlett-Golden, and city commissioner Charles W. Cherry Sr.; (back row) Richard W. Shiver, Sheila McKay, Gwen Azama-Edwards, and Dwayne Taylor. The City Commission meets twice each month and includes the city manager and the city attorney. (Courtesy of City of Daytona Beach.)